For Configuring IP

To Do This	Do This
Configure a WAN service	Use the ENCAPSULATION command in interface specific configuration mode
Create a subinterface for a WAN communication	Use the INTERFACE command in either global or interface specific configuration mode; choose either a point-to-point or point-to-multipoint subinterface
Assign an IP address to an interface	Use the IP ADDRESS command in interface or subinterface specific configuration mode
Assign a secondary address to an interface	Use the IP ADDRESS command with the SECONDARY keyword in interface or subinterface specific configuration mode
Configure a static route	Use the IP ROUTE command in global configuration mode
Configure a default route	Use the IP DEFAULT-NETWORK command in global configuration mode

For Configuring IP Routing Protocols

To Do This	Do This
Configure RIP routing	Start the RIP routing protocol with the ROUTER RIP command in global configuration mode
Select interfaces to participate in the RIP routing process	Use the NETWORK command in routing protocol specific configuration mode
Configure the OSPF routing protocol	Start an instance of the OSPF routing process with the ROUTER OSPF command in global configuration mode
Select one or more interfaces to participate in an OSPF area	Configure the NETWORK AREA command in routing protocol specific configuration mode; use a wildcard mask to select multiple interfaces in a single command line
Summarize OSPF routes on an ABR	Use the AREA RANGE command in routing protocol specific configuration mode
Summarize OSPF routes on an ASBR	Configure the SUMMARY-ADDRESS command in routing protocol specific configuration mode
Configure EIGRP routing	Start an EIGRP routing process for an autonomous system with the ROUTER EIGRP command
Select interfaces to participate in the EIGRP routing process	Use the NETWORK statement in routing protocol specific configuration mode
Summarize routes on any EIGRP router	Configure the IP SUMMARY-ADDRESS command in interface specific configuration mode
Start the BGP routing process	Configure with the ROUTER BGP command in global configuration mode
Initiate BGP routing with an internal or external peer	Use the NEIGHBOR REMOTE-AS command in routing protocol specific configuration mode
Make a route eligible for advertisement to a BGP peer	Use the NETWORK command to match any route currently in the IP forwarding table
Conditionally advertise summarized routes to a BGP peer	Enter the AGGREGATE-ADDRESS command in routing protocol specific configuration mode

For Configuring Routing Protocol Independent Features

To Do This	Do This
Redistribute routing information between a source and destination protocol	Use the REDISTRIBUTE command in routing protocol specific configuration mode for the destination protocol
Filter routes arriving on or sent from an interface	Configure the DISTRIBUTE-LIST command in interface specific configuration mode on the receiving or sending interface
Filter routes transferred between routing protocols	Enter the DISTRIBUTE-LIST command in routing protocol configuration mode for the destination protocol
Prevent routing updates on an interface	Use the PASSIVE-INTERFACE command in routing protocol specific configuration mode
Enable split-horizon on an interface or subinterface	Enter the command IP SPLIT-HORIZON in interface or subinterface specific configuration mode
Disable split-horizon on an interface or subinterface	Configure the command NO IP SPLIT-HORIZON in interface or subinterface specific configuration mode

For Configuring IOS

To Do This	Use This Command in Global Configuration Mode	Use This Command in Routing Protocol Specific Configuration Mode	Use This Command in Interface Specific Configuration Mode
Configure a WAN service			ENCAPSULATION *protocol*
Create a subinterface for a WAN communication	INTERFACE *type number.sub-if* [*point-to-point* I *point-to-multipoint*]		INTERFACE *type number.sub-if* [*point-to-point* I *point-to-multipoint*]
Assign an IP address to an interface			IP ADDRESS *address mask*
Assign a secondary address to an interface			IP ADDRESS *address mask* SECONDARY
Configure a static route	IP ROUTE *address mask type number*		
Configure a default route	IP DEFAULT-NETWORK *address*		
Configure RIP routing and select interfaces	ROUTER RIP	NETWORK *address*	
Configure the OSPF routing protocol and select interfaces	ROUTER OSPF *process-id*	NETWORK *address* AREA *area-id*	
Summarize OSFP routes on an ABR		AREA *area-id* RANGE *address*	
Summarize OSPF routes on an ASBR		SUMMARY-ADDRESS *address*	
Configure EIGRP routing and select interfaces	ROUTER EIGRP *autonomous-system*	NETWORK *address*	
Summarize routes on any EIGRP router			IP SUMMARY-ADDRESS EIGRP *autonomous-system address mask*
Start the BGP routing process	ROUTER BGP *autonomous-system*		
Initiate BGP routing with an internal or external peer		NEIGHBOR *address* REMOTE-AS *autonomous-system*	
Make a route eligible for advertisement to a BGP peer		NETWORK *address mask*	
Conditionally advertise summarized routes to a BGP peer		AGGREGATE-ADDRESS *address mask*	
Redistribute routing information between a source and destination protocol		REDISTRIBUTE *protocol id*	
Filter routes arriving on or exiting an interface			DISTRIBUTE-LIST *list-num* [IN I OUT]
Filter routes transferred between routing protocols		REDISTRIBUTE *protocol id* DISTRIBUTE-LIST *list-num*	
Prevent routing updates on an interface		PASSIVE-INTERFACE *type num*	
Enable split-horizon on an interface or subinterface			IP SPLIT-HORIZON
Disable split-horizon on an interface or subinterface			NO IP SPLIT-HORIZON

Cisco Router Configuration

Answers!
Certified Tech Support

Syngress Media, Inc.

Osborne/**McGraw-Hill**

Berkeley • New York • St. Louis • San Francisco
Auckland • Bogotá • Hamburg • London
Madrid • Mexico City • Milan • Montreal
New Delhi • Panama City • Paris • São Paulo
Singapore • Sydney • Tokyo • Toronto

Osborne/**McGraw-Hill**
2600 Tenth Street
Berkeley, California 94710
U.S.A.

For information on translations or book distributors outside the U.S.A., or to arrange bulk purchase discounts for sales promotions, premiums, or fund-raisers, please contact Osborne/**McGraw-Hill** at the above address.

Cisco Router Configuration Answers! Certified Tech Support

1234567890 DOC DOC 90198765432109

ISBN 0-07-88211943-8

Publisher
Brandon A. Nordin

Associate Publisher and Editor-in-Chief
Scott Rogers

Acquisitions Editor
Gareth Hancock

Editorial Management
Syngress Media, Inc.

Editorial Assistant
Stephane Thomas

Technical Editors
Glenn Lepore, Tony Costa,
Wayne Periman

Copy Editor
Kathleen Faughnan

Proofreader
Pat Mannion

Indexer
David Heiret

Computer Designers
Jean Butterfield, Gary Corrigan,
Mickey Galicia

Illustrators
Robert Hansen, Brian Wells,
Beth Young

Series Design
Mickey Galicia

Contents @ a Glance

Contents

About the Contributors

About Syngress Media

Syngress Media creates books and software for Information Technology professionals seeking skill enhancement and career advancement. Visit the Syngress Web site at www.syngress.com.

Glenn Lepore (CCNA) is a senior network engineer with Niche Networks, LLC in Herndon, VA. He has over 13 years experience in LAN and WAN design, installation, and troubleshooting. His background includes Frame Relay, X.25, TCP/IP, IPX, and SNA. His experience includes Novell and UNIX administration, Web page design, and Internet Service Provider (ISP) network operations. He is working toward CCIE certification as well as MCSE.

Tony Costa (CCIE #4140, MCSE, CNE) started his networking career in 1979 installing Gandalf synchronous modems. Since then he has worked extensively in TCP/IP and IBM SNA networks. He also installed some of the earliest Banyan Vines LANs in the U.S. Department of Defense, and now occasionally assists in replacing them with Microsoft Windows NT-based networks.

Tony spends his weekends at his home in New Mexico. During the week, he teaches Cisco technology to Cisco's engineers, and delivers Cisco IOS router and Cisco Catalyst switch classes to the public through Chesapeake Computer Consultants, Inc.

Prakash Ranade has more than ten years of experience in the application of state-of-the-art computer technologies to the solution of complex engineering problems. His expertise includes systems analysis and requirements definition, operation systems architecture, operations planning, software testing, and conceptual modeling. Through his work at major

American corporations, he has acquired broad experience in technical areas ranging from telecommunications to space science. He has taught computer science and chemical engineering courses at major academic institutions in the United States. Prakash holds an M.S. and a Ph.D. in chemical engineering.

Jesse M. Caulfield is the owner and founder of netthink Corporation, which provides strategic, technical, and management consulting to clients in the telecommunications and Internet industries. netthink Corporation supports voice carriers and international data network providers throughout the world with technical, strategic, and product development services. Prior to founding netthink, Mr. Caulfield developed internetwork systems and data solutions for long-distance provider MCI Telecommunications and the Defense Information Systems Agency. He received his bachelors degree in physics from UCLA in 1994.

Wayne Periman is currently a senior network engineer for Niche Networks, LLC in Herndon, VA. He has 17 years of experience in data communications, many of which were for the United States Air Force. Mr. Periman designed the IP network infrastructures for several Air Force bases, using a variety of schemes, including EIGRP, heterogeneous backbones, and OSPF and IGRP homogeneous backbones. Mr. Periman was the primary advisor in setting up access control lists on distribution and access routers to facilitate the new prototype units' mission. Mr. Periman's expertise is in the area of routing and switching.

ACKNOWLEDGMENTS

Syngress Media would like to thank Bridget Robeson, managing partner of Niche Networks, LLC, for providing us access to some great people. Thanks also to all the incredibly hard-working folks at Osborne/McGraw-Hill, especially Gareth Hancock, Scott Rogers, and Brandon Nordin for being solid team players. In addition, thanks to Stephane Thomas, Emily Rader, and Janet Walden for their help in fine-tuning the book.

Introduction

With 80 percent marketshare, Cisco is the fastest-growing networking technology on the market. This book of questions and answers is designed to capture the most common routing and switching problems that Cisco product engineers encounter. *Cisco Router Configuration Answers!* covers all of the IP routing protocols supported by Cisco Systems. You'll find valuable answers here on everything from the different uses for each type of routing protocol, to configuring each protocol, to monitoring the IP network.

Cisco Router Configuration Answers! is organized into 12 chapters. Each chapter contains questions and answers on specific routing techniques and protocols. Chapter 1 starts with in-depth questions on the top ten Cisco routing and switching topics, including multiple routing protocols, filtering, redistribution, neighbors, compatibility with other vendors, routing databases, and special routing techniques. Answers to questions on interior, system, and exterior routing explain the different categories of routing protocols and their functions. The section on metrics reviews the methods of measurement used by routing protocols to determine the best path to a destination.

Chapter 2 covers the most widely used routing protocols, including RIP, OSPF, IGRP and EIGRP, BGP and EGP, and IP Multicast. Chapter 3 answers questions about configuring Enhanced Interior Gateway Routing Protocol (EIGRP), Cisco's enhanced version of Interior Gateway Routing Protocol (IGRP). Chapter 4 describes configuration of a router in an Open Shortest Path First (OSPF) network. It summarizes various commands used to configure and monitor an OSPF router's performance. Chapter 5 covers the Routing Information Protocol version 1 (RIPv1), the most commonly used interior gateway protocol (IGP). It describes the features added to RIP by the Routing Information Protocol version 2 (RIPv2). Chapter 6 covers IS-IS (Intermediate System-

to-Intermediate System), a link-state, hierarchical routing protocol.

Chapter 7 provides answers to questions about configuring the Border Gateway Protocol (BGP), including questions on BGP support, BGP IP routing support, ISPs and BGP, and monitoring and maintaining BGP. EGP—the first exterior gateway protocol to gain widespread acceptance in the Internet—is covered in Chapter 8. Chapters 9 and 10 cover configuring the Gateway Discovery Protocol (GDP), and ICMP Router Discovery Protocol (IRDP). In Chapter 11 you can get answers on configuring IP Muticast Routing, including the Internet Group Management Protocol (IGMP) and Distance Vector Multicast Routing Protocol (DVMRP). Chapter 12 discusses monitoring the IP Network using routing tables, neighbors, and statistics.

Besides the questions and answers, each chapter contains tips and notes that provide insight, call attention to time-saving steps, warn of potential problems, and explain hard-to-understand items.

Conventions Used in This Book

Cisco Router Configuration Answers! uses several conventions designed to make it easier for you to find the answers you need.

- **ALL CAPITALS**   Are used to indicate router commands in text. For example:
  The SHOW IP ROUTE command
- *Italics*   Are used to indicate variables in router commands. For example:
  OFFSET-LIST *access-list-number*

In addition to those conventions, you will encounter some symbols that are designed to draw your attention to important information: Tips, Notes, and Cautions.

 Tip: *Tips are shortcuts that could help make your life easier as you follow the instructions for configuring a router protocol.*

 Note: *Notes are interesting facts that might enhance your understanding of the subject. File these items away to impress your colleagues!*

 Caution: *Cautions are warnings and reminders of pitfalls to avoid.*

Chapter 1

Top 10 Routing and Switching Topics

Answer Topics!

The Top Ten Routing and Switching Topics @ a Glance

Every protocol forwarder that a router supports has a set of rules that instructs the router how and where to forward the packet to reach its destination. These sets of rules (algorithms) measure various metrics about the type of connection directly attached to the router's interface, and what network assignment has been placed on that interface. The algorithm calculates the values of the metrics and directs the router to forward the packet out of a particular interface because it received information that the best path to the destination address of the packet could be reached through that interface. Some protocol forwarders have multiple routing protocols, including distance vector or link-state. Each routing protocol depends on key information such as addressing, identifying neighbors, discovering routes, selecting routes, and maintaining routing information.

This chapter describes the parameters of the widely used routing protocols such as RIP, OSPF, IGRP, and EIGRP. It is divided into the following sections:

- **Multiple Routing Protocols** explains the differences between distance vector and link-state routing protocols.
- **Filtering** describes how to control traffic on the network using access lists.
- **Redistribution** describes the integration of routing tables from one routing protocol to another.
- **Neighbors** defines how router adjacencies are formed during route discovery.
- **Interior, System, and Exterior Routing** explains the different categories of routing protocols and their functions.
- **Split-Horizon** describes the steps taken to prevent routing loops.
- **Metrics** reviews the methods of measurement used by routing protocols to determine the best path to a destination.
- **Compatibility with Other Vendors** defines the relationship between open routing protocols and proprietary routing protocols.
- **Routing Databases** describes the use of routing tables and why they are important.
- **Special Routing Techniques** describes creating static routes and disabling split-horizon.

MULTIPLE ROUTING PROTOCOLS

 When do you use multiple routing protocols?

You will use multiple routing protocols whenever you need to exchange routing information between two different routing protocols. The route redistribution feature allows this exchange to take place. Multiple routing protocols are desirable when:

- You are migrating from an older Interior Gateway Protocol (IGP) to a new IGP

- You want to use another protocol but need to keep the old one due to older host systems
- You want to terminate the interior route for protection against other routers that do not upgrade or implement a strict filtering policy
- You have a mixed router vendor environment

What is a distance vector routing protocol?

Distance vector routing protocols were designed for use in smaller network environments. The way they learn about routes and maintain routes, for example, is effective for a small network, but would require too much bandwidth in a large network. They detect when a neighboring router is down only when the neighbor does not send its routing table update in 90 seconds. Distance vector routing sends the entire routing table every 30 seconds to update its directly connected neighbors; it compiles a list of networks from neighbors (directly connected or otherwise). Distance vector routing uses hop count as a metric to count the number of routers to the destination.

As an example, Routing Information Protocol (RIP) uses the Bellman-Ford algorithm to determine shortest path. The path with the lowest number of hops is selected. The maximum number of hops is normally limited to 15. Destinations above 15 hops are deemed unreachable.

Examples of distance vector protocols are IP RIP, IPX RIP, AppleTalk RTMP, and IGRP.

What is a link-state routing protocol?

Link-state routing protocols can account for larger network issues, such as network growth, but require more CPU resources because of their complexity. Link-state routing protocols speed up the convergence time (compared to distance vector) because they learn of a failed or new router in less time. Normally, they detect a downed neighbor when a hello packet is not received in 10 seconds. A link-state router sends update packets to its neighbors about all the links it knows. The metric used to determine best path is cost, a numerical value, which is assigned by the operator based on

the bandwidth of the link. The path with the lowest cost is deemed best, with the maximum possible cost almost unlimited because of the Shortest Path First algorithm. If no changes occur in the network, routers will send updates only for routing table entries that have not been updated periodically (from 30 minutes to 2 hours).

Examples of link-state protocols are IP OSPF, IPX NLSP, and IS-IS.

Can a router use both distance vector and link-state routing protocols?

Yes. Each interface can be configured to use a different routing protocol; however, they must also be able to redistribute the routing information to the other routing protocol. (Redistribution is discussed in its own section later in this chapter.)

FILTERING

What are access lists?

Access lists are statements that express a set of rules, imposed by the operator, that give added control for packets inbound to and outbound from the router, but not generated by the router itself. The access lists can permit or deny incoming or outgoing packets to the destination. They operate in sequential and logical order, evaluating packets from the top of the list downward; if the packet matches the first statement, it skips the rest of the statements and is permitted or denied. There can be only one access list per protocol per interface.

What kinds of access lists are supported?

An access list can be identified by its number, which details the protocol and type as described below:

- IP standard access lists use numbers 1–99
- IP extended access lists use numbers 100–199
- IPX standard access lists use numbers 800–899
- IPX extended access lists use numbers 1000–1099
- Appletalk access lists use numbers 600–699

Tip: *You may also use Named Access Lists to identify access lists numbers 1–199 with Cisco IOS Release 11.2 or newer.*

How do I create IP standard access lists?

An IP standard access list is created using the following command:

```
Access-list access list number {permit | deny}
 source [source-mask]
```

In this command:

- **access-list number** Identifies the list to which the entry belongs; a number from 1 to 99
- **permit | deny** Indicates whether this entry allows or blocks traffic from the specified address
- **source** Identifies the source IP address
- **source-mask** Identifies which bits in the address field are matched. Put a 1 in positions indicating "don't care" and a 0 in any position that is to be strictly followed. Wildcards can be used.

The following is a sample of an access list from a router configuration file:

```
Router# show access-lists
Standard IP access list 1
deny 204.59.144.0, wildcard bits 0.0.0.255
permit any
Router#
```

The following is sample output from the SHOW IP ACCESS-LIST command when the name of a specific access list is requested:

```
showcase# show ip access-list Internetfilter
Extended IP access list Internetfilter
permit tcp any 171.69.0.0 0.0.255.255 eq telnet
deny tcp any any
deny udp any 171.69.0.0 0.0.255.255 lt 1024
deny ip any any log
```

 How do I create IP extended access lists?

An IP extended access list is created using:

```
Access-list access list number {permit | deny}
 protocol source [source-mask] destination
 destination-mask [operator operand] [established]
```

In this command:

- **access-list number**   Identifies the list using a number in the range 100–199
- **permit | deny**   Indicates whether this entry allows or blocks the specified address
- **protocol**   IP, TCP, UDP, ICMP, GRE, IGRP
- **source and destination**   Identifies the source and destination IP address
- **source-mask and destination-mask**   Identifies which bits in the address field are matched. Put a 1 in positions indicating "don't care" and a 0 in any position that is to be strictly followed. Wildcards can be used.
- **Operator and operand**   lt, gt, eq, neq (less than, greater than, equal, not equal), and a port number
- **established**   Allows TCP traffic to pass if packet uses an established connection (for example, has ACK bits set)

 Note: *An access list must have conditions that test true for all packets using the access list. A final implied statement covers all packets for which conditions did not test true. This final condition matches all other packets and results in a deny.*

 What command links the access list to the interface?

Use the IP ACCESS-GROUP command to link the access list to an interface:

```
ip access-group access-list-number {in | out}
```

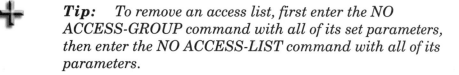

In this command:

- **access-list-number**   Indicates the number of the access list to be linked
- **in | out**   Selects whether the access is applied to the incoming or outgoing interface, without being the default

---

Tip: *To remove an access list, first enter the NO ACCESS-GROUP command with all of its set parameters, then enter the NO ACCESS-LIST command with all of its parameters.*

How do I use named IP access lists?

You may use named IP access lists to delete individual entries from a specific access list. This enables you to modify your access lists without deleting and then reconfiguring them. Named IP access lists are used when:

- You want to identify an access list using an alphanumeric name
- You have more than 99 simple, and 100 extended, access control lists to be configured for a given protocol

---

Note: *You cannot use the same name for multiple access lists, and lists of different types cannot have the same name.*

Why is the location of the access list important?

Where the operator places an access list can reduce unnecessary traffic. Packets that will be denied at a remote destination should not use network resources along the path to the destination. Standard access lists do not specify the destination, and should be placed close to the destination. Extended access lists do specify destination, and should be placed close to the source of the traffic denied.

 ### How can you find out what access lists are configured and their status?

Use the SHOW IP INTERFACE command to display whether access lists are active. Use the SHOW ACCESS-LISTS command to display the contents of all access lists. If you enter the access list name or number, you may view a specific list.

 ### What are the differences between IPX standard access lists and SAP filters?

IPX standard lists can filter source and destination addresses. SAP filters service types and servers on one or more networks. Standard access lists check for source address or for both source and destination, and can use a wildcard mask that operates like the IP wildcard mask. SAP filters can control overhead traffic such as Get Nearest Server (GNS), IPX RIP, and NetWare Link Services Protocol (NLSP).

 ### How do I configure IPX standard access lists?

IPX standard access lists can be configured using the following command:

```
Access-list access-list number {deny | permit}
 protocol source-network [.source-node] [source-node-mask]
 [destination-network] [.destination-node]
 [destination-node-mask]
```

In this command:

- **access-list-number**   Is a number for an IPX filter list from 800–899
- **protocol**   Is the number of the protocol type, which can be 0 for any protocol, 1 for RIP, 4 for SAP, 5 for SPX, 17 for NCP, and 20 for IPX NetBIOS
- **source-network**   Is the source network number, expressed in eight-digit hexadecimal
- **source-node**   Is the node number on the source network represented as a 48-bit value shown in a dotted triplet of four-digit hexadecimal numbers

● **destination-network**   Refers to the network number to which the packet is being sent

● **destination-node**   Is the node on the destination network to which the packet is being sent

The IPX ACCESS-GROUP command links the access lists to an interface:

```
ipx access-group access-list-number
```

The following example creates an extended access list named sal that denies all SPX packets:

```
ipx access-list extended sal
deny spx any all any all log
permit any
```

Following is an example of an IPX standard access list:

```
Hostname Router
!
!
ipx routing 00e0.1e68.5c62
!
interface Ethernet0
ip address 192.168.68.1 255.255.255.0
ipx access-group 800
ipx network 100
!
interface Serial0
ip address 172.16.1.1 255.255.255.252
no fair-queue
!
!
access-list 800 deny 1 200
access-list 800 permit FFFFFFFF
```

How do I configure IPX SAP filters?

SAP filters are created using the following format:

```
access-list access-list-number {deny | permit} network
[.node] [network-mask node-mask]
[service-type [server-name]]
```

The next line would be either:

```
ipx input-sap-filter access-list-number
```

or

```
ipx output-sap-filter access-list-number
```

In this command:

- **access-list-number** Is a number for an IPX filter list from 1000–1099 indicating a SAP filter list
- **network (.node]** Is the Novell source internal network number with optional node number (-1 for all networks)
- **network-mask node-mask** Is the mask to be applied to the network and node. Ones should be in the positions to be masked
- **service-type** Is the SAP service type to filter. Each service type is identified by a hexadecimal number such as: 4= file server, 7=print server, and 24=remote bridge server (router).
- **server-name** Is the name of the server providing the service type

The use of the IPX INPUT | OUTPUT–SAP FILTER command at the interface configuration prompt links the filter to the interface and determines where SAPs are filtered before entry into the SAP table, or filtered during the next update.

The following configuration file shows an IPX SAP filter:

```
Hostname Router
!
!
ipx routing 00e0.1e68.5c62
!
interface Ethernet0
ip address 192.168.68.1 255.255.255.0
ipx input-sap-filter 1000
ipx network 100
!
```

```
interface Serial0
ip address 172.16.1.1 255.255.255.252
no fair-queue
!
!
access-list 1000 deny 1 200 7
access-list 1000 permit FFFFFFFF
```

The following example creates a SAP access list named Merchant that allows only Merchant to be sent in SAP advertisements:

```
ipx access-list sap Merchant
permit 1234 4 Merchant
```

What are the key concepts for AppleTalk access lists?

Access lists for AppleTalk can filter extended networks or cable ranges. You may also select partial cable ranges from within an extended network. Using AppleTalk I, you may specify a single network; with AppleTalk II, you may specify a full or partial cable range. Access lists can control data packets and routing updates using RTMP and ZIP.

How do I configure AppleTalk access lists?

AppleTalk access lists are configured using two formats. To define a full cable range filtering parameter, enter the following:

```
access-list number {permit | deny} cable-range cable-range
```

To define a partial cable range filtering parameter, enter the following:

```
access-list number {permit | deny} within cable range
 cable-range
```

In this command:

- **number**   Is the access list number for AppleTalk (from 600–699)
- **cable-range**   Indicates the specific cable range

The APPLETALK ACCESS-GROUP command links the access list to one or more interfaces:

```
Appletalk access-group access-list-number
```

REDISTRIBUTION

 What is redistribution?

Redistribution allows routes discovered by one routing process to be advertised in the updates of another process. Redistribution allows, for example, routing tables learned from RIP to be imported into the routing tables of OSPF or EIGRP, and vice versa.

 Tip: *You can only redistribute protocols that support the same protocol stack. As an example, IP RIP and OSPF can redistribute between each other because they both support the TCP/IP protocol stack. However, IPX RIP and OSPF cannot, because IPX RIP supports the IPX/SPX protocol stack and OSPF does not. There is an exception: EIGRP supports multiple routing protocols and can be used to redistribute with IP, IPX, and AppleTalk.*

 When is redistribution used?

Redistribution is normally configured on autonomous system routers that have the responsibility of advertising routes learned from one autonomous system to other autonomous systems. If you are using IGRP or EIGRP, redistribution is normally done automatically.

 What is administrative distance?

Administrative distance is the believability of a routing protocol. Each is prioritized in order of most reliability to least reliability, using a value called administrative distance. This is the first criterion a router uses to determine what routing protocol to believe, if routing information to the same destination is provided by two different routing protocols.

What are the administrative distance values?

Table 1-1 displays the administrative distance values for various route sources.

How do I configure redistribution?

Before configuring redistribution, you must first:

1. Determine where to add new protocols.
2. Identify the ASBRs (autonomous system border routers).
3. Determine which protocol is the core and which is the edge.
4. Determine the directions you want to redistribute protocols.

Use the following command to redistribute routing updates (this example is for OSPF):

```
router(config-router)#redistribute protocol [process-id]
    [metric metric-value] [metric-type type-value] [subnets]
```

Route Source	Default Distance
Connected Interfaces	0
Static Route	1
Enhanced IGRP Summary Route	5
External BGP	20
Internal Enhanced IGRP	90
IGRP	100
OSPF	110
IS-IS	115
RIP	120
EGP	140
External Enhanced IGRP	170
Internal BGP	200
Unknown	255

Table 1-1   Administrative Distance Values

In this command:

- **protocol** Is the source protocol from which routes are being redistributed. Keyword values are: bgp, eqp, igrp, isis, ospf, static [ip], connected, and rip.
- **process-id** Is the OSPF process ID
- **metric** Is an optional parameter used to specify which metric is being used for the redistributed route. The default metric is 0. You should use a value that is consistent with the destination protocol.
- **metric-type** Is an optional OSPF parameter that specifies the external link type associated with the default advertised into the OSPF routing domain. Values are 1 for type-1 external routes, or 2 for type-2 external routes. Type-2 is the default.
- **subnets** Is an optional OSPF parameter, which specifies that subnetted routes should be redistributed

---

Note: *You only need to use the REDISTRIBUTE and DEFAULT-METRIC command to redistribute routes between routing protocols that do not automatically perform route distribution.*

NEIGHBORS

 ### Why is identifying neighbors important?

Identifying neighbors in a small network is not a major issue. When a router fails, the other routers can converge in a reasonable amount of time. In large networks, however, the delay in detecting a down router can be disastrous. Knowing the neighbors speeds up the convergence, because routers learn of the failed route sooner, because the hello interval is shorter than the route exchange interval.

Distance vector routing protocols detect a down neighbor only when the neighbor does not send its routing update during the update interval, usually 10–90 seconds. Link-state routing protocols detect a down neighbor when a hello is not received during the update interval, usually 10 seconds.

How do distance vector and link-state protocols discover neighbors?

Routers using distance vector protocols create a routing table (which includes its directly connected networks) and sends the routing table to its directly connected neighbors. The neighbor merges the received routing table into its own and forwards the updated routing table to its neighbors. Routers using link-state protocols create a link-state table that includes entries about the entire network. Each router forwards the entire internetwork, with information about the links that it knows in update packets. As each neighbor receives the update, it copies the content and forwards it to other neighbors. There is no recalculation in the routing table before forwarding.

Note: *IGRP and EIGRP routers multicast hello packets to discover neighbors and to exchange route updates similar to OSPF. EIGRP maintains a neighbor table for each configured network-layer protocol. This includes the neighbors' addresses, the number of packets waiting in queue to be sent, the average time it takes to send and receive packets from the neighbor, and the interval to wait without receiving anything from a neighbor before determining that the link is down.*

INTERIOR, SYSTEM, AND EXTERIOR ROUTING

What is an autonomous system?

An autonomous system is a set of routers and networks under the same administration. It may consist of one router directly connected to one LAN to the Internet, or it may be a corporate network linking several local networks through a corporate backbone. All routers in an autonomous system must be interconnected, running the same routing protocol and assigned the same autonomous system number. Autonomous systems are linked together using an exterior routing protocol such as Border Gateway Protocol (BGP).

What is the difference between interior and exterior routing protocols?

Exterior routing protocols are used to communicate between autonomous systems. Interior routing protocols are used within a single autonomous system.

How do I configure the router to use Routing Information Protocol (RIP)?

Routing Information Protocol is configured using the following commands:

```
router rip
```

starts the RIP routing process

```
network network-number
```

selects participating attached networks

What command do you issue to verify that the RIP routing protocol is enabled?

You issue the SHOW IP PROTOCOL command to verify that the RIP routing protocol is enabled.

What command disables the display of RIP routing updates sent from, and received at, your router?

The NO DEBUG IP RIP command disables the display of the RIP routing updates sent from, and received at, the router.

In the RIP routing table display, how do you determine which networks are discovered by the RIP routing protocol?

The code letter R precedes the networks discovered by the RIP routing protocol.

The code letter C precedes the networks that are directly connected to the router and have been configured with the NETWORK command.

What command do you issue to enable the IGRP routing protocol?

To enable the IGRP routing protocol, issue the following commands:

```
router IGRP autonomous-system
```

which defines IGRP as an IP routing process, and

```
network network-number
```

which selects participating attached networks.

What is Enhanced IGRP?

Enhanced IGRP (EIGRP) is a proprietary protocol that combines the advantages of link-state and distance vector routing protocols. It borrows very little from link-state technology, but is more of an advanced distance vector protocol. It uses a Hello protocol, but route update exchange is distance vector based. It uses a totally different algorithm than distance vector or link-state protocols for the selecting of routes. EIGRP supports IP, IPX, and AppleTalk.

In the IGRP routing table display, how do you determine which networks are discovered by the IGRP routing protocol?

The networks discovered by the IGRP routing protocol are preceded by the code letter I.

The code letter C precedes the networks that are directly connected to the router and have been configured with the NETWORK command.

What is Border Gateway Protocol (BGP)?

BGP enables an interdomain routing system that guarantees the loop-free exchange of routing information between autonomous systems. The classic definition of an autonomous system is a set of routers under a single technical administration, using an IGP and common metrics to route packets to other autonomous systems. Using the term *autonomous system* in connection with BGP stresses the fact that the administration of an autonomous system appears to other autonomous systems to have a single coherent interior routing plan, and presents a consistent picture of those networks that are reachable through it.

What types of session are supported by BGP?

BGP sessions are carried by the Transmission Control Protocol (TCP), a reliable transport mechanism that supports two types of sessions between a router and its neighbors:

- **External BGP (EBGP)** Occurs between routers in two different autonomous systems. Their routers are usually adjacent to one another, sharing the same medial and a subnet.

- **Internal BGP (IBGP)** Occurs between routers in the same autonomous system. and is used to coordinate and synchronize routing policy within the autonomous system. Neighbors may be located anywhere in the autonomous system, even several hops away from one another.

Note: *"The initial data flow is the entire BGP routing table. Incremental updates are sent as the routing table changes. BGP does not require periodic refresh of the entire BGP routing table. Therefore a BGP speaker must retain the current version of the entire BGP routing tables of all of its peers for the duration of the connection. KeepAlive messages are sent periodically to ensure the connection stays active. Notification messages are sent in response to errors or special conditions. If a connection encounters an error condition, a notification message is sent and the connection is closed."*
—Excerpt from RFC 11654, BGP Operations

Does BGP allow redistribution of routing tables?

Yes, since BGP primarily deals with autonomous system pathing rather than routing decisions, it must support the integration of RIP, OSPF, and IGRP routing tables in order to advertise their routes into an autonomous system. BGP is an exterior routing protocol and hence operates somewhat differently from an interior routing protocol. The NETWORK command in BGP creates a route in the BGP routing table only if the route is already present in the IP routing table.

 How do I display all the BGP paths in the database?

To display all the BGP paths in the database, enter this command at the EXEC prompt:

```
show ip bgp paths
```

A sample output for this command would be:

```
Address     Hash      Refcount     Metric    Path
0x297A9C    0         2            0         i
0x30BF84    1         0            0         702 701 ?
0x2F7BC8    2         235          0         ?
0x2FA1D8    3         0            0         702 701 i
```

In this output:

- **Address**   Internal address where the path is stored
- **Hash**   Hash bucket where path is stored
- **Refcount**   Number of routes using that path
- **Metric**   The INTER_AS metric for the path
- **Path**   The AS_PATH for that route, followed by the origin code for that route

SPLIT-HORIZON

 What is split-horizon?

Split-horizon is just one technique used to eliminate routing loops and speed convergence of the network. Split-horizon follows the principle that it is not useful to send information about a route in the direction where the information came from. The split-horizon technique omits any information in the routing update about destinations routed on the link, and relies on routes never being advertised or fading away through some timeout mechanism.

 How are routing loops created?

Routing loops can occur if the networks' slow convergence on a new or modified entry in the routing table causes inconsistent routing entries.

METRICS

 What are metrics?

Metrics represent distance. They are used to select the best path for routing. As each routing algorithm interprets the routing table, it generates a number (metric value) for each path through the network. The smallest number represents the best path.

Metrics can be calculated using a single characteristic of a path, but more complex metrics can be utilized by combining several characteristics. Some of the more commonly used metrics include:

- **Hop count** The number of passages of a packet through the output port of one router
- **Ticks** The delay on a data link (approx. 1/18 of a second)
- **Costs** An arbitrary value based on bandwidth, expense, or other measurement defined by network operator
- **Bandwidth** The data capacity of a link
- **Delay** The length of time required to move a packet from source to destination
- **Load** The amount of activity on a network resource or link
- **Reliability** The bit/error rate of network link
- **Maximum transmission unit (MTU)** The maximum message length in octets that is acceptable to all links on the path

What type of routing metric does IGRP use, and what are the components of that metric?

IGRP uses a composite metric as its routing metric. This metric includes the following components:

- **Bandwidth**   Smallest bandwidth between source and destination
- **Delay**   Cumulative interface delay along the path
- **Reliability**   Worst reliability between source and destination, based on keepalives
- **Loading**   Worst load on a link between source and destination, based on bits per second
- **MTU**   Smallest MTU value in path

Can metrics be modified or adjusted?

The OFFSET-LIST ROUTER subcommand can be used to add a positive offset to incoming and outgoing metrics for networks matching an access list. Full syntax for this command is as follows:

```
offset-list {in|out} offset [access-list]
no offset-list {in|out} offset [access-list]
```

If the argument *LIST* is zero, the argument supplied to *OFFSET* is applied to all metrics. If *OFFSET* is zero, no action is taken. For IGRP, the offset is added to the delay component only. This subcommand is implemented for the RIP and Hello routing protocols as well.

The NO OFFSET-LIST command with the appropriate keyword removes the offset list.

In the following example, a router using IGRP applies an offset of ten to its delay component for all outgoing metrics.

```
offset-list out 10
```

In the next example, the router applies the same offset only to access list 121.

```
offset-list out 10 121
```

 ## What are the five pieces of information every router needs in order to route traffic?

All routers need the following to route traffic:

- **Destination address** The host to which the packet is being sent
- **Identification of neighbors** Who is directly connected to its interfaces
- **Discovery of routes** What networks do its neighbors know about
- **Selecting routes** Which route, learned from its neighbors, offers the best (metric-sensitive) path to the destination address
- **Maintaining routing information** A table kept by the router, storing all route information it learns

COMPATIBILITY WITH OTHER VENDORS

 ## Are the routing protocols supported by Cisco compatible with the routing protocols of other router vendors?

All of the routing protocols supported by Cisco are compatible with other vendors' implementation of those routing protocols, with the exception of Interior Gateway Routing Protocol and Enhanced Interior Gateway Routing Protocol, which are proprietary.

ROUTING DATABASES

 ## What do the entries in the RIP routing table specify?

Each entry in a RIP routing table provides a range of information, including the ultimate destination, the next hop on the way to that destination, and a *metric*. The metric indicates the distance (in number of hops) to the destination. Other information can also be present in the routing table, including various timers associated with the route. A typical RIP routing table is shown in Table 1-2.

SPECIAL ROUTING TECHNIQUES

 ## How do I create static routes?

The IP ROUTE global configuration command is used to establish static routes. A static route is appropriate if the router cannot dynamically build a route to the destination. The command syntax is as follows:

```
ip route network mask {address|interface} [distance]
```

In this command:

- **network**   Is the Internet address of the target network or subnet
- **mask**   Is a network mask that lets you mask network and subnetwork bits
- **address**   Is the Internet address of a router that can reach that network
- **interface**   Is the name of the interface to use for that network
- **distance**   Specifies an administrative distance

Destination	Next Hop	Distance	Timers	Flags
Network A	Router 1	3	11, 12, 13	x, y
Network B	Router 2	5	11, 12, 13	x, y
Network C	Router 1	2	11, 12, 13	x, y

Table 1-2   A Typical RIP Routing Table

Static routes that point to an interface (using the argument INTERFACE) are advertised via RIP and IGRP regardless of whether REDISTRIBUTE STATIC commands were specified for those routing protocols. This is because static routes that point to an interface are considered in the routing table to be connected and hence lose their static nature. However, if you define a static route to an interface that is not one of the networks defined in a NETWORK command, neither RIP nor IGRP will advertise the route.

In the following example, packets for network 131.108.0.0 will be routed to the router at 131.108.6.6:

```
ip route 131.108.0.0 255.255.0.0 131.108.6.6
```

 ## When should split-horizon be disabled?

Routers that are connected to broadcast-type IP networks, and use distance vector routing protocols, employ the split-horizon mechanism to prevent routing loops. Split-horizon blocks information about routes from being advertised by a router out any interface from which that information originated. This optimizes data flow among multiple routers, particularly when links are broken. However, with nonbroadcast networks such as Frame Relay and SMDS, situations can arise for which this behavior is less than ideal.

Use the NO IP SPLIT-HORIZON interface subcommand to disable the split-horizon mechanism:

```
ip split-horizon
no ip split-horizon
```

Chapter 2

IP Routing Protocols

Answer Topics!

IP Routing Protocols @ a Glance

What are routing protocols? They are the processes by which an item gets from one location to another. Everyday items such as the mail, telephone calls, and trains get routed. To be able to route anything, the entity that performs the routing needs to know several key pieces of information:

- the destination address of the item to be routed
- a source from which it can learn the paths to the destination
- any alternative routes to the destination
- the best path to the destination
- a way of confirming that the paths are the most current

This type of information is what a routing protocol provides to a router. Each routing protocol uses a slightly different algorithm to obtain the information. This chapter describes the most widely used routing protocols:

- **RIP** covers the configuration aspects of the Routing Information Protocols.

- **OSPF** describes the configuration, monitoring, and displaying OSPF parameters.

- **IGRP and EIGRP** presents various configurations of IGRP and EIGRP.

- **BGP and EGP** discusses the use of Exterior Gateway Protocols.

- **IP Multicast** covers the protocols supported by IP Multicast.

RIP

 ### What is the Routing Information Protocol and how does it work?

The Routing Information Protocol uses broadcast User Datagram Protocol (UDP) data packets to exchange routing information. Each router sends routing information updates every 30 seconds; this process is termed *advertising*. If a router does not receive an update from another router for 180 seconds or more, it marks the routes served by the nonupdating router as being unusable. If there is still no update after 240 seconds, the router removes all routing table entries for the nonupdating router.

 ### What metric does RIP use to determine reachability?

The measure, or metric, that RIP uses to rate the value of different routes is the *hop count*. The hop count is the number of routers that can be traversed in a route. A directly connected network has a metric of zero; an unreachable network has a metric of 16. This small range of metrics makes RIP unsuitable as a routing protocol for large networks. If the router has a default network path, RIP advertises a route that links the router to the pseudo-network 0.0.0.0. The network 0.0.0.0 does not exist, but RIP treats 0.0.0.0 as a network to implement the default routing feature.

 ### How do I configure RIP and disable RIP?

To create a routing process for RIP, use the ROUTER RIP global configuration command:

```
router rip
```

Use the NO ROUTER RIP command to shut down the routing process:

```
no router rip
```

How do I redistribute RIP updates into HELLO updates?

In this situation, consider a wide-area network, using RIP, which needs to advertise routes to another network using HELLO as the routing protocol. The following commands should be entered:

```
router hello
network 192.168.23.0
redistribute rip
default-metric 10000
distribute-list 10 out rip
```

In this command:

- **router** Starts a HELLO routing process
- **network** Specifies network 192.168.23.0 (the network to receive HELLO routing information)
- **redistribute** Specifies that RIP-derived routing information be advertised in the HELLO routing updates
- **default-metric** Assigns a HELLO delay of 10,000 to all RIP-derived routes
- **distribute-list** Instructs the router to use access list 10 (not defined in this example) to limit the entries in each outgoing HELLO update. The access list prevents unauthorized advertising of university routes to the regional network.

Note: *The example could have specified automatic conversion between the RIP and HELLO metrics. However, in the interest of routing table stability, it is not desirable to do so. Instead, this example limits the routing information exchanged to availability information only.*

Can the update timers for RIP be adjusted or modified?

When you need to adjust RIP network timers, use the TIMERS BASIC router configuration command.

```
timers basic update invalid holddown flush
```

In this command:

- **update**   Is the rate in seconds at which updates are sent. This is the fundamental timing parameter of the routing protocol. The default is 30 seconds.

- **invalid**   Describes the interval of time (in seconds) after which a route is declared invalid; it should be at least three times the value of *update*. A route becomes invalid when there is an absence of updates that refresh the route. The route then enters holddown. The route is marked inaccessible and advertised as unreachable. However, the route is still used for forwarding packets. The default is 180 seconds.

- **holddown**   Is the interval (in seconds) during which routing information regarding better paths is suppressed. It should be at least three times the value of update. A route enters into a holddown state when an update packet is received that indicates the route is unreachable. The route is marked inaccessible and advertised as unreachable. However, the route is still used for forwarding packets. When holddown expires, routes advertised by other sources are accepted and the route is no longer inaccessible. The default is 180 seconds.

- **flush**   Describes the amount of time in seconds that must pass before the route is removed from the routing table; the interval specified should be greater than the invalid value. If it is less than this sum, the proper holddown interval cannot elapse, which results in a new route being accepted before the holddown interval expires. The default is 240 seconds.

To restore the default timers, use the NO form of this command.

```
no timers basic
```

What is the command to change RIP's version?

To specify a RIP version used globally by the router, use the VERSION router configuration command.

```
router rip
version {1 | 2}
```

In this command:

- **1** specifies RIP version 1
- **2** specifies RIP version 2

Use the NO form of this command to restore the default value.

```
no version
```

What are the key characteristics of RIP?

RIP's characteristics are:

- It is a distance vector routing protocol.
- Hop count is used as the metric for path selection.
- The maximum allowable hop count is 16.
- Routing updates are broadcast every 30 seconds by default.
- It is capable of load balancing over multiple paths.

How do I display active RIP updates?

The DEBUG IP RIP command displays RIP routing updates as they are sent and received. The NO DEBUG IP RIP command turns off the display.

 What command do you issue to display the current state of RIP?

You should issue the SHOW IP ROUTE command to display the current state of RIP.

 In the RIP routing table, how do you determine which networks are discovered by the RIP routing protocol?

The code letter R precedes networks discovered by RIP. The code letter C precedes the networks that are directly connected to the router and have been configured with the NETWORK command. Figure 2-1 shows the output of routes that have been discovered by RIP and directly connected networks.

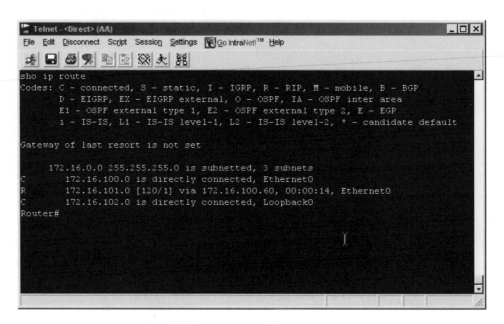

Figure 2-1 Output of routes that have been discovered by RIP and directly connected networks

How does RIP maintain its routing information?

When routers learn about changes in the internetwork, the routers update their routing tables with the change and send their entire routing tables to their neighbors.

Once a routing table has been received, routers incorporate it into their own routing tables, run the Bellman-Ford algorithm, and forward their updated routing tables. This process is not completed until all routers in the internetwork converge. If there are no changes in the network, each router normally sends out its routing table to its neighbor every 60 seconds.

OSPF

What is OSPF?

Open Shortest Path First (OSPF) is a link-state technology developed by the Internet Engineering Task Force (IETF) in 1988. As an interior gateway protocol, it was written to address the needs of large, scalable internetworks that RIP could not handle. These addressed needs were:

- **Speed of convergence**   Convergence is faster because routing changes are flooded immediately and computed in parallel
- **Support for variable length subnet masks**   Supports subnet masking and VLSMs
- **Network reachability**   No reachability limitations
- **Use of bandwidth**   OSPF multicasts its routing updates and only sends when there is a change in the network
- **Method for path selection**   OSPF uses a cost value which is based on the speed of the connection

 ## How does OSPF maintain its routing information?

When OSPF routers learn about a change in the internetwork, OSPF updates its link-state table and sends an update to the routers that are adjacent. The adjacent router receives the update, adds it to the link-state table, and then runs the OSPF algorithm to select the best paths. When there are no changes, the routers send updates only for those route entries that have not been updated for a specified period—typically from 30 minutes to two hours.

 ## What are the OSPF router types?

The router types configurable in OSPF are:

- **Internal routers**   Have all interfaces in the same area
- **Backbone routers**   May sit on the perimeter of the backbone area or may be a backbone-only router
- **Area border routers**   Have interfaces attached to multiple areas
- **Autonomous Systems Boundary Router**   Can have at least one interface into another autonomous system or can be a router that redistributes static routes into OSPF

 Note: *A router can be more than one router type. If a router interconnects to the backbone and another area, as well as to a non-OSPF network, it would be both an ABR and ASBR.*

 ## How do I configure OSPF area parameters?

Configurable OSPF parameters include authentication, defining stub areas, and assigning specific costs to the default summary route. The command AREA *area-id* AUTHENTICATION enables authentication for an OSPF area. In this command AUTHENTICATION allows password-based protection against unauthorized access to an area.

The command AREA *area-id* STUB defines an area to be a stub area. Stub areas are areas into which information on external routes is not sent. Instead, there is a default external route generated by the area border communication server into the stub area for destinations outside the autonomous system (AS).

The command AREA *area-id* DEFAULT-COST *cost* assigns a specific cost to the default summary route used for the stub area.

How do I configure OSPF on the router?

To enable OSPF you must create an OSPF routing process by specifying the range of IP addresses to be associated with the routing process, and assign area IDs to be associated with that range of IP addresses. The steps to enable OSPF are:

1. Enter global configuration mode.
2. Enable OSPF routing with the command ROUTER OSPF *ospf-process-id*.
3. Define an interface on which OSPF runs, and define the area ID for that interface with the command NETWORK *address wildcard-mask* AREA *area-id*.

Note: *There are no special commands or syntax to configure a router as an ABR. The router assumes this role automatically when it is configured with multiple areas (ABRs) or with multiple routing protocols (OSPF and RIP, or EIGRP). For ASBR routers, static routes to interfaces are redistributed automatically. You must manually redistribute routes from other protocols such as RIP, EIGRP, or a second OSPF process.*

What would be a typical configuration enabling OSPF and redistributing RIP routes?

The sample configuration that follows is a simple OSPF configuration that enables OSPF routing process 9011,

attaches Ethernet 0 to area 0.0.0.0, and redistributes RIP into OSPF, and OSPF into RIP:

```
interface ethernet 0
 ip address 192.168.1.1 255.255.255.0
 ip ospf cost 1
interface ethernet 1
 ip address 192.169.1.1 255.255.255.0
router ospf 9000
 network 192.168.0.0 0.0.255.255 area 0.0.0.0
 redistribute rip metric 1 subnets
router rip
 network 192.169.0.0
 redistribute ospf 9011
 default-metric 1
```

What would be a typical configuration for an OSPF internal router, ABR, and ASBR?

The sample configuration that follows assigns four area IDs to four IP address ranges. In this example, OSPF routing process 112 is initialized, and four OSPF areas are defined: 2, 3, 4, and 0. Areas 2, 3, and 4 mask specific address ranges, while Area 0 enables OSPF for all other networks.

```
router ospf 112
 network 172.38.10.0 0.0.0.255 area 2
 network 172.40.0.0 0.0.255.255 area 3
 network 172.39.30.0 0.0.0.255 area 4
 network 0.0.0.0 255.255.255.255 area 0
```

Interface Ethernet0 is in Area 2:

```
interface ethernet 0
    ip address 172.38.10.3 255.255.255.0
```

Interface Ethernet1 is in Area 3:

```
interface ethernet 1
    ip address 172.40.1.5 255.255.255.0
```

Interface Ethernet2 is in Area 3:

```
interface ethernet 2
    ip address 172.40.2.5 255.255.255.0
```

Interface Ethernet3 is in Area 4:

```
interface ethernet 3
     ip address 172.39.30.7 255.255.255.0
```

Interface Ethernet4 is in Area 0:

```
interface ethernet 4
     ip address 172.39.1.1 255.255.255.0
```

Interface Ethernet5 is in Area 0:

```
interface ethernet 5
     ip address 10.1.0.1 255.255.0.0
```

Each NETWORK AREA router configuration command is evaluated sequentially, so the order of these commands in the configuration is important.

Consider the first NETWORK AREA command. Area ID 2 is configured for the interface on which subnet 172.38.10.0 is located. Assume that a match is determined for interface Ethernet 0. Interface Ethernet 0 is attached to Area 2 only.

The second NETWORK AREA command is evaluated next. For Area 3, the same process is then applied to all interfaces (except interface Ethernet 0). Assume that a match is determined for interface Ethernet 1. OSPF is then enabled for that interface and Ethernet 1 is attached to Area 3.

This process of attaching interfaces to OSPF areas continues for all NETWORK AREA commands. Note that the last NETWORK AREA command in this example is a special case. With this command, all available interfaces (not explicitly attached to another area) are attached to Area 0.

What are the five OSPF packet types?

The five OSPF packet types are:

- **Hello** Sent at regular intervals to establish and maintain neighbor relationships
- **Database description** Describe the contents of the topological database, and are exchanged when an adjacency is being initialized

- **Link state request** Request pieces of a neighbor's topological database. They are exchanged after a router has discovered (through examination of database description packets) that parts of its topological database are out of date.

- **Link state update** Are responses to link-state request packets. They are also used for the regular dispersal of LSAs. Several LSAs may be included within a single packet.

- **Link state acknowledgment** Acknowledge link-state update packets. Link-state update packets must be explicitly acknowledged to ensure that link-state flooding throughout an area is a reliable process.

What are LSAs and why are they important?

LSAs are link-state advertisements that can be included in the link-state update (LSU), which is the routing information update sent by, and received from, OSPF routers. There are four types of LSAs:

- **Router links advertisements (RLA)** Describe the collected states of the router's links to a specific area. A router sends an RLA for each area to which it belongs. RLAs are flooded throughout the entire area, and no further.

- **Network links advertisements (NLA)** Describe all the routers that are attached to a multiaccess network, and are flooded throughout the area containing the multiaccess network.

- **Summary links advertisements (SLA)** Summarize routes to destinations outside an area, but within the AS. They are generated by area border routers, and are flooded throughout the area. Only intra-area routes are advertised into the backbone. Both intra-area and inter-area routes are advertised into the other areas.

● **AS external links advertisements**   Describe a route to a destination that is external to the AS. AS external links advertisements are originated by AS boundary routers. This type of advertisement is the only type that is forwarded everywhere in the AS; all others are forwarded only within specific areas.

How many metrics can OSPF support?

OSPF supports one or more metrics. If only one metric is used, it is considered to be arbitrary, and TOS (type of service) is not supported. If more than one metric is used, TOS is optionally supported through the use of a separate metric (and, therefore, a separate routing table) for each of the eight combinations created by the three IP TOS bits (the delay, throughput, and reliability bits). For example, if the IP TOS bits specify low delay, low throughput, and high reliability, OSPF calculates routes to all destinations based on this TOS designation.

Note: *TOS (type of service), also called COS (class of service), is used by subarea nodes to determine the optimal route to establish a given session. A COS definition comprises a virtual route number and a transmission priority field.*

IGRP AND EIGRP

What is IGRP?

IGRP can be considered a distance vector routing protocol, although it also has been referred to as a hybrid routing protocol. It has several features that differentiate it from other distance vector protocols, such as RIP. Some of these features include scalability, fast response to networks changes, sophisticated metric, and multiple paths.

Note: *IGRP does not support variable-length subnet masking.*

What are the metrics used by IGRP to determine best path?

IGRP does not have RIP's hop-count limitation. It uses a composite metric to select the best path, including such elements as:

- **Bandwidth** The smallest bandwidth between source and destination
- **Delay** The cumulative interface delay along the path
- **Reliability** Based on keepalives, the worst reliability between source and destination
- **Loading** Based on bits per second, the worst load on a link between source and destination
- **Maximum transmission unit (MTU)** The smallest MTU value in the path

---

Tip: *The path that has the smallest metric value is the best route. By default, only bandwidth and delay are used in the IGRP metric.*

How do I configure IGRP?

To configure IGRP, use the following command:

```
Router igrp autonomous-system
network network-number
```

For example:

- **ROUTER IGRP 110** Enables the IGRP process for AS 110
- **NETWORK 10.0.0.0** Associates network 10.0.0.0 with IGRP routing
- **NETWORK 128.185.0.0** Associates network 128.185.0.0 with IGRP routing

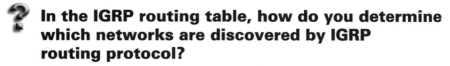

In the IGRP routing table, how do you determine which networks are discovered by IGRP routing protocol?

The networks discovered by the IGRP routing protocol are preceded by the code letter I. The networks that are directly connected to the router and have been configured with the network command are preceded by the code letter C.

What command displays the IGRP routing updates transactions sent from the router?

The DEBUG IP IGRP TRANSACTION command displays the IGRP routing updates transactions sent from the router.

How do I control traffic distribution for multiple routes to the same destination?

You can use the TRAFFIC-SHARE router configuration command to control traffic distribution among routes, when there are multiple routes for the same destination network that have different costs.

```
traffic-share {balanced | min}
```

To disable this function, use the NO form of the command:

```
[no] traffic share {balanced | min}
```

In these commands:

- **balanced**   Distributes traffic proportionately to the ratios of the metrics
- **min**   Uses routes that have minimum costs

Tip: *By default traffic is distributed proportionately to the ratios of the metrics.*

This command applies to IGRP and Enhanced IGRP routing protocols only. With the default setting, routes that have higher metrics represent less-preferable routes and get less traffic. Configuring TRAFFIC-SHARE MIN causes the Cisco IOS software to divide traffic only among the routes with the best metric. Other routes will remain in the routing table, but will receive no traffic.

In the following example, only routes of minimum cost will be used:

```
router igrp 4
traffic-share min
```

What is Enhanced IGRP?

EIGRP takes advantage of link-state and distance vector routing protocols. It is a Cisco proprietary protocol that is defined as a hybrid.

In addition to TCP/IP, what other protocols does EIGRP support?

EIGRP supports IPX from Novell, AppleTalk, and TCP/IP, all at the same time.

What are the advantages of using EIGRP?

Several advantages of using EIGRP are:

- **Rapid Convergence** Using the Diffusing Update Algorithm (DUAL). Each router configured to use EIGRP stores backup routes (only when feasible) to adapt quickly to alternate routes. If no alternative exists, EIGRP will query its neighbors to discover one. These queries are forwarded until an alternative router is found or it is determined that no alternative path exists.

- **Reduced bandwidth usage** Due to the fact that EIGRP does not make periodic updates. It sends partial updates when the path or metric changes for that route.

The DUAL algorithm sends an update (rather than the entire table) about only the link that changes, and only to the routers that need it.

● **Multiple network layer support**   EIGRP supports AppleTalk, IP, and Novell NetWare with the use of protocol-dependent modules (PDM), which are responsible for network layer-specific protocol requirements.

What are the components of EIGRP and what are their responsibilities?

The components of Enhanced IGRP are:

● **Neighbor discovery/recovery**   Routers use this process to learn about routers that exist on directly attached networks. This process is also used by routers to determine when neighbors become unreachable or inoperative. Router discovery/recovery is achieved with low overhead through the use of small hello packets. When hello packets are received, the router determines that a neighbor is alive and functioning. Once this status is determined, the neighboring routers can exchange routing information.

● **The reliable transport protocol**   This protocol is used to ensure that EIGRP packets sent to all neighbors are guaranteed and in order. Intermixed transmission of multicast and unicast packets is also supported. Reliable transmission is not needed for all Enhanced IGRP packets. Some packets, such as update packets requiring acknowledgment, require reliability. In the case of other packets, such as hello packets sent to neighbors on a multiaccess network with multicast capability, reliability is not necessary. Instead, Enhanced IGRP will send a single multicast hello with an indication in the packet informing the receivers that the packet need not be acknowledged. Reliable transport has a provision to send multicast packets quickly when there are unacknowledged packets pending. This will ensure that

convergence time remains low when varying-speed links exist.

● **The DUAL finite-state machine** This is the decision process used for all route computations. Routes that are advertised by all neighbors are tracked. Distance information (AKA metric) is used by DUAL to determine the most efficient, loop-free paths. Routes selected by DUAL are inserted into a routing table based on feasible successors. A neighboring router that has the least-cost path to a destination guaranteed not to be part of a routing loop is defined as a successor. A recomputation occurs when no feasible successors exist, but there are neighbors advertising the destination. This process determines a new successor. The convergence time is affected by the time it takes to recompute the route. Recomputation should be avoided even though the process is not processor-intensive. DUAL will test for feasible successors when a change in topology occurs. If feasible successors are found, it will use any it finds in order to avoid unnecessary recomputation.

● **Protocol-dependent modules** These are used for tasks that are network layer protocol-specific. The Enhanced IGRP module is responsible for sending and receiving Enhanced IGRP packets encapsulated in IP. It is also responsible for parsing Enhanced IGRP packets and informing DUAL of the new information received. DUAL is used to make routing decisions within IP Enhanced IGRP, with the results stored in the IP routing table. Redistributing routes that are learned by other routing protocols is handled by IP Enhanced IGRP.

What commands are used to monitor and display routing statistics about the EIGRP processes?

Various routing statistics can be displayed by entering:

```
show ip eigrp interfaces [interface] [as-number]
```

which displays information about interfaces configured for Enhanced IGRP,

```
show ip eigrp neighbors [type number]
```

which displays the IP Enhanced IGRP-discovered neighbors,

```
show ip eigrp topology
[autonomous-system-number |[[ip-address] mask]]
```

which displays the IP Enhanced IGRP topology table for a given process, and

```
show ip eigrp traffic [autonomous-system-number]
```

which displays the number of packets sent and received for all or a specified IP Enhanced IGRP process.

How do I configure IPX using EIGRP?

The following example configures two interfaces for Enhanced IGRP routing in autonomous system 10:

```
ipx routing
interface ethernet 0
ipx network 5
interface serial 0
ipx network 15
ipx router eigrp 10
network 5
network 15
```

How do I use EIGRP to control the bandwidth used by SAP updates?

The following configuration assumes that an Ethernet interface has neighbors that are all configured for Enhanced IGRP. You want to reduce the bandwidth used by SAP packets by sending SAP updates incrementally. To do this, you would configure the interface as follows:

```
ipx routing
interface ethernet 0
ipx network 5
ipx sap-incremental eigrp 10
interface serial 0
ipx network 15
ipx router eigrp 10
network 5
network 15
```

If you wanted to send only incremental SAP updates on a serial line that is configured for Enhanced IGRP, but periodic RIP updates, use the following commands:

```
ipx routing
interface ethernet 0
ipx network 5
interface serial 0
ipx network 15
ipx sap-incremental eigrp 10 rsup-only
ipx router eigrp 10
network 5
network 15
```

BGP AND EGP

 ## What are BGP and EGP?

Exterior Gateway Protocol (EGP) was used to connect two autonomous systems together. It separates each routing domain from the other. EGP has been replaced with Border Gateway Protocol (BGP).

The Border Gateway Protocol's primary function is to exchange network reachability information with other BGP systems, including information about the list of autonomous system paths. This information can be used to construct a graph of autonomous system connectivity, from which routing loops can be pruned, and with which autonomous system-level policy decisions can be enforced.

 Note: *BGP Version 4 supports classless interdomain routing (CIDR), which lets you reduce the size of your routing tables by creating aggregate routes, resulting in supernets. CIDR eliminates the concept of network classes within BGP and supports the advertising of IP prefixes. OSPF, Enhanced IGRP, ISIS-IP, and RIP can carry CIDR routes.*

What are the types of BGP sessions?

BGP sessions are carried by TCP and support two types of sessions between a router and its neighbor:

- **External BGP (EBGP)**   Occurs between routers in two different autonomous systems. These routers normally share a common link and subnet.

- **Internal BGP (IBGP)**   Occurs between routers in the same autonomous system. It is used to coordinate and synchronize routing policy. Neighbors can be located anywhere in the autonomous system.

"The initial data flow is the entire BGP routing table. Incremental updates are sent as the routing table changes. BGP does not require periodic refresh of the entire BGP routing table. Therefore, a BGP speaker must retain the current version of the entire BGP routing table of all of its peers for the duration of the connection. KeepAlive messages are sent periodically to ensure liveness of the connection. Notification messages are sent in response to errors or special conditions. If a condition encounters an error condition, a notification message is sent and the connection is closed."

—RFC 1654, BGP Operations

 ## How does BGP select paths?

A single autonomous path is selected by the BGP process to use and be passed along to the router's BGP peers. The default BGP implementation used in Cisco routers is reasonable, but can be overridden through the use of administrative weights. The algorithm for path selection is as follows:

1. Do not consider the next hop if not accessible.

2. Larger administrative weights are considered first.

3. The route with higher local preference is used if routes have the same administrative weight.

4. The route the local router originates is used, if the routes have the same local preference.

5. The shorter autonomous system path is preferred.

6. The lowest origin code is preferred if the routes have the same path length.

7. The lowest multiexit discriminator (MED) is preferred when the origin codes are the same and all the paths are from the same autonomous system.

8. External paths are preferred over internal if the MEDs are the same.

9. The closest neighbor path is preferred when IGP synchronization is disabled and only internal paths remain.

10. The lowest IP address value for the BGP router ID is preferred.

 ## How do I enable BGP on the router?

To enable BGP, enter the command:

```
router bgp autonomous-system
```

in which *autonomous-system* identifies the local autonomous system.

To allow BGP advertisement of an IGP route if it is already in the IP table, enter the command:

```
network network-number
```

in which *network-number* identifies an IP network to be advertised by BGP.

To activate a BGP session, enter the command:

```
neighbor ip-address remote-as autonomous system
```

In this command:

● **ip address**   Identifies the peer router

● **autonomous-system**   Identifies the autonomous system of the peer router

 Tip: *If this is the same as the local autonomous system, the session will be internal; if the autonomous systems are different, the session will be external.*

What would be a typical configuration of BGP neighbors?

In the following example, a BGP router is assigned to autonomous system 103, and two networks are listed as originating in the autonomous system. Then the addresses of three remote routers (and their autonomous systems) are listed. The router being configured will share information about networks 192.168.0.0 and 209.56.74.0 with the neighbor routers. The first router listed is in a different autonomous system; the second NEIGHBOR command specifies an internal neighbor (with the same autonomous system number) at address 192.168.234.2; and the third NEIGHBOR command specifies a neighbor on a different autonomous system.

```
router bgp 103
network 192.168.0.0
network 192.31.7.0
neighbor 192.168.200.1 remote-as 171
neighbor 192.168.234.2 remote-as 103
neighbor 150.136.64.19 remote-as 69
```

What commands monitor and display BGP statistics?

You can display specific statistics such as the contents of BGP routing tables, caches, and databases. Information provided can be used to determine resource utilization and solve network problems. You can also display information about node reachability and discover the routing path your device's packets are taking through the network. To display various routing statistics, enter the following commands:

```
show ip bgp cidr-only
```

which displays all BGP routes that contain subnet and supernet network masks,

```
show ip bgp community community-number [exact]
```

which displays routes that belong to the specified communities,

```
show ip bgp community-list community-list-number [exact]
```

which displays routes that are permitted by the community list,

```
show ip bgp filter-list access-list-number
```

which displays routes that are matched by the specified autonomous system path access list,

```
show ip bgp inconsistent-as
```

which displays the routes with inconsistent originating autonomous systems,

```
show ip bgp regexp regular-expression
```

which displays the routes that match the specified regular expression entered on the command line,

```
show ip bgp [network] [network-mask] [subnets]
```

which displays the contents of the BGP routing table,

```
show ip bgp neighbors [address]
```

which displays detailed information on the TCP and BGP connections to individual neighbors,

```
show ip bgp neighbors [address] [received-routes | routes |
advertised-routes | paths regular-expression | dampened-routes]
```

which displays routes learned from a particular BGP neighbor,

```
show ip bgp paths
```

which displays all BGP paths in the database,

```
show ip bgp peer-group [tag] [summary]
```

which displays information about BGP peer groups, and

```
show ip bgp summary
```

which displays the status of all BGP connections.

Can the incoming data from a BGP neighbor be modified?

The following configuration example shows how you can use route maps to modify incoming data from a neighbor. Any route received from 192.168.1.1 that matches the filter parameters set in autonomous system access list 200 will have its weight set to 200 and its local preference set to 250, and it will be accepted.

```
router bgp 156
neighbor 192.168.1.1 route-map fix-weight in
neighbor 192.168.1.1 remote-as 1
route-map fix-weight permit 10
match as-path 200
set local-preference 250
set weight 200
ip as-path access-list 200 permit ^690$
ip as-path access-list 200 permit ^1800
```

Since there are different versions of BGP, how do I configure the necessary version number?

By default, BGP sessions begin using BGP version 4 and negotiate downward to earlier versions if necessary. To prevent negotiation and force the BGP version used to communicate with a neighbor, perform the following task in router configuration mode:

```
neighbor {ip-address | peer-group-name} version value
```

This command specifies the BGP version to use when communicating with a neighbor.

IP MULTICAST

What protocols are supported by IP multicast routing?

The Cisco router supports the following protocols to implement IP multicast routing:

- **Internet Group Management Protocol (IGMP)** Used between hosts on a LAN and the router(s) on that LAN to track multicast groups of which the hosts are members.

- **Protocol Independent Multicast (PIM)** Used between routers so that they can track which multicast packets to forward to each other and to their directly connected LANs.

- **Distance Vector Multicast Routing Protocol (DVMRP)** The protocol used on the MBONE (the multicast backbone of the Internet). The Cisco IOS software supports PIM-to-DVMRP interaction.

- **Cisco Group Management Protocol (CGMP)** A protocol used on routers connected to Cisco Catalyst switches to perform tasks similar to those performed by IGMP.

Chapter 3

Configuring Enhanced IGRP (EIGRP)

Answer Topics!

Configuring Enhanced IGRP (EIGRP) @ a Glance

Enhanced Interior Gateway Routing Protocol (EIGRP), developed by Cisco, is an enhanced version of Interior Gateway Routing Protocol (IGRP). Although it is based on a distance vector algorithm similar to IGRP, it provides better convergence through the use of the Diffusing Update Algorithm (DUAL). The implementation of DUAL allows for a loop-free environment and also allows network elements to synchronize with each other simultaneously. This chapter describes configuration of a router in an EIGRP network. It summarizes various commands used to configure and monitor EIGRP router performance.

This chapter explores the following areas:

- **EIGRP IP Support** describes the features offered by EIGRP and shows how routers can be configured in an IP environment.

- **Concepts and Terminology of EIGRP** defines key terms used in describing the operation and components of EIGRP.

- **Basic Components of EIGRP** describes the components included in EIGRP that interoperate to implement the routing protocol.

- **EIGRP IPX SAP Support** describes how Service Advertisement Protocol (SAP) is supported by EIGRP in a Novell IPX network environment.

- **Monitoring EIGRP** focuses on network monitoring activities and provides examples of how router performance can be monitored.

EIGRP IP SUPPORT

What are the features offered by the Enhanced IGRP?

- **Increased network width** Whereas IP RIP is limited to 15 hops, the largest possible number of hops in an EIGRP environment is 224

- **Automatic redistribution of routes** EIGRP routes can be redistributed into IGRP, and IGRP routes can also be redistributed into EIGRP

Is EIGRP a distance vector or a link-state routing protocol?

EIGRP adds several new features not found in any other routing protocol and improves those that are present in others. EIGRP has been described as a hybrid routing protocol because it shares aspects of the distance vector protocols and the link-state protocols. For instance, EIGRP sends updates only to directly connected neighbors like traditional distance vector protocols, but does so in a reliable fashion, which is a feature of the link-state protocols.

Like the distance vector protocols, EIGRP sends route information rather than link-state information in its updates, but the information need not be sent to all routers in an autonomous system. Instead, EIGRP introduces the concept of a diffusing routing calculation that shares detailed information regarding the best loop-free path to a given destination, and up to five alternate loop-free paths only with directly connected neighboring routers. The Diffusing Update Algorithm reduces the quantity of routing protocol overhead traffic to a fraction of that sent by older distance vector protocols.

EIGRP looks like a distance vector protocol in its use of the split-horizon rule to control transmission of routing protocol information back to the originator of the information. Split-horizon is a technique that prevents routing loops and the "count to infinity" problem inherent in early distance vector protocols.

Like link-state protocols, EIGRP avoids the "ships in the night" routing problem by sending routing protocol information in reliable fashion. The protocol uses a proprietary mechanism to guarantee ordered delivery of some of its messages. The EIGRP update and query/reply packets are sent using Cisco's Reliable Transport Protocol (RTP), which guarantees sequenced delivery of the packet through an acknowledgment of sequence numbers included in the packet. Other packet types—the hello packet and the acknowledgment packet—are sent unreliably by RTP.

CONCEPTS AND TERMINOLOGY OF EIGRP

Like any complex protocol, EIGRP uses a number of terms in specific ways to describe its operation and components. In this section, we will define some of the terms routinely tossed about by students of EIGRP.

What is a successor router?

A successor is any router that is one hop closer to some destination network. Think of a successor router as the next hop along the path to some destination.

What is distance?

Routing protocols in general represent the topology of an internetwork by the metric associated with each network. Using this representation, the protocol makes decisions about the best path to choose when forwarding packets to any given destination. That is, the metric allows the protocol to compare two or more possible paths to some destination and choose the best path. The EIGRP protocol (and its predecessor, IGRP) uses a composite metric called distance to represent an internetwork's topology.

Distance describes the desirability of a particular path between a given router and some destination network. It is defined as a weighted-sum of five factors:

- Bandwidth
- Delay
- Reliability
- Load
- MTU
- Hop count

 What is the bandwidth component of EIGRP distance?

The bandwidth factor in the metric is actually the minimum bandwidth in the path between the router (where this metric calculation is carried out) and the destination network itself. LAN interfaces know their bandwidth automatically. Serial interfaces are a bit more problematic. Since the physical bandwidth for a serial interface may exceed the committed information rate (CIR) provisioned by your carrier, the physical clock rate on the interface is not always an appropriate bandwidth for the purposes of metric calculation. A serial link running at T1 or below clock rate always sees 1.544 Mbps bandwidth regardless of what the CIR or physical clock rate might be. Since EIGRP metric calculation depends to a great degree on correct link bandwidth parameters, and since the calculated metric determines how EIGRP forwards traffic, it makes sense to ensure that an appropriate metric is chosen. Figure 3-1 shows how the BANDWIDTH interface command is used to make this happen.

 What is the delay component of EIGRP distance?

The delay characteristic associates each router interface type with a typical delay value and sums these delays across the path from source router to destination network. Each unit of the delay parameter itself represents 39.1 nanoseconds of delay. Some sample default interface delays that you should be aware of are shown in Table 3-1.

Interface	Bandwidth	Delay
Ethernet	10 Mbps	25600 (1 ms)
Serial T1	1.544 Mbps	512000 (20,000 ms)
Serial DS0	64 kbps	512000 (20,000 ms)
Serial DS0	56 kbps	512000 (20,000 ms)

Table 3-1 Typical Interface Delay Values

Figure 3-1 Configuring link bandwidth for EIGRP metric calculation

Notice that all the serial interface default delay values are the same. It turns out that all serial interfaces that run at E1 speed (2.048 Mbps) or less are treated the same in terms of delay.

What is the reliability component of EIGRP distance?

If you wish, EIGRP can adjust the distance metric dynamically based on the reliability of updates arriving on router interfaces. The reliability component of distance is represented in an eight-bit counter and is interpreted as the numerator of a fraction whose denominator is always 255. Thus, a perfectly reliable interface would be represented with a reliability component of 255, while a 50 percent reliable interface would be represented with a reliability component of 127.

 ## What is the load component of EIGRP distance?

Load, like reliability, is an optional component of metric that can be used to adjust the distance metric for an EIGRP route. It resembles the reliability component in another way as well. Load is also represented by the numerator of a fraction whose denominator is 255. A saturated router would have a load component of 255, while a lightly loaded router would have a component of 1. The load parameter figures into the EIGRP metric calculation in such a way that a heavily loaded router makes a certain path through an internetwork less desirable.

 ## How is EIGRP distance calculated?

By default, only two of the four EIGRP distance components are used in the metric calculation. Unless you have changed them, the load and reliability factors are not part of the EIGRP metric. The load and reliability components are excluded by introducing constant multipliers in the distance formula, and setting the multipliers associated with them to 0.

The formula for EIGRP distance calculation looks like this:

$$\text{Metric} = 256 \times ((K1 \times \text{Bandwidth}) + ((K2 \times \text{Bandwidth})/(256 - \text{Load})) + (K3 \times \text{Delay}))$$

If you wish to include the reliability as part of the metric, the "K" constant multiplier is set to 1 and the formula becomes:

$$\text{Distance} = \text{Metric} \times (K5 / (\text{Reliability} + K4))$$

Otherwise, the distance is given by:

$$\text{Distance} = \text{Metric}$$

You can modify the default EIGRP constant multipliers using the command:

```
Router(config-router)#metric weights 0 1 0 1 0 0
```

In this command, the first parameter represents the type of service (ToS, always set to 0), and the remaining five represent the constants K1–K5. Figure 3-2 shows you how to use the IOS Help facility to explore the options of the METRIC WEIGHTS command.

What is feasible distance?

The feasible distance (FD) is a parameter used by the DUAL algorithm to determine which of many possible routes to a particular destination network might include a routing loop. FD is defined as the current best distance from the calculating EIGRP router to the particular destination network.

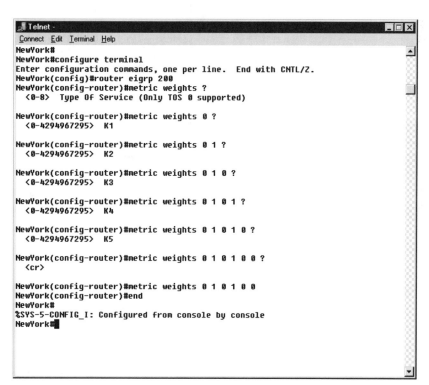

Figure 3-2   EIGRP distance constants and the METRIC WEIGHTS command

 ### What are the feasibility criteria?

The feasibility criteria comprise a test performed by EIGRP on alternative routes to a destination network. The DUAL algorithm compares the metric advertised by routers offering alternative paths to a destination network and allows immediate fail-over to an alternate route whose advertised distance is less than the feasible distance.

All alternative paths are compared to FD. If another router advertises to us a distance smaller than the FD, it is safe to assume that this alternate path could not possibly include our router. If it did, the advertised distance would be larger than the FD. If the distance advertised to us is less than our current FD to some destination, then EIGRP assumes the path does not pass through our router. Because the path does not pass through our own router, it is guaranteed loop-free.

BASIC COMPONENTS OF EIGRP

EIGRP includes several components that interoperate to implement the routing protocol. The components include a neighbor discovery and recovery process, the Reliable Transport Protocol, the Diffusing Update Algorithm, and several protocol-dependent modules.

 ### What is the neighbor discovery and recovery process?

A neighbor discovery/recovery process is one of the components of EIGRP. It is responsible for determining which routers receive EIGRP update information from a given router. The process is implemented using a Hello protocol to establish a neighbor relationship between two directly connected routers. In a multiaccess network environment such as Ethernet, a full mesh of neighbor relationships exists. Contrast this with the use of designated router and backup designated router roles as implemented in OSPF.

The hello packet is sent at approximately five-second intervals except on nonbroadcast multiaccess (NBMA) WAN interfaces, ATM switched virtual circuits, and ISDN Primary

Rate Interface links, where it is sent at approximately 60-second intervals. The packet is sent to the multicast destination address 224.0.0.10 to minimize its impact on non-Cisco routers or host computers that may hear it. It is sent with the IP Time To Live (TTL) field set to a value of 1 in order to prevent it from being incorrectly forwarded by non-Cisco routers. When an EIGRP router receives a hello message on one of its interfaces, it notes the holdtime specified by that neighbor. This is the period of time that the receiving router will maintain the neighbor relationship in the absence of subsequent hello messages. If the neighbor fails to send another hello message within the holdtime period, it is declared down and update messages are sent.

The neighbor relationship is key to implementation of reliability in EIGRP. When update or query/reply packets are transmitted, the sending router waits for each neighbor to respond in acknowledgement. Should a neighbor fail to respond, the sender declares the neighbor down and removes all routes advertised by that neighbor. The Active timer parameter controls how long the sending router waits for a reply message after sending a query. Early implementations set the Active timer to one minute by default. In EIGRP version 2, the default Active timer is three minutes.

What is RTP?

The process that sends messages for EIGRP is called the Reliable Transport Protocol. It is another component of EIGRP. RTP implements an OSI Layer 4-like service that allows EIGRP to transmit information over IP, IPX, or AppleTalk as appropriate to the topology in question. For packets that are sent reliably, RTP includes in the EIGRP packet header a pair of sequence numbers. In the first, EIGRP writes a number representing the place of the packet in the sequence. In the second, EIGRP writes a number representing the last packet received from a particular neighbor. Using this information and the neighbor table, RTP can reschedule transmission of lost packets and detect packets that may arrive out of order.

 What are protocol-dependant modules?

The EIGRP components that allow one routing process to maintain routing information for IP, IPX, and AppleTalk are called the protocol-dependent modules. Each of the three routed protocols that EIGRP manages uses a different scheme to number the networks in an internetwork. In IP for instance, the network plus the subnet portion of a 32-bit IP address distinguishes a particular piece of wire from all others in the internetwork. With IPX a 32-bit, fixed-length network number performs the same function. AppleTalk uses one or more 16-bit cable numbers grouped in sequential order to identify a particular physical network. It is the responsibility of the appropriate protocol-dependant module to create the proper updates, queries, and acknowledgements when routing traffic for a particular routed protocol.

 What is DUAL?

A third EIGRP component, the Diffusing Update Algorithm, accounts in large part for the fast convergence time relative to other routing protocols. Using DUAL, the routing protocol maintains two tables: a neighbor table and a topology table. The neighbors are learned from hello packets. The topology table represents all the networks that exist in the autonomous system. It is built from update packets sent by neighbors. The successor table lists, for a given destination network, all the neighboring routers that can provide a guaranteed loop-free alternate path to the destination network. These data structures give EIGRP the capability, in many cases, to choose immediately an alternate path to some destination network, should we experience a failure of the primary path. Because of DUAL, convergence times are close to the hello interval for most internetwork topologies.

 How does DUAL work?

The central premise of DUAL is that a router may use an alternate path to any destination when a primary path fails, so long as the alternate path can be guaranteed loop-free.

When this criterion is satisfied, the algorithm considers it feasible to converge immediately on a new routing solution without first informing other routers of its decision to do so. In fact, if the newly converged routing solution does not specifically change the calculated distance to reach the destination network in question, the router need never inform its neighbors about the new routing solution.

Any one of several events can cause EIGRP to compute a new routing solution to reach some destination network.

● Receipt of an update message that changes the distance to the destination network

● A neighboring router declared down because its hello messages do not arrive

● A change in a local link's distance

● Receipt of query or reply messages

EIGRP first performs a local computation. In the local computation, each possible path to the destination in question is evaluated for feasibility. If an alternate route meets the feasibility criteria (which is to say, the alternate path can be guaranteed not part of a routing loop), EIGRP may immediately begin to use it for forwarding traffic. In the local computation, no traffic need be sent to neighboring routers, so we consider the route to have remained passive throughout the computation.

If no feasible alternate path can be found, it is not a certainty that a loop-free alternate path does not exist. An alternate successor router may simply have a slower link in its path to the destination, or there may be more hops in the alternate path than in the preferred path. Consider Figure 3-3, for example. Router Zanker provides two alternate paths from router Tasman to router Frisco, should the more direct paths fail. Since router Tasman, using the feasibility criteria, cannot guarantee that an alternate path through Zanker will be loop-free, it must actively query Zanker to ensure that this is the case.

When a router makes a route active, it sends a query message to all neighbors listed in the topology table and

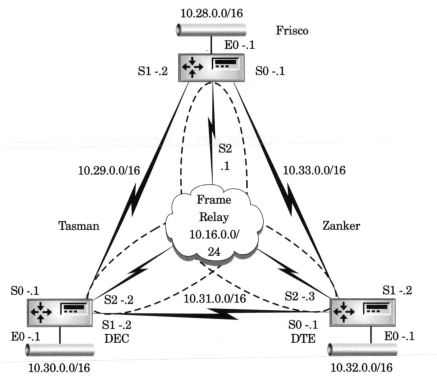

Figure 3-3 Example EIGRP topology

requests their best distance to the listed destination network. Each neighbor that hears the query performs a local computation in an effort to determine if it has a feasible successor to the destination. If so, the neighbor formulates a reply message and sends it to the requesting router. If not, the neighbor makes the route active and sends a query to all of its neighbors.

The original requesting router waits for reply messages from all neighbors for a period of three minutes by default. This period, called the active time, imposes a maximum time that a non-responsive router can keep a route in the active state. When the active time expires, the requesting router declares the neighboring router down and uninstalls its relationship.

When all outstanding replies have been received or adjacent neighbors have been declared down, a new route can be chosen and traffic can continue to flow along the path.

 ## How does EIGRP learn routes?

When hello packets are sent by an EIGRP router, the receiver uses them to construct a neighbor table. Later the router will send update packets to inform the neighbor about the networks it can reach and their distance from the sender. This information is incorporated into the topology table. Consider the simple network illustrated in Figure 3-3. Here router Tasman considers routers Frisco and Zanker its neighbors because it hears hello packets arriving over all of its serial interfaces.

When all three routers are configured for EIGRP, router Tasman hears hello messages from routers Frisco and Zanker. Using the information in the hello messages, Tasman will build a neighbor table that looks like Figure 3-4. Because the neighbor relationship is formed interface-by-interface, it is possible for all three of Zanker's serial interfaces to show up

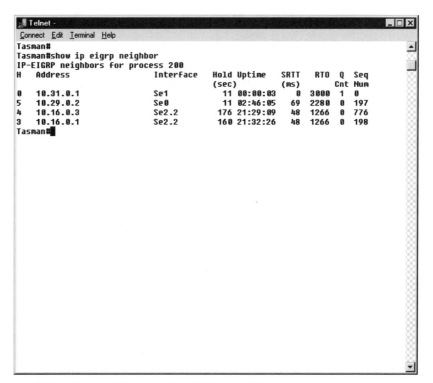

Figure 3-4 Router Tasman's neighbor table

independently in the neighbor table. Contrast this behavior with the OSPF router LSA, which represents all networks connected to a given OSPF router in a single OSPF packet. To see the neighbor table on your routers, use the IOS privileged EXEC mode command:

```
Tasman#show ip eigrp neighbor
```

In Figure 3-5, we use the privileged EXEC mode command:

```
Tasman#show ip eigrp topology
```

This command examines the topology table created through EIGRP update messages, following formation of the neighbor relationship. Each entry in the table represents

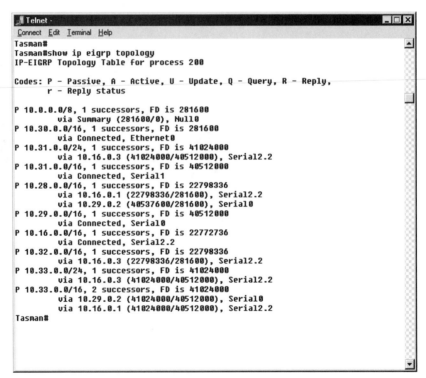

Figure 3-5 Router Tasman's topology table

a subnet in the internetwork. The table lists, for example, subnet 10.28.0.0 as available through neighbor Frisco. Listed along with the subnet we see the network or networks through which the destination subnet can be reached. The topology table stores the feasible distance.

Since the feasible distance is the best distance to a given destination network, this path is also recorded as the EIGRP route to the destination network in question. To see the routing information derived from the EIGRP topology table, use the privileged EXEC mode commands:

```
Tasman#show ip route
```

and

```
Tasman#show ip eigrp route
```

What are the commands necessary to configure an EIGRP routing process?

The command to configure EIGRP is:

```
router eigrp autonomous-system
```

This is a global configuration mode command.

To specify a set of networks for the EIGRP process, the following command is used:

```
network network-number
```

The *network-number* is the ID of the classful summarization of the network directly connected to the router. This includes specific subnets that are configured on matching interfaces. This is a command in router configuration mode.

The following commands will configure a router for EIGRP process 201 and connect networks 173.24.35.0 and 164.121.0.0

```
router eigrp  201
network  173.24.35.0
network  164.121.0.0
```

 Note: *The command NETWORK ALL can be used to configure EIGRP for all networks on a router.*

How do I configure and verify EIGRP in an internetwork?

It is possible to configure EIGRP in an internetwork and verify correct operation in a stepwise fashion, to limit the work required to correct any problems. To illustrate the process, let's establish the slightly more complex internetwork in Figure 3-6.

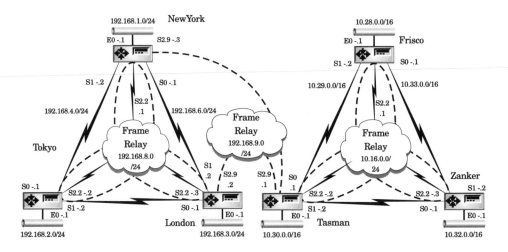

Figure 3-6 Feasible distance prevents routing loops

The following two illustrations show the configuration steps to set up EIGRP on router NewYork:

```
Telnet -                                                          _ □ ×
Connect  Edit  Terminal  Help
router1>
router1>enable
Password:
router1#configure terminal
Enter configuration commands, one per line.  End with CNTL/Z.
router1(config)#hostname NewYork
NewYork(config)#interface e0
NewYork(config-if)#ip address 192.168.1.1 255.255.255.0
NewYork(config-if)#no shutdown
NewYork(config-if)#
%LINEPROTO-5-UPDOWN: Line protocol on Interface Ethernet0, changed state to up
%LINK-3-UPDOWN: Interface Ethernet0, changed state to up
NewYork(config-if)#interface s1
NewYork(config-if)#ip address 192.168.4.2 255.255.255.0
NewYork(config-if)#clock rate 64000
NewYork(config-if)#bandwidth 64
NewYork(config-if)#no shutdown
NewYork(config-if)#
%LINK-3-UPDOWN: Interface Serial1, changed state to up
%LINEPROTO-5-UPDOWN: Line protocol on Interface Serial1, changed state to up
NewYork(config-if)#interface s0
NewYork(config-if)#ip address 192.168.6.1 255.255.255.0
NewYork(config-if)#bandwidth 64
NewYork(config-if)#no shutdown
NewYork(config-if)#
NewYork(config-if)#
%LINK-3-UPDOWN: Interface Serial0, changed state to up
%LINEPROTO-5-UPDOWN: Line protocol on Interface Serial0, changed state to up
NewYork(config-if)#
```

```
Telnet -                                                          _ □ ×
Connect  Edit  Terminal  Help
NewYork(config-if)#
NewYork(config-if)#interface s2
NewYork(config-if)#encapsulation frame-relay
NewYork(config-if)#frame-relay lmi-type ansi
NewYork(config-if)#interface s2.2 multipoint
NewYork(config-subif)#ip address 192.168.8.1 255.255.255.0
NewYork(config-subif)#frame-relay interface-dlci 212
NewYork(config-fr-dlci)#frame-relay interface-dlci 213
NewYork(config-fr-dlci)#interface s2.9
NewYork(config-subif)#ip address 192.168.9.3 255.255.255.0
NewYork(config-subif)#frame-relay interface-dlci 215

NewYork(config-fr-dlci)#no shutdown
NewYork(config-if)#
%FR-5-DLCICHANGE: Interface Serial2 - DLCI 215 state changed to ACTIVE
%FR-5-DLCICHANGE: Interface Serial2 - DLCI 215 state changed to INACTIVE
%LINEPROTO-5-UPDOWN: Line protocol on Interface Serial2.9, changed state to down
NewYork(config-if)#exit
NewYork(config)#router eigrp 200
NewYork(config-router)#network 192.168.1.0
NewYork(config-router)#network 192.168.4.0
NewYork(config-router)#network 192.168.6.0
NewYork(config-router)#network 192.168.8.0
NewYork(config-router)#network 192.168.9.0
NewYork(config-router)#end
NewYork#
%SYS-5-CONFIG_I: Configured from console by console
NewYork#
```

After configuring NewYork, we can view the neighbor table using the privileged EXEC mode command:

```
NewYork#show ip eigrp neighbors
```

We aren't surprised that the neighbor display in Figure 3-7 is empty, since we haven't yet configured the other routers. It is instructive to view the debug reports provided by the IP routing processes. When we use the IOS debug service to see the EIGRP hello packets, we notice that none is coming in.

In Figure 3-8, we look at the simple topology table composed only of the links selected for EIGRP processing by the NETWORK statements shown previously in the

```
Telnet -                                                          _ □ ×
Connect  Edit  Terminal  Help
NewYork#
NewYork#show ip eigrp neighbors
IP-EIGRP neighbors for process 200
NewYork#debug ip packet detail
IP packet debugging is on (detailed)
NewYork#
Jan 23 12:21:49: IP: s=192.168.4.2 (local), d=224.0.0.10 (Serial1), len 60, send
ing broad/multicast, proto=88
Jan 23 12:21:51: IP: s=192.168.1.1 (local), d=224.0.0.10 (Ethernet0), len 60, se
nding broad/multicast, proto=88
Jan 23 12:21:52: IP: s=192.168.6.1 (local), d=224.0.0.10 (Serial0), len 60, send
ing broad/multicast, proto=88
Jan 23 12:21:53: IP: s=192.168.4.2 (local), d=224.0.0.10 (Serial1), len 60, send
ing broad/multicast, proto=88
Jan 23 12:21:55: IP: s=192.168.1.1 (local), d=224.0.0.10 (Ethernet0), len 60, se
nding broad/multicast, proto=88
Jan 23 12:21:57: IP: s=192.168.6.1 (local), d=224.0.0.10 (Serial0), len 60, send
ing broad/multicast, proto=88
Jan 23 12:21:58: IP: s=192.168.4.2 (local), d=224.0.0.10 (Serial1), len 60, send
ing broad/multicast, proto=88
Jan 23 12:22:00: IP: s=192.168.1.1 (local), d=224.0.0.10 (Ethernet0), len 60, se
nding broad/multicast, proto=88
Jan 23 12:22:01: IP: s=192.168.6.1 (local), d=224.0.0.10 (Serial0), len 60, send
ing broad/multicast, proto=88
Jan 23 12:22:03: IP: s=192.168.4.2 (local), d=224.0.0.10 (Serial1), len 60, send
ing broad/multicast, proto=88
Jan 23 12:22:05: IP: s=192.168.1.1 (local), d=224.0.0.10 (Ethernet0), len 60, se
nding broad/multicast, proto=88
Jan 23 12:22:06: IP: s=192.168.6.1 (local), d=224.0.0.10 (Serial0), len 60, send
ing broad/multicast, proto=88
Jan 23 12:22:07: IP: s=192.168.4.2 (local), d=224.0.0.10 (Serial1), len 60, send
ing broad/multicast, proto=88
Jan 23
```

Figure 3-7   Router NewYork's EIGRP neighbors

```
Telnet -                                                          _ □ X
Connect  Edit  Terminal  Help
NewYork#
NewYork#show ip eigrp topology
IP-EIGRP Topology Table for process 200

Codes: P - Passive, A - Active, U - Update, Q - Query, R - Reply,
       r - Reply status

P 192.168.1.0/24, 1 successors, FD is 281600
         via Connected, Ethernet0
P 192.168.4.0/24, 1 successors, FD is 40512000
         via Connected, Serial1
P 192.168.6.0/24, 1 successors, FD is 40512000
         via Connected, Serial0
NewYork#
```

Figure 3-8   Router NewYork's EIGRP topology table

configuration of router NewYork. You notice that the topology
table lists a feasible distance of 281600 for the Ethernet 0,
connected destination network 192.168.1.0/24. This value
represents the metric for the directly connected Ethernet.
When we finish configuring the group of routers shown in
Figure 3-6, we will see many possible routes to any given
network. Each router will compare the distance to each
network offered by various paths and compare it to the FD,
which is the current best distance.

If some newly advertised distance is less than the current
FD, it indicates to the router that the new path cannot
possibly include the current path. Otherwise, the new path
would have a distance greater than the current FD. We will
illustrate this point more fully after we configure router

Tokyo for EIGRP. The following two illustrations show the
configuration statements to set up router Tokyo:

```
router2>
router2>enable
Password:
router2#configure terminal
Enter configuration commands, one per line.  End with CNTL/Z.
router2(config)#hostname Tokyo
Tokyo(config)#interface e0
Tokyo(config-if)#ip address 192.168.2.1 255.255.255.0
Tokyo(config-if)#no shutdown
Tokyo(config-if)#int
%LINEPROTO-5-UPDOWN: Line protocol on Interface Ethernet0, changed state to uper
fa
%LINK-3-UPDOWN: Interface Ethernet0, changed stat
Tokyo(config-if)#interface s0
Tokyo(config-if)#ip address 192.168.4.1 255.255.255.0
Tokyo(config-if)#bandwidth 64
Tokyo(config-if)#no shutdown
Tokyo(config-if)#interface s1
Tokyo(config-if)#ip address 192.168.5.2 255.255.255.0
Tokyo(config-if)#clock rate 64000
Tokyo(config-if)#bandwidth 64
Tokyo(config-if)#no shutdown
Tokyo(config-if)#
Tokyo(config-if)#
```

```
Tokyo(config-if)#
Tokyo(config-if)#interface s2
Tokyo(config-if)#encapsulation frame-relay
Tokyo(config-if)#frame-relay lmi-type ansi
Tokyo(config-if)#interface s2.2 multipoint
Tokyo(config-subif)#ip address 192.168.8.2 255.255.255.0
Tokyo(config-subif)#frame-relay interface-dlci 221
Tokyo(config-fr-dlci)#frame-relay interface-dlci 223
Tokyo(config-fr-dlci)#exit
Tokyo(config)#
Tokyo(config)#router eigrp 200
Tokyo(config-router)#network 192.168.4.0
Tokyo(config-router)#network 192.168.5.0
Tokyo(config-router)#network 192.168.8.0
Tokyo(config-router)#network 192.168.2.0
Tokyo(config-router)#end
Tokyo#
%SYS-5-CONFIG_I: Configured from console by console
Tokyo#
```

With both NewYork and Tokyo configured, we notice a strange thing in the neighbor table. Looking at Figure 3-9, we see that NewYork considers both of Tokyo's interfaces as separate neighbors.

In NewYork's topology table, Figure 3-10, we see that the FD from NewYork to Tokyo's Ethernet (192.168.2.0/24) is given by the Frame Relay interface Serial 2.2. Observe the parameters in parentheses in the lines referring to network 192.168.2.0/24.

```
P 192.168.2.0/24, 1 successors, FD is 22798336
          via 192.168.8.2 (22798336/281600), Serial2.2
          via 192.168.4.1 (40537600/281600), Serial1
```

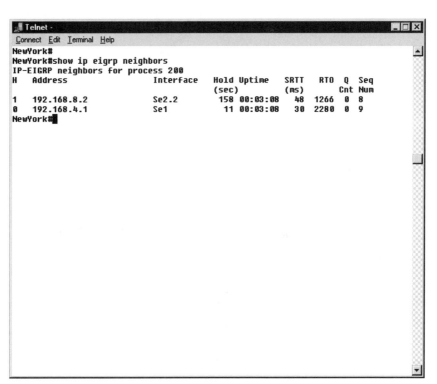

Figure 3-9 EIGRP neighbors' table on router NewYork

```
Telnet -                                                          _ □ X
Connect  Edit  Terminal  Help
NewYork#                                                              ▲
NewYork#show ip eigrp topology
IP-EIGRP Topology Table for process 200

Codes: P - Passive, A - Active, U - Update, Q - Query, R - Reply,
       r - Reply status

P 192.168.8.0/24, 1 successors, FD is 22772736
        via Connected, Serial2
        via Connected, Serial2.2
P 192.168.1.0/24, 1 successors, FD is 281600
        via Connected, Ethernet0
P 192.168.2.0/24, 1 successors, FD is 22798336
        via 192.168.8.2 (22798336/281600), Serial2.2
        via 192.168.4.1 (40537600/281600), Serial1
P 192.168.4.0/24, 1 successors, FD is 40512000
        via Connected, Serial1
NewYork#█
```

Figure 3-10 EIGRP topology table on router NewYork

The Frame Relay link has the lowest metric, so its distance becomes the feasible distance. The metric along this path is the first number in the parentheses, 22798336. The distance advertised by the neighboring router is the second number, 281600.

We observe similar results on router Tokyo as it considers the two communication paths to router NewYork as different neighbors, and treats them as alternative paths. In Figure 3-11 we see the EIGRP neighbor table on router Tokyo.

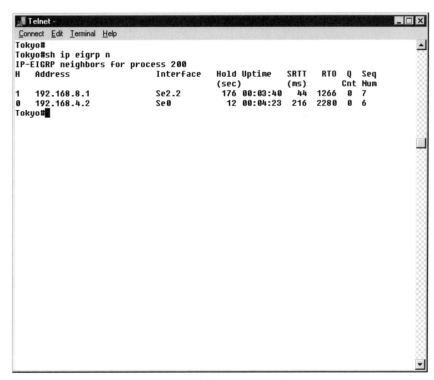

Figure 3-11   EIGRP neighbor table on router Tokyo

Figure 3-12 displays the EIGRP topology table on router Tokyo.

Since the Frame Relay link will be shared by traffic between all the routers, the configured bandwidth on router NewYork's Frame Relay interface should reflect a less desirable path than the other serial interfaces. In Figure 3-13, we correct the situation by reducing the bandwidth on each Frame Relay subinterface to 32 kbps. Now, when we display the topology table we see that the Frame Relay interface no longer has the same distance as the other link to router Tokyo.

```
Telnet -                                                    _ □ ×
Connect  Edit  Terminal  Help
Tokyo#
Tokyo#sh ip eigrp topology
IP-EIGRP Topology Table for process 200

Codes: P - Passive, A - Active, U - Update, Q - Query, R - Reply,
       r - Reply status

P 192.168.8.0/24, 1 successors, FD is 22772736
        via Connected, Serial2.2
P 192.168.1.0/24, 1 successors, FD is 22798336
        via 192.168.8.1 (22798336/281600), Serial2.2
        via 192.168.4.2 (40537600/281600), Serial0
P 192.168.2.0/24, 1 successors, FD is 281600
        via Connected, Ethernet0
P 192.168.4.0/24, 1 successors, FD is 40512000
        via Connected, Serial0
Tokyo#
```

Figure 3-12   EIGRP topology table on router Tokyo

```
Telnet -                                                    _ □ ×
Connect  Edit  Terminal  Help
NewYork#
NewYork#configure terminal
Enter configuration commands, one per line.  End with CNTL/Z.
NewYork(config)#interface s2.2
NewYork(config-subif)#bandwidth 32
NewYork(config-subif)#interface s2.9
NewYork(config-subif)#bandwidth 32
NewYork(config-subif)#end
NewYork#
%SYS-5-CONFIG_I: Configured from console by console
NewYork#show ip eigrp topology
IP-EIGRP Topology Table for process 200

Codes: P - Passive, A - Active, U - Update, Q - Query, R - Reply,
       r - Reply status

P 192.168.8.0/24, 1 successors, FD is 80512000
        via Connected, Serial2.2
P 192.168.1.0/24, 1 successors, FD is 281600
        via Connected, Ethernet0
P 192.168.2.0/24, 1 successors, FD is 22798336
        via 192.168.4.1 (40537600/281600), Serial1
        via 192.168.8.2 (80537600/281600), Serial2.2
P 192.168.4.0/24, 1 successors, FD is 40512000
        via Connected, Serial1
NewYork#
```

Figure 3-13   Corrected bandwidth for Frame Relay subinterfaces

We continue the configuration example with router London. The following two illustrations show the configuration:

```
Telnet -                                                    _ □ ×
Connect  Edit  Terminal  Help
router3>
router3>enable
Password:
router3#configure terminal
Enter configuration commands, one per line.  End with CNTL/Z.
router3(config)#hostname London
London(config)#interface e0
London(config-if)#ip address 192.168.3.1 255.255.255.0
London(config-if)#no shutdown
London(config-if)#i
%LINEPROTO-5-UPDOWN: Line protocol on Interface Ethernet0, changed state to upnt
 s0
%LINK-3-UPDOWN: Interface Ethernet0, changed state
London(config-if)#interface s0
London(config-if)#ip address 192.168.5.1 255.255.255.0
London(config-if)#bandwidth 64
London(config-if)#no shutdown
London(config-if)#
%LINK-3-UPDOWN: Interface Serial0, changed state to up
%LINEPROTO-5-UPDOWN: Line protocol on Interface Serial0, changed state to up
London(config-if)#interface s1
London(config-if)#ip address 192.168.6.2 255.255.255.0
London(config-if)#bandwidth 64
London(config-if)#clock rate 64000
London(config-if)#no shutdown
London(config-if)#
%LINK-3-UPDOWN: Interface Serial1, changed state to up
%LINEPROTO-5-UPDOWN: Line protocol on Interface Serial1, changed state to up
London(config-if)#
```

```
Telnet - 208.244.110.94                                     _ □ ×
Connect  Edit  Terminal  Help
London(config-if)#
London(config-if)#interface s2
London(config-if)#encapsulation frame-relay
London(config-if)#frame-relay lmi-type ansi
London(config-if)#interface s2.2 multipoint
London(config-subif)#ip split-horizon
London(config-subif)#ip address 192.168.8.3 255.255.255.0
London(config-subif)#frame-relay interface-dlci 232
London(config-fr-dlci)#frame-relay interface-dlci 231
London(config-fr-dlci)#interface s2
London(config-if)#interface s2.9
% Incomplete command.

London(config)#interface s2.9 point-to-point
London(config-subif)#ip address 192.168.9.2 255.255.255.0
London(config-subif)#frame-relay interface-dlci 235
London(config-fr-dlci)#
%LINEPROTO-5-UPDOWN: Line protocol on Interface Serial2.9, changed state to down
London(config-fr-dlci)#exit
London(config)#router eigrp 200
London(config-router)#network 192.168.3.0
London(config-router)#network 192.168.6.0
London(config-router)#network 192.168.8.0
London(config-router)#network 192.168.9.0
London(config-router)#end
London#
%SYS-5-CONFIG_I: Configured from console by console
London#
```

Figure 3-14 shows the new EIGRP topology table on router London.

When we configure the Frame Relay link to connect the groups of routers, we see the benefit of using the feasibility criteria for preventing routing loops. Let's look at the example

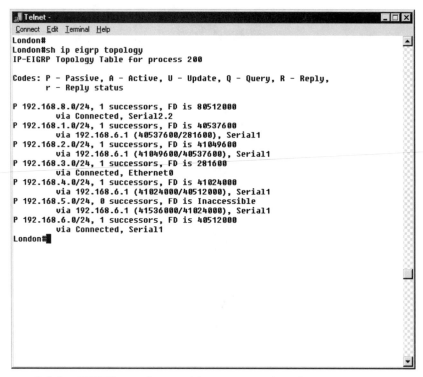

Figure 3-14 EIGRP topology table on router London

of router Tasman, configured as shown in the following two illustrations:

```
Telnet -                                                                    _ □ ✕
Connect  Edit  Terminal  Help
router5>en
Password:
router5#configure terminal
Enter configuration commands, one per line.  End with CNTL/Z.
router5(config)#hostname Tasman
Tasman(config)#interface e0
Tasman(config-if)#ip address 10.30.0.1 255.255.0.0
Tasman(config-if)#no shutdown
Tasman(config-if)#
%LINEPROTO-5-UPDOWN: Line protocol on Interface Ethernet0, changed state to up
Tasman(config-if)#interface s0
Tasman(config-if)#ip address 10.29.0.1 255.255.0.0
Tasman(config-if)#bandwidth 64
Tasman(config-if)#no shutdown
Tasman(config-if)#interface s1
Tasman(config-if)#ip address 10.31.0.2 255.255.0.0
Tasman(config-if)#clock rate 64000
Tasman(config-if)#bandwidth 64
Tasman(config-if)#no shutdown
Tasman(config-if)#
%LINK-3-UPDOWN: Interface Serial1, changed state to down
Tasman(config-if)#█
```

```
Telnet -                                                                    _ □ ✕
Connect  Edit  Terminal  Help
Tasman(config-if)#
Tasman(config-if)#interface s2
Tasman(config-if)#encapsulation frame-relay
Tasman(config-if)#frame-relay lmi-type ansi
Tasman(config-if)#interface s2.2 multipoint
Tasman(config-subif)#ip split-horizon
Tasman(config-subif)#ip address 10.16.0.2 255.255.0.0
Tasman(config-subif)#frame-relay interface-dlci 254
Tasman(config-fr-dlci)#frame-relay interface-dlci 256
Tasman(config-fr-dlci)#interface s2
Tasman(config-if)#interface s2.9 multipoint
Tasman(config-subif)#ip split-horizone
                                      ^
% Invalid input detected at '^' marker.

Tasman(config-subif)#ip split-horizon
Tasman(config-subif)#ip address 192.168.9.1 255.255.255.0
Tasman(config-subif)#frame-relay interface-dlci 251
Tasman(config-fr-dlci)#frame-relay interface-dlci 253
Tasman(config-fr-dlci)#interface s2
Tasman(config-if)#no shutdown
Tasman(config-if)#
%LINEPROTO-5-UPDOWN: Line protocol on Interface Serial2.2, changed state to down
%LINEPROTO-5-UPDOWN: Line protocol on Interface Serial2.9, changed state to down
%LINK-3-UPDOWN: Interface Serial2, changed state to up
%LINEPROTO-5-UPDOWN: Line protocol on Interface Serial2.9, changed state to up
%LINEPROTO-5-UPDOWN: Line protocol on Interface Serial2.2, changed state to up
Tasman(config)#
Tasman(config)#
Tasman(config)#router eigrp 200
Tasman(config-router)#network 192.168.9.0
Tasman(config-router)#network 10.0.0.0
Tasman(config-router)#end
Tasman#
```

After configuring router Tasman, we can observe the operation of the feasibility criteria in Figure 3-15. Notice that the only duplicate routes accepted into the topology table are those with identical distance metrics.

```
Telnet -                                                            _ □ ✕
Connect  Edit  Terminal  Help

Tasman#sh ip eigrp top
IP-EIGRP Topology Table for process 200

Codes: P - Passive, A - Active, U - Update, Q - Query, R - Reply,
       r - Reply status

P 10.0.0.0/8, 1 successors, FD is 281600
          via Summary (281600/0), Null0
P 10.30.0.0/16, 1 successors, FD is 281600
          via Connected, Ethernet0
P 10.31.0.0/16, 1 successors, FD is 40512000
          via Connected, Serial1
P 10.29.0.0/16, 1 successors, FD is 40512000
          via Connected, Serial0
P 192.168.8.0/24, 2 successors, FD is 81024000
          via 192.168.9.3 (81024000/80512000), Serial2.9
          via 192.168.9.2 (81024000/80512000), Serial2.9
P 192.168.9.0/24, 1 successors, FD is 22772736
          via Connected, Serial2.9
P 192.168.1.0/24, 1 successors, FD is 22798336
          via 192.168.9.3 (22798336/281600), Serial2.9
P 192.168.2.0/24, 1 successors, FD is 41049600
          via 192.168.9.3 (41049600/40537600), Serial2.9
P 192.168.3.0/24, 1 successors, FD is 22798336
          via 192.168.9.2 (22798336/281600), Serial2.9
P 192.168.4.0/24, 1 successors, FD is 41024000
          via 192.168.9.3 (41024000/40512000), Serial2.9
P 192.168.5.0/24, 1 successors, FD is 41536000
          via 192.168.9.3 (41536000/41024000), Serial2.9
P 192.168.6.0/24, 2 successors, FD is 41024000
          via 192.168.9.3 (41024000/40512000), Serial2.9
          via 192.168.9.2 (41024000/40512000), Serial2.9
Tasman#
Tasman#█
```

Figure 3-15 EIGRP topology table on router Tasman

In similar fashion, we configure router Frisco as shown in the next two illustrations:

```
Telnet -                                                          _ □ ✕
Connect  Edit  Terminal  Help
router4>en
Password:
router4#conf t
Enter configuration commands, one per line.  End with CNTL/Z.
router4(config)#host Frisco
Frisco(config)#interface e0
Frisco(config-if)#ip address 10.28.0.1 255.255.0.0
Frisco(config-if)#no shutdown
%LINEPROTO-5-UPDOWN: Line protocol on Interface Ethernet0, changed state to up
%LINK-3-UPDOWN: Interface Ethernet0, changed s
Frisco(config-if)#interface s0
Frisco(config-if)#ip address 10.33.0.1 255.255.0.0
Frisco(config-if)#bandwidth 64
Frisco(config-if)#no shutdown
Frisco(config-if)#
%LINK-3-UPDOWN: Interface Serial0, changed state to down
Frisco(config-if)#interface s1
Frisco(config-if)#ip address 10.29.0.2 255.255.0.0
Frisco(config-if)#clock rate 64000
Frisco(config-if)#bandwidt 64
Frisco(config-if)#no shutdown
Frisco(config-if)#
%LINK-3-UPDOWN: Interface Serial1, changed state to up
%LINEPROTO-5-UPDOWN: Line protocol on Interface Serial1, changed state to up
Frisco(config-if)#
```

```
Telnet -                                                          _ □ ✕
Connect  Edit  Terminal  Help
Frisco(config-if)#
Frisco(config-if)#interface s2
Frisco(config-if)#encapsultation frame-relay
                            ^
% Invalid input detected at '^' marker.

Frisco(config-if)#
Frisco(config-if)#interface s2
Frisco(config-if)#encapsulation frame-relay
Frisco(config-if)#frame-relay lmi-type ansi
Frisco(config-if)#interface s2.2 multipoint
Frisco(config-subif)#ip split-horizon
Frisco(config-subif)#ip address 10.16.0.1 255.255.0.0
Frisco(config-subif)#frame-relay interface-dlci 245
Frisco(config-fr-dlci)#frame-relay interface-dlci 246
Frisco(config-fr-dlci)#exit
Frisco(config)#router eigrp 200
Frisco(config-router)#network 10.0.0.0
Frisco(config-router)#end
Frisco#
%SYS-5-CONFIG_I: Configured from console by console
```

The topology table of router Frisco, shown in Figure 3-16, reveals the reason that EIGRP routers require significant memory configurations. Notice that unlike OSPF, where a given router maintains a detailed database representing the topology of the local area only, the EIGRP topology table by default includes all destinations in the internetwork.

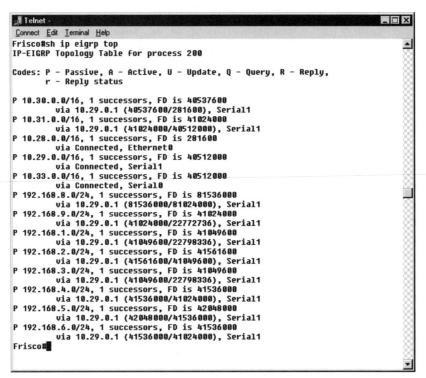

Figure 3-16 EIGRP topology table on router Frisco

We complete the example by configuring router Zanker as shown in the following two illustrations:

```
Telnet -                                                    _ □ X
Connect  Edit  Terminal  Help
router6>en
Password:
router6#configure terminal
Enter configuration commands, one per line.  End with CNTL/Z.
router6(config)#host Zanker
Zanker(config)#interface e0
Zanker(config-if)#ip address 10.32.0.1 255.255.0.0
Zanker(config-if)#no shutdown
Zanker(config-if)#
%LINEPROTO-5-UPDOWN: Line protocol on Interface Ethernet0, changed state to up
%LINK-3-UPDOWN: Interface Ethernet0, changed state to up
Zanker(config-if)#interface s0
Zanker(config-if)#ip address 10.33.0.1 255.255.0.0
Zanker(config-if)#band 64
Zanker(config-if)#no shutdown
Zanker(config-if)#
%LINK-3-UPDOWN: Interface Serial0, changed state to up
%LINEPROTO-5-UPDOWN: Line protocol on Interface Serial0, changed state to up
Zanker(config-if)#interface s1
Zanker(config-if)#ip address 10.29.0.2 255.255.0.0
Zanker(config-if)#clock rate 64000
Zanker(config-if)#bandwidth 64
Zanker(config-if)#no shutdown
Zanker(config-if)#
%LINK-3-UPDOWN: Interface Serial1, changed state to up
%LINEPROTO-5-UPDOWN: Line protocol on Interface Serial1, changed state to up
Zanker(config-if)#
```

```
Telnet -                                                    _ □ X
Connect  Edit  Terminal  Help
Zanker(config-if)#
Zanker(config-if)#interface s2
Zanker(config-if)#encapsulation frame-relay
Zanker(config-if)#frame-relay lmi-type ansi
Zanker(config-if)#interface s2.2 multipoint
Zanker(config-subif)#ip split-horizon
Zanker(config-subif)#ip address 10.16.0.3 255.255.0.0
Zanker(config-subif)#frame-relay interface-dlci 264
Zanker(config-fr-dlci)#frame-relay interface-dlci 265
Zanker(config-fr-dlci)#exit
Zanker(config)#
Zanker(config)#router eigrp 200
Zanker(config-router)#network 10.0.0.0
Zanker(config-router)#end
Zanker#
%SYS-5-CONFIG_I: Configured from console by console
Zanker#
```

In Figure 3-17 we observe the entire topology table for our sample internetwork.

How do I reduce the size of the EIGRP topology table?

You can use route summarization to reduce the size of the EIGRP topology table. Notice in the example internetwork of Figure 3-18 that we can create summary addressing between the groups of three routers to reduce the size of the topology tables.

To reconfigure the network from the previous example to implement EIGRP summarization, we use the interface mode configuration command:

```
NewYork(config-if)#ip summary-address eigrp 200
```

It is not necessary to suppress the more specific route when configuring summarization. EIGRP summarization automatically replaces updates for the specific routes with the summary.

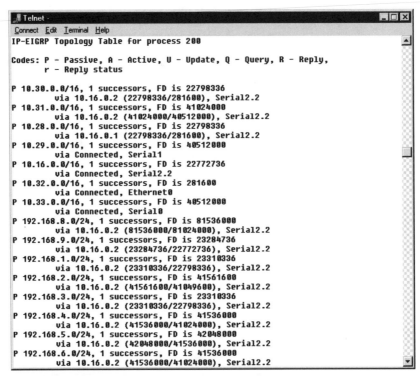

Figure 3-17   EIGRP topology table on router Zanker

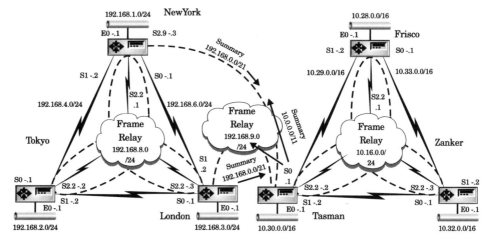

Figure 3-18   Two-way summarization

In Figure 3-19 we configure summarization on router NewYork. Notice in the IP routing table that the summary route is represented as a route to interface Null0.

```
Telnet -
Connect Edit Terminal Help
NewYork#
NewYork#configure terminal
Enter configuration commands, one per line.  End with CNTL/Z.
NewYork(config)#interface s2.9
NewYork(config-subif)#ip summary-address eigrp 200 192.168.0.0 255.255.248.0
NewYork(config-subif)#end
NewYork#
%SYS-5-CONFIG_I: Configured from console by console
NewYork#
NewYork#show ip route
Codes: C - connected, S - static, I - IGRP, R - RIP, M - mobile, B - BGP
       D - EIGRP, EX - EIGRP external, O - OSPF, IA - OSPF inter area
       N1 - OSPF NSSA external type 1, N2 - OSPF NSSA external type 2
       E1 - OSPF external type 1, E2 - OSPF external type 2, E - EGP
       i - IS-IS, L1 - IS-IS level-1, L2 - IS-IS level-2, * - candidate default
       U - per-user static route, o - ODR

Gateway of last resort is not set

C    192.168.8.0/24 is directly connected, Serial2.2
C    192.168.9.0/24 is directly connected, Serial2.9
C    192.168.4.0/24 is directly connected, Serial1
D    192.168.5.0/24 [90/41024000] via 192.168.4.1, 00:01:16, Serial1
C    192.168.6.0/24 is directly connected, Serial0
C    192.168.1.0/24 is directly connected, Ethernet0
D    192.168.2.0/24 [90/40537600] via 192.168.4.1, 00:01:16, Serial1
D    192.168.3.0/24 [90/40537600] via 192.168.6.2, 00:01:17, Serial0
D    192.168.0.0/21 is a summary, 00:00:12, Null0
NewYork#
```

Figure 3-19   Summary address configuration on router NewYork

We perform similar configuration on router London to ensure that router Tasman sees only summarized updates from the 192.168.0.0 portion of our internetwork. Figure 3-20 demonstrates the configuration steps.

When we create the summary address on routers NewYork and London, EIGRP discontinues update messages regarding the more specific network numbers. In Figure 3-21, we observe that no update traffic is sent to remove the old, more specific routes. Notice for example, that the new summary route 192.168.0.0/21 exists alongside the more specific 192.168.1.0/24 route.

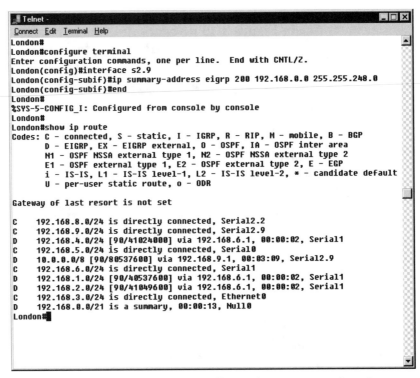

Figure 3-20 Summary address configuration on router London

```
Telnet -                                                              _ □ ×
Connect  Edit  Terminal  Help
Tasman#
Tasman#show ip route
Codes: C - connected, S - static, I - IGRP, R - RIP, M - mobile, B - BGP
       D - EIGRP, EX - EIGRP external, O - OSPF, IA - OSPF inter area
       N1 - OSPF NSSA external type 1, N2 - OSPF NSSA external type 2
       E1 - OSPF external type 1, E2 - OSPF external type 2, E - EGP
       i - IS-IS, L1 - IS-IS level-1, L2 - IS-IS level-2, * - candidate default
       U - per-user static route, o - ODR

Gateway of last resort is not set

D    192.168.8.0/24 [90/81024000] via 192.168.9.3, 00:05:42, Serial2.9
                    [90/81024000] via 192.168.9.2, 00:05:43, Serial2.9
C    192.168.9.0/24 is directly connected, Serial2.9
D    192.168.4.0/24 [90/41024000] via 192.168.9.3, 00:09:34, Serial2.9
     10.0.0.0/8 is variably subnetted, 8 subnets, 2 masks
D       10.0.0.0/8 is a summary, 00:05:43, Null0
C       10.30.0.0/16 is directly connected, Ethernet0
C       10.31.0.0/16 is directly connected, Serial1
D       10.28.0.0/16 [90/22798336] via 10.16.0.1, 01:01:34, Serial2.2
C       10.29.0.0/16 is directly connected, Serial0
C       10.16.0.0/16 is directly connected, Serial2.2
D       10.32.0.0/16 [90/22798336] via 10.16.0.3, 01:01:35, Serial2.2
D       10.33.0.0/16 [90/41024000] via 10.29.0.2, 01:01:35, Serial0
                     [90/41024000] via 10.16.0.1, 01:01:35, Serial2.2
                     [90/41024000] via 10.16.0.3, 01:01:35, Serial2.2
D    192.168.6.0/24 [90/41024000] via 192.168.9.3, 00:05:44, Serial2.9
                    [90/41024000] via 192.168.9.2, 00:05:44, Serial2.9
D    192.168.1.0/24 [90/22798336] via 192.168.9.3, 00:09:35, Serial2.9
D    192.168.3.0/24 [90/22798336] via 192.168.9.2, 00:05:43, Serial2.9
D    192.168.0.0/21 [90/22798336] via 192.168.9.3, 00:05:44, Serial2.9
                    [90/22798336] via 192.168.9.2, 00:05:44, Serial2.9
Tasman#
```

Figure 3-21   Summary and specific routes on router Tasman

We see in Figure 3-22 that only the summary route is published by EIGRP on routers London and NewYork after disabling EIGRP auto-summarization and clearing the old routes with the following commands starting in privileged EXEC mode:

```
Tasman#configure terminal
Tasman(config)#router eigrp 200
Tasman(config-rotuer)#no auto-summary
Tasman(config-router)#end
Tasman#clear ip route *
```

```
Telnet -                                                              _ □ ×
Connect  Edit  Terminal  Help
Tasman#
Tasman#clear ip route *
Tasman#show ip route
Codes: C - connected, S - static, I - IGRP, R - RIP, M - mobile, B - BGP
       D - EIGRP, EX - EIGRP external, O - OSPF, IA - OSPF inter area
       N1 - OSPF NSSA external type 1, N2 - OSPF NSSA external type 2
       E1 - OSPF external type 1, E2 - OSPF external type 2, E - EGP
       i - IS-IS, L1 - IS-IS level-1, L2 - IS-IS level-2, * - candidate default
       U - per-user static route, o - ODR

Gateway of last resort is not set

D    192.168.8.0/24 [90/81024000] via 192.168.9.2, 00:00:05, Serial2.9
                    [90/81024000] via 192.168.9.3, 00:00:06, Serial2.9
C    192.168.9.0/24 is directly connected, Serial2.9
     10.0.0.0/8 is variably subnetted, 8 subnets, 2 masks
D       10.0.0.0/8 is a summary, 00:00:06, Null0
C       10.30.0.0/16 is directly connected, Ethernet0
C       10.31.0.0/16 is directly connected, Serial1
D       10.28.0.0/16 [90/22798336] via 10.16.0.1, 00:00:06, Serial2.2
C       10.29.0.0/16 is directly connected, Serial0
C       10.16.0.0/16 is directly connected, Serial2.2
D       10.32.0.0/16 [90/22798336] via 10.16.0.3, 00:00:06, Serial2.2
D       10.33.0.0/16 [90/41024000] via 10.16.0.1, 00:00:07, Serial2.2
                     [90/41024000] via 10.29.0.2, 00:00:07, Serial0
                     [90/41024000] via 10.16.0.3, 00:00:07, Serial2.2
D    192.168.0.0/21 [90/22798336] via 192.168.9.2, 00:00:07, Serial2.9
                    [90/22798336] via 192.168.9.3, 00:00:07, Serial2.9
Tasman#
```

Figure 3-22   Summary route only on router Tasman

When we compare the size of the summarized EIGRP topology table for router Zanker in Figure 3-23 with the full topology table in Figure 3-17, we understand the usefulness of summarization in managing the memory consumed by EIGRP.

What task is necessary to transition from IGRP to EIGRP?

If routers on a network are configured for IGRP, and it is necessary to make a transition to EIGRP, then some routers are designated as transition routers, on which both IGRP and EIGRP are configured. On routers that are running both IGRP and EIGRP with the same autonomous system number, routes from both processes are redistributed automatically. Once the network has stabilized, IGRP can be removed, leaving EIGRP as the primary routing protocol.

```
Telnet -                                                       _ □ ×
Connect  Edit  Terminal  Help
Zanker#
Zanker#show ip eigrp topology
IP-EIGRP Topology Table for process 200

Codes: P - Passive, A - Active, U - Update, Q - Query, R - Reply,
       r - Reply status

P 10.30.0.0/16, 1 successors, FD is 22798336
        via 10.16.0.2 (22798336/281600), Serial2.2
P 10.31.0.0/16, 1 successors, FD is 41024000
        via 10.16.0.2 (41024000/40512000), Serial2.2
P 10.28.0.0/16, 1 successors, FD is 22798336
        via 10.16.0.1 (22798336/281600), Serial2.2
P 10.29.0.0/16, 2 successors, FD is 41024000
        via 10.16.0.1 (41024000/40512000), Serial2.2
        via 10.16.0.2 (41024000/40512000), Serial2.2
P 10.16.0.0/16, 1 successors, FD is 22772736
        via Connected, Serial2.2
P 10.32.0.0/16, 1 successors, FD is 281600
        via Connected, Ethernet0
P 10.33.0.0/16, 1 successors, FD is 40512000
        via Connected, Serial0
P 192.168.8.0/24, 1 successors, FD is 81536000
        via 10.16.0.2 (81536000/81024000), Serial2.2
P 192.168.9.0/24, 1 successors, FD is 23284736
        via 10.16.0.2 (23284736/22772736), Serial2.2
P 192.168.0.0/21, 1 successors, FD is 23310336
        via 10.16.0.2 (23310336/22798336), Serial2.2
Zanker#
```

Figure 3-23 EIGRP topology table on router Zanker with summarization

How are the metric computations in EIGRP tuned?

The tuning of metric computations is achieved by using the command:

```
metric weights tos k1 k2 k3 k4 k5
```

In this command, *tos* stands for type of service. At present, only a value of 0 is supported. The numerical constants k1, k2, k3, k4, and k5 have default values of:

- k1 = 1
- k2 = 0
- k3 = 1
- k4 = 0
- k5 = 0

If k5 = 0, then metric is computed as follows:

metric = {k1 × bandwidth + [(k2 × bandwidth)/(256 - load)] + k3 × delay}

If k5 is not equal to zero, then:

metric = metric × {k 5 /(reliability + k4)}

 ## What does an offset to routing metrics mean?

An offset to a routing metric is a mechanism to increase the value of a routing metric.

The following command is used to specify an offset to a metric:

```
offset-list access-list-number|name in|out
 offset(type number)
```

This command is used in the router configuration command mode.

An offset list with an interface type and interface number is called an extended offset list. An extended offset list takes precedence over an offset list that is not extended.

An example of an offset list that is not extended is:

```
Offset-list 55 in 15
```

This command applies an offset of 15 to the delay component incoming metrics of access list 55.

An example of extended offset-list is:

```
offset-list 65 in 15 ethernet 1
```

This command applies an offset of 15 to routes learned from Ethernet interface 1.

 What is the command sequence used for authentication purposes in configuring an EIGRP?

```
ip authentication mode eigrp
ip authentication key-chain eigrp
exit
key-chain name-of-chain
key number
key-string text
accept-lifetime start-time [infinite|end-time|duration seconds]
end-lifetime start-time [infinite|end-time|duration seconds]
```

EIGRP IPX SAP SUPPORT

 What is a Service Advertisement Protocol?

SAP is a Novell proprietary protocol. SAP advertises the NetWare services offered to clients on a Novell IPX network. A service has a service type number associated with it. The NetWare servers broadcast the SAP packets every 60 seconds by default. Cisco routers enable SAP by default for interfaces configured for IPX. The router builds its SAP table from the information in SAP updates from NetWare servers and other routers.

 What is a Get Nearest Server (GNS) message?

GNS messages are IPX messages sent by the NetWare clients to search for the servers that can offer the services needed by the clients. A Cisco router can advertise to clients the IPX address of a service, if the service happens to be in the router's SAP table.

 What is the purpose of a SAP filter?

The purpose of SAP filter is to limit the amount of traffic sent on, and received by, the router. Assume that there are

60 NetWare devices on a network. Further assume that each device will typically advertise 12 services. Thus, the total number of SAP services will be (60 × 12) = 720. There are 7 SAPs associated with a SAP packet. Thus there will be approximately 103 SAP packets. A SAP packet containing 7 SAPs will require 488 bytes including IPX and related information (each SAP entry is 64 bytes long). The total bandwidth requirement will be approximately (488 × 103) = 50264 bytes. This represents 402112 bits. Assuming a rate of 64 kbps, this means that the SAP traffic will use approximately 6.3 seconds. If the SAP updates are sent every 60 seconds by default, then the SAP traffic utilizes the entire bandwidth approximately 10.5 percent of the time. This represents a significant waste of the bandwidth.

Sending only the incremental SAP updates minimizes the use of bandwidth by SAP traffic.

 Note: *The default for the incremental SAP update feature is "turned off" for LAN interfaces. For WAN interfaces, "turned on" is the default. If incremental updates are enabled and there is no peer router, then periodic updates are sent. Incremental SAP updates are sent when a peer router becomes known.*

 ## What commands are used for implementation of SAP in an IPX environment?

Table 3-2 describes the commands used for implementation of SAP in an IPX environment, as well as the command mode and purpose associated with each command.

 Note: *The delay parameter in assigning metric weights is a 32-bit number and is stored in increments of 39.1 nanoseconds. A delay value of FFFFFFFF means that the network cannot be reached.*

Command	Command Mode	Purpose
DENY	Access-list configuration	Allow SAP filtering
DISTRIBUTE-SAP-LIST IN	Router Configuration	Filter services received in updates
DISTRIBUTE-SAP-LIST OUT	Router Configuration	Filter services from being advertised on the outgoing packets
IPX ROUTER-SAP-FILTER	Interface Configuration	Filter SAP received on an interface
IPX SAP	Global Configuration	Specify static SAP entries
IPX SAP-INCREMENTAL-EIGRP	Interface Configuration	Send SAP updates only when changes occur in the SAP tables
IPX SAP-MAX-PACKETSIZE	Interface Configuration	Configure maximum packet size for SAP updates
IPX SAP-MULTIPLIER	Interface Configuration	Specify the interval at which the SAP entry ages out
IPX SAP-QUEUE MAXIMUM	Global Configuration	Specify maximum queue length of the input SAP requests that are pending
IPX-INPUT-SAP-FILTER	Interface Configuration	Control which services are added to Cisco IOS SAP table
IPX OUTPUT-SAP-DELAY	Interface Configuration	Specify packet delay for SAP updates sent on an interface
IPX OUTPUT-SAP-FILTER	Interface Configuration	Specify which services are sent in a SAP on an interface

Table 3-2   Commands Used for Implementation of SAP in an IPX Environment

How are input and output SAP filters configured?

Refer to Figure 3-24 as the configuration of input and output SAP filters is described in the following text.

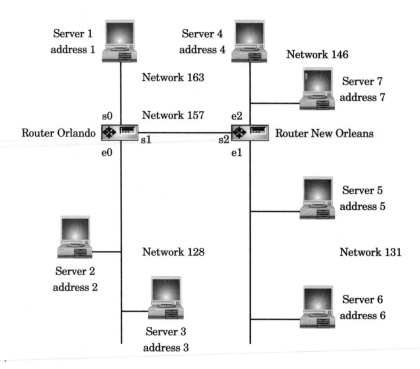

Figure 3-24 Example of SAP filtering

EXAMPLE OF SAP INPUT FILTER For Router New Orleans:

```
access-list  400  deny address 5
access-list  400  -1
interface  ethernet 1
   ipx network 131
   ipx input-sap-filter 400
interface  ethernet 2
   ipx network 146
interface  serial 2
   ipx network  157
```

These commands will deny Server 5 acceptance on interface e1. Consequently, Server 5 cannot be advertised by router New Orleans.

EXAMPLE OF SAP OUTPUT FILTER   For Router New Orleans:

```
access-list  400  deny address 5
access-list   400  -1
interface  ethernet 1
   ipx network 131
interface  ethernet 2
   ipx network 146
   ipx output-sap-filter 400
interface   serial 2
   ipx network  157
```

The router cannot advertise Server 5 on interface e2 to Network 146. It can advertise Server 5 on interfaces s2 and e1.

Caution: *If SAP updates are disabled on a LAN interface, and if all the nodes out of the interface are not EIGRP configured, then there will be a loss of SAP information on other nodes.*

MONITORING EIGRP

What are the important commands used to monitor an EIGRP network?

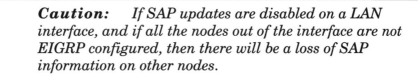

- SHOW IP EIGRP INTERFACES *{interface} {as-number}*
- SHOW IP EIGRP NEIGHBORS *{type number}*
- SHOW IP EIGRP TOPOLOGY *{autonomous-system-number} | {{ip-address}mask}}*
- SHOW IP EIGRP TRAFFIC *{autonomous-system-number}*

 ## What does a typical output from the command SHOW IP EIGRP INTERFACES look like?

The output from SHOW IP EIGRP INTERFACES for process 201 is as follows:

```
Router> show ip eigrp interfaces
IP EIGRP Interfaces for process 201
                     Xmit Queue  Mean  Pacing Time  Multicast   Pending
Interfaces   Peers  Un/Reliable  SRIT  Un/Reliable  Flow Timer  Routes
Et0          0      0/0          15    5/55         0           0
SE0:1.12     1      0/0          0     0/16         15          1
```

Table 3-3 describes the fields shown in the preceding output.

 ## What does a typical output from the command SHOW IP EIGRP NEIGHBORS look like?

The output from SHOW IP EIGRP NEIGHBORS for process 201 is as follows:

```
Router# show ip eigrp neighbors
IP-EIGRP neighbors for process 210
   Address       Interface   Holdtime   Uptime    Q      Seq    SRIT   RTO
                             (secs)     (h:m:s)   Count  Num    (ms)   (ms)
   140.55.92.33  Ethernet0   25         1:20:45   0      29     8      24
   140.55.94.41  Ethernet1   8          0:20:05   0      12     11     20
```

Field	Description
Interfaces	Interface over which EIGRP is configured
Peers	Number of directly connected EIGRP neighbors
Xmit Queue Un/Reliable	Number of packets remaining in the unreliable and reliable transmit queues
Mean SRTT (Smooth Round Trip Time)	Mean SRTT in seconds. Time in milliseconds it takes for an EIGRP packet to be sent to a neighbor and for the local router to receive an acknowledgment of that packet.
Pacing Time Un/Reliable	Pacing time used to determine when EIGRP unreliable and reliable packets should be sent out the interface
Multicast Flow Timer	Maximum number of seconds in which router will send multicast EIGRP packets
Pending Routes	Number of routes in the packets sitting in the transmit queue

Table 3-3   Field Description for the Output from SHOW IP EIGRP INTERFACES

Table 3-4 describes the fields shown in the preceding output.

What does a typical output from the command SHOW IP EIGRP TOPOLOGY look like?

The output from SHOW IP EIGRP TOPOLOGY for process 215 is as follows:

```
Router # show ip eigrp topology
IP-EIGRP Topology Table for process 215
Codes: P - Passive, A - Active, U - Update, Q - Query, R - Reply, r | status
P 151.74.76.0  255.255.255.0  2 successors,  FD is ethernet 1
        via   151.74.76.34 (5101/7502) , Ethernet 0
        via   151.74.77.44 (5101/7502) , Ethernet 1
        via   151.74.76.55 (5101/7502) , Ethernet 0
```

Field	Description
Process 210	Autonomous system number specified in the router configuration command
Address	IP address of the EIGRP neighbor
Interface	Interface on which the router is receiving hello packets from the peer
Holdtime	Time in seconds that the IOS will wait to hear from the peer before announcing it down. If the peer is using a default for holdtime, then this number will be less than 15. If the peer is using a non-default hold time, then that value is shown.
Uptime	Elapsed time in hours, minutes, and seconds since the router first heard from its peer
Q count	Number of EIGRP packets (update, query, and reply) that the IOS is waiting to send
Seq Num	Sequence number of the last update, query, or reply packet that was received from a neighbor
SRTT	Smooth Round Trip Time. Time in milliseconds it takes for an EIGRP packet to be sent to a neighbor and for the local router to receive an acknowledgment of that packet.
RTO	Retransmission timeout in milliseconds. The amount of time the software waits before retransmitting the packet from the queue.

Table 3-4   Field Description for the Output from SHOW IP EIGRP NEIGHBORS

Table 3-5 describes the fields shown in the preceding output.

 Note: *Administrative distance can have a numerical value between 0 and 255. An administrative distance of 255 indicates that the source of routing information should be ignored.*

Field	Description
Codes	State of the topology table entry
P - Passive	No EIGRP computations are being performed for this destination
A - Active	EIGRP computations are being performed for this destination
U - Update	Indication that an update packet has been sent to this destination
Q - Query	Indication that a query packet has been sent to this destination
R - Reply	Indication that a reply packet has been sent to this destination
R - Reply status	Indicates that the software is waiting for a reply after sending a query
151.74.76.0	Destination IP address
255.255.255.0	Destination subnet mask
successors	Number of remaining hops in the IP routing table
FD	Feasible distance
replies	Number of replies that are still outstanding. This parameter is received only when the destination is in an active state.
state	EIGRP state of the destination. This value can be 0, 1, 2, or 3. This applies only when the destination is in an active state.
via	IP address of the peer who advertised this destination to the software. The first N entries are the current successors. The remaining entries are feasible successors.
5101/7502	5101: EIGRP metric representing the cost to the destination 7502: EIGRP metric that the peer has advertised
Ethernet0	Interface from which the information was learned

Table 3-5   Field Description for the Output from SHOW IP EIGRP TOPOLOGY

What does a typical output from the command SHOW IP EIGRP TRAFFIC look like?

The output from SHOW IP EIGRP TRAFFIC for process 220 is as follows:

```
Router# show ip eigrp traffic
IP-EIGRP Traffic Statistics for process 220
Hellos sent/received:  310/420
Updates sent/received:  21/15
Queries sent/received:  5/4
Replies sent/received: 4/5
Acks sent/received:  34/21
```

Table 3-6 describes the fields shown in the preceding output.

 Note: *Traffic on networks having different costs for multiple routes can be controlled using a TRAFFIC SHARE command for load balancing. This command is used only for IGRP and EIGRP.*

Field	Description
process 220	Autonomous system number
Hellos sent/received	Number of hello packets that were sent and received
Updates sent/received	Number of update packets that were sent and received
Queries sent/received	Number of query packets that were sent and received
Replies sent/received	Number of reply packets that were sent and received
Acks sent/received	Number of acknowledgment packets that were sent and received

Table 3-6   Field Description for the Output from SHOW IP EIGRP TRAFFIC

Chapter 4

Configuring OSPF

Answer Topics!

Configuring OSPF @ a Glance

Open Shortest Path First (OSPF) is a link-state TCP/IP routing protocol. OSPF is based on the concept of autonomous system (AS) and areas within an autonomous system. OSPF supports the concept of hierarchical area routing in a "hub and spoke" network topology. This chapter describes configuration of a router in an OSPF network. It summarizes various commands used to configure and monitor an OSPF router's performance.

This chapter explores the following areas:

Area Border Routers describes the concept of Areas and Area Border Routers.

Route Summarization explains how route summarization can be used to reduce the size of the link-state database, thus utilizing the bandwidth more efficiently.

Stub and Totally Stubby Areas describes how to configure stubby areas on a router in an OSPF environment.

Monitoring focuses on network monitoring activities and provides examples of how router performance can be monitored.

Virtual Links defines virtual links and why they are needed.

Not So Stubby Area (NSSA) defines NSSA and how it is different from stub areas.

Bringing It All Together provides examples of configuring routers in an OSPF environment using the information learned in previous sections.

AREA BORDER ROUTERS

 What are the characteristics of an OSPF network?

- OSPF is a link-state routing protocol.
- It uses area border routers.
- It has a backbone area.

> **Note:** *The types of networks defined in the OSPF domain are: point-to-point, broadcast, non-broadcast, point-to-multipoint, stub, and demand.*

What is an area border router?

In OSPF the network is generally identified as an autonomous system. An autonomous system is further divided into several areas. An area border router connects two or more areas within the same autonomous system. This means that one interface of an ABR will be in one area, and the other interface will be in a different area.

What is a backbone area?

A backbone area in OSPF is the area to which area border routers are connected. Generally the only way to get from one area to the another is through the backbone area.

What types of routers may be seen in an OSPF network?

There are four kinds of routers that describe the OSPF network:

- **Backbone router**   Has the interface connected only to the backbone
- **Area border router**   Has interfaces connected to multiple areas
- **Internal router**   Has directly connected interfaces within the same area
- **Autonomous System Boundary Router**   Connects two autonomous systems

 What topological data is contained in an area border router?

The ABR keeps topological data for each area to which the ABR is connected.

How do you define an area over which the OSPF is applicable?

There are two commands necessary to define an OSPF over an area.

```
ROUTER OSPF process-id

NETWORK address wild-card mask AREA area
```

The first command enables OSPF routing. This is a global configuration mode command. The second command defines the area over which the OSPF runs. This command is a router configuration mode command. An example is shown below:

```
interface ethernet 0
  ip address 129.122.35.2  255.255.255.0
router ospf 210
  network  129.122.35.0  0.0.0.255 area 100
  network  129.122.0.0.  0.0.255.255 area 101
  network  0.0.0.0     255.255.255.255   area 0
```

This example defines three areas: 100, 101, and 0.

ROUTE SUMMARIZATION

What is route summarization?

Route summarization is the aggregation of routes created by ABRs and ASBRs and advertised to adjacent routers. If the area contains network numbers that are contiguous, then ABRs and ASBRs can be configured to advertise a summary route by specifying the range of network numbers. Route summarization reduces the size of the link-state database. Route summarization is achieved by the following command:

```
AREA  area-id RANGE address mask
```

This command is a router configuration mode command.

 How can multiple area routers be configured using an AREA RANGE command?

The following commands allow ABR to advertise one summary route to areas for all subnetworks on 94.0.0.0 and for all hosts on 194.31.123.0.

```
network  94.0.0.0 0.255.255.255 area 94.0.0.0
network  194.31.123.0 0.0.0.255 area  200
area 94.0.0.0  range  94.0.0.0 255.0.0.0
area  200 range 194.31.123.0 255.255.255.0
```

 Can the AREA RANGE command be disabled?

The default mode for the area range command is "disabled." Thus, by specifying the AREA RANGE command, one can enable the route summarization.

 Can the AREA RANGE command be used with any type of router?

No. The AREA RANGE command can be used only with the area border routers.

 What is route redistribution?

Route redistribution means OSPF can import routes from other protocols.

STUB AND TOTALLY STUBBY AREAS

 What are stub areas?

Stub areas are the areas that do not receive information on external routes. The ABR creates a default external route into the stub area for destinations outside the autonomous systems in which the stub area is located.

 What command is used to define a stub area?

The command to define a stub area is:

```
AREA area-id STUB
```

This command is a router configuration mode command. The *area-id* can be either a decimal value or an IP address.

What option can be used to prevent ABR from sending summary link-state advertisements into the stub area?

A NO-SUMMARY option is used to prevent ABR from sending summary link-state advertisements into the stub area. Thus the command would be:

```
AREA area-id STUB NO-SUMMARY
```

Caution: *The NO AREA* area-id *command will nullify all area options, including AREA AUTHENTICATION, AREA DEFAULT-COST, AREA NSSA, AREA RANGE, AREA STUB, and AREA VIRTUAL-LINK.*

What is the DEFAULT-COST option used for?

The DEFAULT-COST option is used only on an area border router. It provides the metric for the summary default route created by an ABR into stub area.

How would one specify a default cost to a stub network?

The following commands assign a default cost of 50 to a stub network 75.0.0.0.

```
router ospf 300
network 75.0.0.0  0.255.255.255 area 42
area  42 stub
area 42 default-cost 50
```

What command can be used to enable authentication into an OSPF area?

AREA area-id AUTHENTICATION enables authentication for an OSPF area.

AREA area-id AUTHENTICATION MESSAGE-DIGEST enables MD5 authentication for an OSPF area. The key identifier for a MESSAGE-DIGEST parameter must be the

same for all neighboring routers in a network. The key has no default value.

 Caution: *The AUTHENTICATION-KEY parameter in the AREA area-id command is used to assign a password to a router. A separate password can be assigned to each network on a given interface. All neighboring routers and servers on a given network must use the same password.*

MONITORING

 ### What does monitoring OSPF mean?

Monitoring an OSPF network means obtaining information that can be used to determine resource utilization. It also means resolving network troubles. This is accomplished by displaying statistics on the contents of the databases, caches, and routing tables.

What tasks are associated with monitoring an OSPF network?

- Display of general information about routing processes
- Display of general information about databases
- Display of internal routing tables for ABR and ASBR
- Display of interface-related information
- Display of OSPF neighbor information
- Display of virtual link-related information

What is the purpose of a loopback interface?

Loopback interfaces are used to increase the stability of the routing table, because loopback interfaces never go down. In general, OSPF uses the highest IP address in use on a physical or virtual interface configured on a router, when a loopback interface is not used or incorrectly configured. In the event of the loss of an interface, a router needs to recalculate a new router ID. This causes all of the routers in the same table to rebuild their link-state database. The use of a loopback interface when OSPF is the routing of choice is highly recommended.

What is the command used to display information about routing processes?

The command is SHOW IP OSPF. This is an EXEC mode command. Typical output might be:

```
Router#  show ip ospf
rip with metric mapped to 4
igrp 4 with metric mapped to 155
Number of areas in this router is 4
Area 175.64.125.00
Number of interfaces in this area is 2
Area has simple password authentication
SPF algorithm executed 4 times
Area ranges are
Link State Update Interval is 0:10:00 and due in 0:04:28
Link State Age Interval is 0:15:00 and due in  0:10:29
```

Table 4-1 explains the fields in this output.

Field	Description
Routing process ospf 175.64.125.00.	Process ID and OSPF router ID
Supports only single...	Number of types of services supported (in this example only type 0)
It is an area border router...	Tells that this is an ABR. Allowed values: internal router, ABR, autonomous system router
Summary Link Update Interval	Specifies summary link update interval type in hours:minutes:seconds and tells when next update is due
External Link Update Interval	Specifies external link update interval type in hours:minutes:seconds and tells when next update is due
Redistributing External Routes from	External routes that are redistributed and are listed by protocol
Number of areas	Tells how many areas are in this router
Link State Update Interval	Lists router and network link-state update interval in hours:minutes:seconds and tells when next update is due
Link State Age Interval	Lists max-aged update deletion interval and time until next update of the database in hours:minutes:seconds

Table 4-1   The Fields in the Output of SHOW IP OSPF

Note: Link-state advertisements (LSAs), used in a
link-state protocol, are analogous to routing updates used in
distance vector protocols. LSA is triggered by a change in the
state of a physical link and is therefore considered event
driven. A router that has just been added in the network must
announce itself through a series of OSPF messages such as
hello and LSA using multicast addresses.

What is typical output of a SHOW IP OSPF BORDER-ROUTERS command?

The output from SHOW IP OSPF BORDER-ROUTERS is
as follows:

```
Router# show ip ospf border-routers
OSPF Process 175 internal routing table
Destination      Next Hop        Cost    Type    Rte Type    Area      SPF No
171.75.45.122    155.32.126.55 15       ABR     Intra       0.0.0.4 4
199.200.34.78    212.54.36.2   10       ASBR    Inter       0.0.0.7 7
```

Table 4-2 explains the fields in this output.

What is typical output of a SHOW IP OSPF DATABASE command?

The output from SHOW IP OSPF DATABASE is as follows:

```
Router# show ip ospf database
OSPF  Router with ID (171.75.45.122) (autonomous system 175)
           Router Link States (Area 100)
Link ID          ADV Router      Age     Seq#        Checksum    Link count
171.75.45.122    171.75.45.122   250     0x8000005   0x51C6      3
                 Net Link States
201.154.32.55    189.42.31.73    1500    0x80000032  0xB108
```

Field	Description
Destination	Destination router ID
Next Hop	ID of next router towards destination
Cost	Cost of this route
Type	Router type of the destination router. It can be an ABR or ASBR.
Rte Type	Type of this route. It can be intra-area or inter-area.
Area	Area ID of the area that this route is learned from
SPF No	Internal number of the SPF calculation that installs this route

Table 4-2 The Fields in the Output of SHOW IP OSPF BORDER-ROUTERS

 ## What is typical output for the SHOW IP OSPF DATABASE EXTERNAL command?

The output from SHOW IP OSPF DATABASE EXTERNAL is as follows:

```
Router# show ip ospf database external
OSPF router with id (202.198.155.124) (Autonomous system 201)
 Displaying AS External Link States
 LS age:    120
 Options:   (No TOS capability)
 LS type: AS External Link
 Link State ID:  189.123.0.0 (External Network Number)
 Advertising Router: 189.123.211.7
 LS sequence number:  80000032
 Checksum: 0x60C5
 Length:  48
 Network mask:  255.255.0.0
 Metric Type : 2
TOS: 0
Metric: 2
Forward Address:  126.210.2.3
External Route Tag: 0
```

Table 4-3 explains the fields in this output.

 ## What is typical output for the SHOW IP OSPF DATABASE NETWORK command?

The output from SHOW IP OSPF DATABASE NETWORK is as follows:

```
Router# show ip ospf database network
OSPF router with id (202.198.155.124) (Process ID 400)
 Displaying Net Link States (Area 0.0.0.0)
 LS age: 780
 Options:  (No TOS capability)
 LS type: Network Links
 Link State ID:  189.123.0.0 (Designated Router address)
 Advertising Router:  189.123.211.7
 LS sequence number:  80000032
 Checksum: 0x60C5
 Length:  48
 Network mask:  255.255.255.0
 Attached Router:  154.129.3.1
 Attached router:    154.129.3.4
```

Table 4-4 explains the fields in this output.

Field	Description
OSPF router with id	Router ID
Autonomous system	Autonomous system OSPF process ID
LS age	Link-state age
Options	Type of service options (type 0 only)
LS type	Link-state type
Link State ID	Link-state ID (external network number)
Advertising Router	Advertising router's ID
LS sequence number	Link-state sequence
Checksum	Link-state checksum
Length	Length of the link-state advertisement in bytes
Network mask	Network mask
Metric Type	External type
TOS	Type of service
Metric	Metric for the link state
Forward Address	Forwarding address where the data for the destination will be forwarded. If this address is 0.0.0.0, then the data is forwarded to the originator of the advertisement.
External Route Tag	This is a 32-bit field attached to the external router

Table 4-3   The Fields in the Output of SHOW IP OSPF DATABASE EXTERNAL

Field	Description
OSPF router with id	Router ID
Process ID 400	OSPF process ID
LS age	Link-state age
Options	Type of service options (type 0 only)
LS type	Link-state type
Link State ID	Link-state ID (external network number)
Advertising Router	Advertising router's ID
LS sequence number	Link-state sequence
Checksum	Link-state checksum
Length	Length of the link-state advertisement in bytes
Network mask	Network mask
Attached router	IP address of the router attached to the network

Table 4-4   The Fields for the Output of SHOW IP OSPF DATABASE NETWORK

What is typical output for the SHOW IP OSPF DATABASE ROUTER command?

The output from SHOW IP OSPF DATABASE ROUTER is as follows:

```
Router# show ip ospf database router
OSPF router with id (202.198.155.124) (Process ID 400)
   Displaying Router Link States (Area 0.0.0.0)
 LS age: 1200
 Options:  (No TOS capability)
 LS type: Router Links
Link State ID:  189.123.56.35
Advertising Router:   189.123.56.35
 LS sequence number:  80000032
 Checksum: 0x60C5
 Length:  80
AS Boundary Router
189 Number of Links: 3
Link connected to: another router
Link ID:  189.123.56.35
Link Data: 189.123.56.35
Number of TOS metrics: 0
TOS 0 Metrics: 1
```

Table 4-5 explains the fields in this output.

Field	Description
OSPF router with id	Router ID
Process ID 400	OSPF process ID
LS age	Link-state age
Options	Type of service options (type 0 only)
LS type	Link-state type
Link State ID	Link-state ID (external network number)
Advertising Router	Advertising router's ID
LS sequence number	Link-state sequence
Checksum	Link-state checksum
Length	Length of the link-state advertisement in bytes

Table 4-5   The Fields in the Output of SHOW IP OSPF DATABASE ROUTER

Field	Description
AS Boundary Router	Router type
Number of Links	Number of active links
Link ID	Link ID
Link Data	Router interface address
TOS	Type of service

Table 4-5 The Fields in the Output of SHOW IP OSPF DATABASE ROUTER
(continued)

 ### What is typical output for the SHOW IP OSPF INTERFACE SUMMARY command?

The output from SHOW IP OSPF INTERFACE SUMMARY is as follows:

```
Router# show ip ospf interface ethernet 2
Ethernet 2 is up, line protocol is up
Internet address is 196.125.45.31, Mask 255.255.255.0  Area 0.0.0.0
AS 400, Router ID 153.21.22.23.24, Network type BROADCAST,  cost: 15
Transmit Delay is 2 sec., State OTHER, Priority 1
Designated Router is  196.125.45.31, Interface Address : 196.125.45.31
Backup Designated Router id 196.125.45.56 Interface Address 196.125.45.56
Time intervals configured, hello 20 , dead 80, wait 30 retransmit 25
Hello due in 0:0: 12
Neighbor count is 6, Adjacent neighbor count is 3
   Adjacent with neighbor 196.125.45.56
   Adjacent with neighbor   196.125.45.31
```

Table 4-6 explains the fields in this output.

VIRTUAL LINKS

 ### Why are virtual links necessary?

Virtual links are required in case of a break in the continuity of the backbone area. The two end points of a virtual link are ABRs.

 ### Where should a virtual link be configured?

The virtual link must be configured between an existing ABR and another router that does not have a direct connection to the backbone.

Field	Description
Ethernet	Interface type
Internet address	Interface IP address
AS	Autonomous system number
Router ID	Router ID
Network type	Network type
cost	Link-state cost
Transmit Delay	Transmit delay in seconds
Designated Router	Designated router ID with interface address
Backup Designated	Backup designated router ID with interface address
Time intervals configured	Value of time interval parameters in seconds
Neighbor count	Number of neighboring networks

Table 4-6   The Fields in the Output of SHOW IP OSPF INTERFACE SUMMARY

 How is virtual link configured?

Use the following command to configure a virtual link:

```
AREA area-id VIRTUAL-LINK router-id
```

An example of this command would be:

```
router ospf 300
network 79.0.0.0 0.255.255.255 area 79.0.0.0
area 79.0.0.0 virtual-link 79.8.7.6
```

The parameter *area-id* is the area ID of the transit area through which the virtual link must pass. In this case it is 79.0.0.0. The number 79.8.7.6 is the router ID associated with the virtual link neighbor.

What optional parameters are allowed in the AREA VIRTUAL-LINK command?

The optional parameters allowed in the AREA *area-id* VIRTUAL-LINK *router-id* command are:

- HELLO-INTERVAL
- RETRANSMIT-INTERVAL

- TRANSMIT-DELAY
- DEAD-INTERVAL
- AUTHENTICATION-KEY
- MESSAGE-DIGEST-KEY

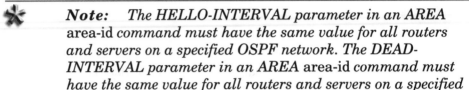

Note: *The HELLO-INTERVAL parameter in an AREA area-id command must have the same value for all routers and servers on a specified OSPF network. The DEAD-INTERVAL parameter in an AREA area-id command must have the same value for all routers and servers on a specified OSPF network.*

NOT SO STUBBY AREA (NSSA)

NSSA is an area which does not flood type 5 link-state advertisements (LSAs) from the core area into the NSSA.

How is the NSSA different from the stub area?

Whereas the stub area cannot import external routes, the Not So Stubby Area has the limited capability of importing external autonomous system routes into the area.

How are external routes imported into NSSA?

NSSA imports Type 7 autonomous system external routes by redistribution. The Type 7 link-state advertisements are translated into Type 5 link-state advertisements.

Who should implement NSSA?

An Internet Service Provider can implement NSSA to simplify administration. An administrator with a need to connect a central OSPF site to a remote site running a different protocol can also use it. The purpose of the stub area is to reduce the size of the link-state database by reducing the number of type 5 link-state advertisements (LSAs). The administrator will not be able to configure an ASBR in the stubby area because the ASBR will send out type 7 LSAs,

that can be converted to a type 5 when an ABR forwards them to the backbone area.

How is NSSA configured?

The command used to define NSSA is the following router configuration mode command:

```
AREA area-id NSSA
```

NSSA is not defined by default.

What optional parameters are allowed in the command to define NSSA?

The NO-REDISTRIBUTION parameter is used with the NSSA ABR in order to import routes into the normal areas and not into NSSA. The full command would be:

```
AREA area-id NSSA [NO-REDISTRIBUTION]
[default-information-originate]
```

How is NSSA defined?

An example of defining NSSA would be as follows:

```
router  ospf 200
redistribute eigrp subnets
network 143.25.68.0 0.0.0.255 area 101
area 101 nssa
```

What commands are used in global command mode?

Table 4-7 shows the commands used in global command and router configuration modes, along with a brief description of the purpose of each command.

What commands are used in the router configuration mode?

Table 4-8 shows the commands used in the router configuration mode, along with a brief description of the purpose of each command.

Command	Command Mode	Purpose
IP OSPF NAME-LOOKUP	Global configuration	Configure OSPF to report router ID as FQDN using Domain Name System (DNS)
ROUTER OSPF *process-id*	Global configuration	Configure an OSPF routing process on a router
AREA *area-id* NSSA	Router configuration	Configure an area as a Not So Stubby Area
AREA *area-id* RANGE *address-mask*	Router configuration	Summarize routes at an area boundary
AREA *area-id* STUB	Router configuration	Configure area as a stub area
AREA *area-id* VIRTUAL LINK *router-id*	Router configuration	Define a virtual link

Table 4-7   Global Commands

 Note: *Cisco Router's default cost assignment uses the bandwidth of a link. Different vendors use different procedures to configure bandwidth. In order for Cisco routers to be compatible with another vendor's product, the costs assigned to all interfaces on a link should agree with each other. This is done on a Cisco router by modifying the cost by using the IP OSPF COST command.*

Command	Command Mode	Purpose
AREA *area-id* AUTHENTICATION	Router configuration	Enable authentication for an OSPF area
AREA *area-id* DEFAULT-COST *cost*	Router configuration	Specify cost for a default summary route sent into a stub area
AREA *area-id* NSSA	Router configuration	Configure an area as a Not So Stubby Area
AREA *area-id* RANGE *address-mask*	Router configuration	Summarizes routes at an area boundary
AREA *area-id* STUB	Router configuration	Configures area as a stub area
AREA *area-id* VIRTUAL LINK *router-id*	Router configuration	Define a virtual link
DEFAULT-INFORMATION ORIGINATE	Router configuration	Generate a default route into an OSPF routing domain

Table 4-8   Router Configuration Commands

Command	Command Mode	Purpose
DEFAULT-METRIC *number*	Router configuration	Sets default metric values
NEIGHBOR *ip-address*	Router configuration	Configure router interconnecting to broadcast networks
NETWORK *address wildcard-mask* AREA *area-id*	Router configuration	Define the interface on which OSPF is running and define the areas for the interfaces
OSPF AUTO-COST REFERENCE-BANDWIDTH *ref-bw*	Router configuration	Control the automatic calculation of link cost by reference bandwidth.
OSPF LOG-ADJ-CHANGES	Router configuration	Configure router to send a syslog message when the state of a neighbor changes
SUMMARY-ADDRESS *address-mask*	Router configuration	Create aggregate addresses for OSPF
TIMERS SPF *spf-delay spf-holdtime*	Router configuration	Set delay time between when OSPF receives a topology change and OSPF starts a Shortest Path first calculation

Table 4-8   Router Configuration Commands *(continued)*

 ## What commands are used in the interface configuration mode?

Table 4-9 shows the commands used in the interface configuration mode, along with a brief description of the purpose of each command.

Command	Command Mode	Purpose
IP OSPF AUTHENTICATION-KEY *password*	Interface configuration	Assign passwords to be used by neighboring routers
IP OSPF COST *cost*	Interface configuration	Specify the cost of sending packets on an interface
IP OSPF DEAD-INTERVAL *seconds*	Interface configuration	Set the time for how long the hello packets must not be seen before declaring that the neighboring router is down
IP OSPF DEMAND-CIRCUIT	Interface configuration	Treat the interface as an OSPF demand circuit

Table 4-9   Interface Configuration Commands

Command	Command Mode	Purpose
IP OSPF HELLO-INTERVAL *seconds*	Interface configuration	Specify the interval between hello packets sent on an interface
IP OSPF MESSAGE-DIGEST-KEY KEY-ID *md5 key*	Interface configuration	Enable OSPF MD5 authentication
IP OSPF NETWORK	Interface configuration	Configure an OSPF network to a type other than the default network
IP OSPF PRIORITY *number*	Interface configuration	Set the router priority for Designated Router election on a multiaccess network.
IP OSPF RETRANSMIT-INTERVAL *seconds*	Interface configuration	Specify time between link-state advertisement retransmissions for adjacencies for an interface
IP OSPF TRANSMIT-DELAY *seconds*	Interface configuration	Set the time it takes to transmit a link-state update packet on an interface

Table 4-9　Interface Configuration Commands *(continued)*

 What are the commands used in the EXEC command mode?

Table 4-10 shows the commands used in the EXEC command mode, along with a brief description of the purpose of each command.

 Note:　At a minimum, configuration of an OSPF router can be implemented with default parameters. One interface must be set to be in Area 0 for network statements to be accepted.

Command	Command Mode	Purpose
SHOW IP OSPF	EXEC	Show general information about the OSPF process
SHOW IP OSPF BORDER-ROUTERS	EXEC	Show an internal routing table
SHOW IP-OSPF DATABASE	EXEC	Display information related to the OSPF database
SHOW IP-OSPF INTERFACE	EXEC	Display interface information
SHOW IP OSPF-NEIGHBOR	EXEC	Display OSPF neighbor information
SHOW IP OSPF VIRTUAL-LINKS	EXEC	Display information related to virtual links

Table 4-10   EXEC Commands

BRINGING IT ALL TOGETHER

What would be an example of configuring OSPF routers?

Figure 4-1 shows the conceptual network with area border routers and backbone areas.

```
Router Boston  Internal Router
interface ethernet 0
ip address 124.113.1.1 255.255.255.0
router ospf  200
network  124.113.0.0 area  1
Router New York - Internal Router
interface ethernet 1
ip address 124.113.1.2   255.255.255.0
router ospf  200
network  124.113.0.0 area  1
Router Philadelphia :  Area Border Router
interface ethernet 2
ip address 124.113.1.3   255.255.255.0
interface serial 1
ip address 124.113.2.1   255.255.255.0
router ospf  200
network  124.113.1.0  0.0.0.255   area  1
network  124.113.2.0  0.0.0.255   area  0
Router Washington, DC  - Internal Router
interface ethernet 3
ip address 124.113.2.2   255.255.255.0
```

```
interface serial 2
ip address 15.0.0.1  255.255.255.0
router ospf  200
network  124.113.2.0   0.0.0.255    area  0
network  15.0.0.0   0.255.255.255   area  0
Router Atlanta - ASBR
interface ethernet 5
ip address 15.0.0.2  255.255.255.0
interface serial 3
ip address 25.0.0.5  255.255.255.0
router ospf  200
network 15.0.0.0   0.255.255.255    area  0
redistribute rip 200 metric 2 metric-type 2
 router rip 200
  network 124.113.00
  network 15.0.0.0
  neighbor 25.0.0.2 remote-as 41
```

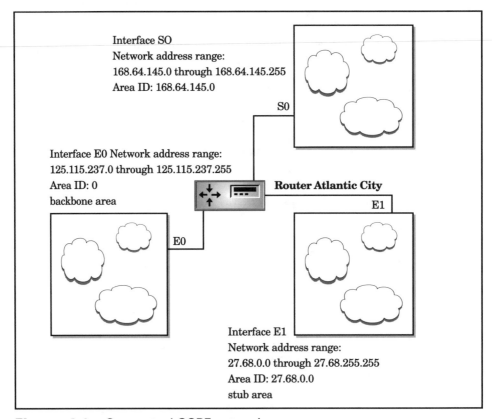

Figure 4-1 Conceptual OSPF network

What would be an example of configuring an area border router?

Figure 4-2 is an example of an area border router.

OSPF network is on 125.115.0.0 in autonomous system 150. IGRP is on autonomous system 175 on network 125.115.0.0

```
Interface serial 0
 ip address  168.64.145.150  255.255.255.0
 ip ospf authentication-key  ijklmnop
 ip ospf cost 25
!
interface ethernet  0
ip address 125.115.237.150 255.255.255.0
ip ospf authentication-key qrstuvw
ip ospf cost 15
!
interface ethernet  1
ip address 27.68.0.150 255.255.0.0
ip ospf authentication-key efghijklm
ip ospf cost 30
 ip ospf retransmit-interval 15
 ip osp dead-interval 70
!
router ospf 150
network 168.64.145.0  0.0.0.255  area 168.64.145.0
network 27.0.0.0  0.255.255.255  area 27.0.0.0
network 125.115.0.0 0.0.255.255 area 0
area 0 authentication
area 27.0.0.0  stub
area 27.0.0.0 authentication
area 27.0.0.0 default-cost 10
area 168.64.145.0 authentication
area 27.0.0.0 range 27.0.0.0  255.0.0.0
area 168.64.145.0 range  168.64.145.0  255.255.255.0
area 0 range 125.115.237.0  255.255.255.0
area 0 range 125.115.250.0  255.255.255.0
redistribute igrp 175 metric-type 4 metric 2 tag 175
subnets
redistribute rip  metric-type 1 metric 1 tag 175
router igrp 175
 network 125.115.0.0
!
!        rip for 168.64.110.0
```

```
!
router rip
 network 168.64.110.0
 redistribute igrp 175 metric 2
 redistribute ospf 150 metric 1
```

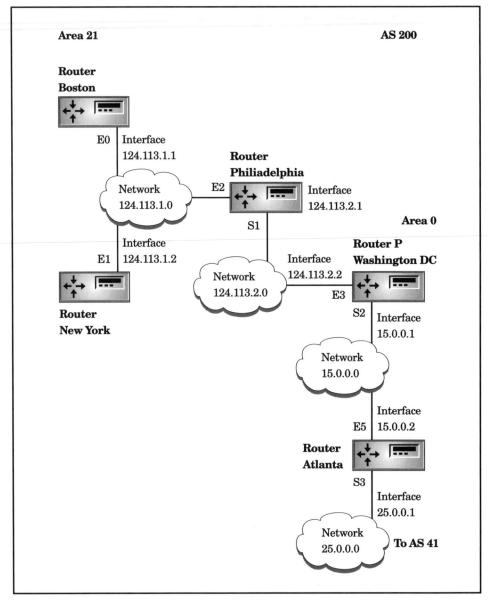

Figure 4-2 Area border router

Chapter 5

Configuring RIP

Answer Topics!

Configuring RIP @ a Glance

The Routing Information Protocol version 1 (RIPv1) is the most commonly used interior gateway protocol (IGP). It was created for use in small, homogeneous networks.

The Routing Information Protocol version 2 provides additional features to the earlier version. Both are classical distance vector routing protocols.

RIP uses broadcast User Datagram Protocol (UDP) data packets to exchange routing information between routers. RIP sends routing information updates every 30 seconds. If a router does not receive an update from another router for 180 seconds or more, it marks the routes as being unusable. If there is still no update after 240 seconds, the router removes all routing table entries for the router not responding.

RIP uses hop count as a metric to rate the value of different routes. The hop count is the number of routers that can be traversed in a route. A directly connected network has a metric of zero; an unreachable network has a metric of 16. This small range of metrics makes RIP an unsuitable routing protocol for large networks.

Cisco's implementation of RIP version 2 supports plain text and MD5 authentication, route summarization, classless interdomain routing (CIDR), and variable-length subnet masks (VLSMs).

This chapter is divided into the following sections:

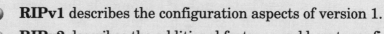

RIPv1 describes the configuration aspects of version 1.

RIPv2 describes the additional features and how to configure them.

Triggered RIP reviews the configuration aspects of triggered RIP.

Compatibility reviews the compatibility issues with other routing protocols.

RIPV1

 ### How do I configure RIP or disable RIP?

To create a routing process for RIP, use the ROUTER RIP global configuration command:

```
router rip
```

Use the NO ROUTER RIP command to turn the RIP routing process off.

```
no router rip
```

 ### How do I allow unicast updates for RIP?

Since RIP is a broadcast protocol, in order for routing updates to reach nonbroadcast networks, you must configure the router to permit the exchange of routing information. This is accomplished through the use of the NEIGHBOR command.

 ### How do I apply offsets to routing metrics?

Offset lists are used to increase incoming and outgoing metrics to routes learned via RIP. This provides a local mechanism for increasing the value of routing metrics. As an option, you can limit the offset list with either an access list or an interface.

```
offset-list [access-list-number | name] {in | out}
 offset [type number]
```

In this command:

- **offset-list [access-list-number | name]** Applies an offset to routing metrics
- **access-list-number | name** Is the standard access list number or name to be applied. Access list number 0 indicates all access lists. If offset is 0, no action is taken. For IGRP, the offset is added to the delay component only.

- **in**   Applies the access list to incoming metrics
- **out**   Applies the access list to outgoing metrics
- **offset**   Is the positive offset to be applied to metrics for networks matching the access list. If the offset is 0, no action is taken.
- **type**   Is the interface type to which the offset-list is applied
- **number**   Is the interface number to which the offset-list is applied

How do I adjust the timers of the routing protocol?

Routing protocols use several timers to determine such variables as the frequency of routing updates, the length of time before a route becomes invalid, and other parameters. These timers can be adjusted to tune routing protocol performance to better suit your networking needs. The following timers may be adjusted:

- The rate (time in seconds between updates) at which routing updates are sent
- The interval of time after which a route is declared invalid
- The interval during which routing information regarding better paths is suppressed
- The amount of time that must pass before a route is removed from the routing table
- The amount of time for which routing updates will be postponed

You may also tune the IP routing support in the software to enable faster convergence of the various IP routing algorithms, resulting in quicker fallback to redundant routers. The total effect is to minimize disruptions to end users of the network in situations where quick recovery is essential. To adjust routing protocol timers, use:

```
timers basic update invalid holddown flush
```

In this command:

- **update** Is the rate in seconds at which updates are sent. This is the fundamental timing parameter of the routing protocol. The default is 30 seconds.

- **invalid** Is the interval of time in seconds after which a route is declared invalid; it should be at least three times the value of *update*. A route becomes invalid when there is an absence of updates that refresh the route. The route then enters holddown. The route is marked inaccessible and advertised as unreachable. However, the route is still used for forwarding packets. The default is 180 seconds.

- **holddown** Is the interval in seconds during which routing information regarding better paths is suppressed. It should be at least three times the value of *update*. A route enters into a holddown state when an update packet is received that indicates the route is unreachable. The route is marked inaccessible and advertised as unreachable. However, the route is still used for forwarding packets. When holddown expires, routes advertised by other sources are accepted and the route is no longer inaccessible. The default is 180 seconds.

- **flush** Is the amount of time in seconds that must pass before the route is removed from the routing table; the interval specified should be greater than the *invalid* value. If it is less than this value, the proper holddown interval cannot elapse, which results in a new route being accepted before the holddown interval expires. The default is 240 seconds.

What is an example of using the TIMERS command?

In the following example, updates are broadcast every seven seconds. If a router is not heard from in 18 seconds, the route is declared unusable. Further information is suppressed for an additional 18 seconds. At the end of the suppression period, the route is flushed from the routing table.

```
router rip
timers basic 7  18  18  30
```

> *Note:*   *By setting a short update period, you run the risk of congesting slow-speed serial lines; however, this is not a big concern on faster-speed Ethernets and T1-rate serial lines. Also, if you have many routes in your updates, you can cause the routers to spend an excessive amount of time processing updates.*

How do I specify a particular RIP version?

The router software, by default, receives RIP version 1 and version 2 packets, but sends only version 1 packets. You can configure the software to receive and send only version 1 packets. You can also configure the software to receive and send only version 2 packets.

```
version {1 | 2}
```

How do I specify which version will send on specific interfaces?

You can configure a particular interface to control which RIP version an interface sends by entering the following commands at the interface configuration mode:

```
ip rip send version 1
```

which configures an interface to send only RIP version 1,

```
ip rip send version 2
```

which configures an interface to send only RIP version 2, and

```
ip rip send version 1 2
```

which configures an interface to send RIP versions 1 and 2.

Can the update timers for RIP be restored to their default settings?

When you need to adjust RIP network timers, use the TIMERS BASIC router configuration command (described earlier in this chapter). To restore the default timers, use the NO form of this command.

```
no timers basic
```

 ## How do I redistribute RIP updates into HELLO updates?

In this situation, consider a wide-area network using RIP, which needs to advertise routes to another network using HELLO as the routing protocol. The following commands should be entered:

```
router hello
network 192.168.23.0
redistribute rip
default-metric 10000
distribute-list 10 out rip
```

In these commands:

- **router**   Is a HELLO routing process
- **network**   Specifies that network 192.168.23.0 is the network to receive HELLO routing information
- **redistribute**   Specifies that RIP-derived routing information be advertised in the HELLO routing updates
- **default-metric**   Assigns a HELLO delay of 10,000 to all RIP-derived routes
- **distribute-list**   Instructs the router to use access list 10 (not defined in this example) to limit the entries in each outgoing HELLO update. The access list prevents unauthorized advertising of university routes to the regional network.

 Note: *The example could have specified automatic conversion between the RIP and HELLO metrics. However, in the interest of routing table stability, it is not desirable to do so. Instead, this example limits the routing information exchanged to availability information only.*

How do I specify which version will receive on specific interfaces?

To control how packets received from an interface are processed, perform one of the following tasks in interface configuration mode:

```
ip rip receive version 1
```

which configures an interface to accept only RIP version 1,

```
ip rip receive version 2
```

which configures an interface to accept only RIP version 2, and

```
ip rip receive version 1 2
```

which configures an interface to accept RIP version 1 or 2.

How do I enable and disable split-horizon?

Split-horizon blocks information about routes from being advertised by a router out of any interface from which that information originated. This method optimizes communications among multiple routers when links are broken. Split-horizon should not be used for nonbroadcast networks such as Frame Relay or SMDS. If an interface is configured with secondary IP addresses, and split-horizon is enabled, updates might not be sourced by every secondary address. One routing update is sourced per network number unless split-horizon is disabled. In interface configuration mode, use the following command to enable split-horizon:

```
ip split-horizon
```

To disable split-horizon, use:

```
no ip split-horizon
```

Note: *Split-horizon for Frame Relay and SMDS encapsulation is disabled by default. Split-horizon is not disabled by default for interfaces using any of the X.25 encapsulations. For all other encapsulations, split-horizon is enabled by default. In general, changing the state of the default is not recommended unless you are certain that your application requires making a change in order to advertise routes properly.*

Tip: *If split-horizon is disabled on a serial interface (and that interface is attached to a packet-switched network), you must disable split-horizon for all routers in any relevant multicast group on that network.*

 ## When would I configure interpacket delay?

Interpacket delay is the period of time, measured in milliseconds, between packets in a multiple-packet RIP update. If you have a high-end router sending to a low-speed router, you might want to add interpacket delay to RIP updates, in the range of 8–50 milliseconds. Enter the following command in router configuration mode:

```
output-delay delay
```

 ## How do I define neighbors using RIP?

To define a neighboring router with which to exchange routing information, use this form of the NEIGHBOR router configuration command.

```
neighbor ip-address
```

To remove an entry, use the NO form of this command.

```
no neighbor ip-address
```

In these commands, *ip-address* is the IP address of a peer router.

 ## What command allows the operator to specify a list of networks for RIP routing?

The NETWORK router configuration command allows the operator to specify a list of networks for the RIP routing process.

```
network network-number
```

The NO NETWORK command removes a network from the list.

```
no network network-number
```

In these commands, *network-number* is the IP address of the network of directly connected networks.

What command disables sending RIP updates on an interface?

The PASSIVE-INTERFACE router configuration command disables sending routing updates on an interface.

```
passive-interface interface
```

The NO PASSIVE-INTERFACE command reenables sending routing updates on the specified interface.

```
no passive-interface interface
```

In these commands, *interface* is the specified interface. The particular subnet will continue to be advertised to other interfaces. Updates from other communication servers on that interface continue to be received and processed.

 How do I redistribute using RIP?

The REDISTRIBUTE router configuration command redistributes routes from one routing domain into another routing domain.

```
redistribute protocol [process-id]
 {level-1 | level-1-2 | level-2} [metric metric-value]
[metric-type type-value]
 [match internal | external 1 | external 2]
[tag tag-value] [route-map map-tag]
[weight weight] [subnets]
```

The NO form of this command ends redistribution of information when you supply the appropriate arguments, or disables any of the specified keywords.

```
no redistribute protocol [process-id]
 {level-1 | level-1-2 | level-2} [metric metric-value]
[metric-type type-value]
 [match internal | external 1 | external 2]
[tag tag-value] [route-map map-tag]
 [weight weight] [subnets]
```

In these commands:

● **protocol** Is the source protocol from which routes are being redistributed. It can be one of the following keywords: bgp, egp, igrp, ospf, static [ip], connected, and rip. The keyword static [ip] is used to redistribute IP static routes. The keyword connected refers to routes, which are established automatically by virtue of having enabled IP on an interface. For routing protocols such as OSPF, these routes will be redistributed as external to the AS.

● **metric metric-value** Is the metric used for the redistributed route. If a value is not specified for this option, and no value is specified using the DEFAULT-METRIC router configuration command, the default metric value is 0. Use a value consistent with the destination protocol.

● **external type-value** Is the external route type to be redistributed into other routing domains: 1=Type 1 external route. 2=Type 2 external route. The default is internal.

● **route-map** Is the route map that should be interrogated to filter the importation of routes from this source routing protocol to the current routing protocol. If not specified, all routes are redistributed. If this keyword is specified, but no route map tags are listed, no routes will be imported.

What command defines the conditions for redistributing?

The ROUTE-MAP global configuration command defines the conditions for redistributing routes from one routing protocol into another. Each ROUTE-MAP command has a list of MATCH and SET commands associated with it. The MATCH commands specify the match criteria—the conditions under which redistribution is allowed for the current route-map. The SET commands specify the set actions—the particular redistribution actions to perform if the criteria enforced by the MATCH commands are met.

```
route-map map-tag {permit | deny} sequence-number
```

The NO ROUTE-MAP command deletes the route map.

```
no route-map map-tag {permit | deny} sequence-number
```

In these commands:

- **map-tag**　Defines a meaningful name for the route map. The REDISTRIBUTE router configuration command uses this name to reference this route map. Multiple route maps may share the same map tag name.

- **permit**　If the match criteria are met for this route map, and PERMIT is specified, the route is redistributed as controlled by the set actions. If the match criteria are not met, and PERMIT is specified, the next route map with the same map tag is tested. If a route passes none of the match criteria for the set of route maps sharing the same name, it is not redistributed by that set.

- **deny**　If the match criteria are met for the route map, and DENY is specified, the route is not redistributed, and no further route maps sharing the same map tag name will be examined.

- **sequence-number**　Is the number that indicates the position a new route map is to have in the list of route maps already configured with the same name. If given with the NO form of this command, it specifies the position of the route map that should be deleted.

How do I display the status of the routing table?

The SHOW IP ROUTE command is used to display the current state of the routing table.

```
show ip route
  [address [mask]] | [protocol [process-id]]
```

In this command, all of the following parameters are optional:

- **address**　Is the address about which routing information should be displayed

- **mask**　Is the argument for a subnet mask

- **protocol**   Is the argument for a particular routing protocol, or *static* or *connected*
- **process-id**   Identifies the particular routing protocol process

What do the fields displayed by SHOW IP ROUTE mean?

The following sample is an output from the SHOW IP ROUTE command when entered without an address.

```
cs# show ip route
Codes: I - IGRP derived, R - RIP derived,
 O - OSPF derived
C - connected, S - static, E - EGP derived,
 B - BGP derived
* - candidate default route, IA - OSPF inter
 area route
 E1 - OSPF external type 1 route, E2 - OSPF external
 type 2 route
Gateway of last resort is 131.119.254.240 to
 network 129.140.0.0
O E0 150.150.0.0 [160/5]
 via 131.119.254.6, 0:01:00, Ethernet0
E    192.67.131.0 [200/128]
 via 131.119.254.244, 0:02:22, Ethernet0
O E0 192.68.132.0 [160/5]
 via 131.119.254.6, 0:00:59, Ethernet0
O E0 130.130.0.0 [160/5]
 via 131.119.254.6, 0:00:59, Ethernet0
E    128.128.0.0 [200/128]
 via 131.119.254.244, 0:02:22, Ethernet0
E    129.129.0.0 [200/129]
 via 131.119.254.240, 0:02:22, Ethernet0
E    192.65.129.0 [200/128]
 via 131.119.254.244, 0:02:22, Ethernet0
E    131.131.0.0 [200/128]
 via 131.119.254.244, 0:02:22, Ethernet0
E    192.75.139.0 [200/129]
 via 131.119.254.240, 0:02:23, Ethernet0
E    192.16.208.0 [200/128]
 via 131.119.254.244, 0:02:22, Ethernet0
E    192.84.148.0 [200/129]
 via 131.119.254.240, 0:02:23, Ethernet0
E    192.31.223.0 [200/128]
```

```
 via 131.119.254.244, 0:02:22, Ethernet0
E    192.44.236.0 [200/129]
 via 131.119.254.240, 0:02:23, Ethernet0
E    140.141.0.0 [200/129]
 via 131.119.254.240, 0:02:22, Ethernet0
E    141.140.0.0 [200/129]
 via 131.119.254.240, 0:02:23, Ethernet0
```

In this output:

- **O** Indicates the protocol that derived the route. Possible values include:
  - I (IGRP derived)
  - R (RIP derived)
  - O (OSPF derived)
  - C (connected)
  - S (static)
  - E (EGP derived)
  - B (BGP derived)

- **E2** Indicates the type of route. Possible values include:
  - * (candidate default route)
  - IA (OSPF interarea route)
  - E1 (OSPF external type 1 route)
  - E2 (OSPF external type 2 route)

- **150.150.0.0** Indicates the address of the remote network

- **[160/5]** The first number in the brackets is the administrative distance of the information source. The second number is the metric for the route.

- **via 131.119.254.6** Specifies the address of the next communication server to the remote network

- **0:01:00** Specifies the last time the route was updated (in hours:minutes:seconds)

- **Ethernet 2** Specifies the interface through which the specified network can be reached

- ***** Is the round-robin pointer. It indicates the last path used when a packet was forwarded. The pointer applies to nonfast-switched packets only. The asterisk gives no indication as to which path will be used next when forwarding a nonfast-switched packet, except when the paths are of equal cost.

 ## What does the information from the SHOW IP ROUTE SUMMARY command mean?

The following ouptut is a sample from the SHOW IP ROUTE SUMMARY command:

```
cs# show ip route summary
Route                                            Memory
Source    Networks    Subnets    Overhead    (bytes)
connected        0          3         126        360
static           1          2         126        360
igrp 109       747         12       31878      91080
internal         3                                360
Total          751         17       32130      92160
cs#
```

In this output:

- **Route Source** Routing protocol name, or *connected* or *static* or *internal*

- **internal** Those routes that are in the primary routing table merely as markers to hold subnet routes. These routes are not owned by any routing protocol. There should be one of these internal routes for each subnetted network in the routing table.

- **Networks** The number of Class A, B, or C networks that are present in the routing table for each route source

- **Subnets** The number of subnets that are present in the routing table for each route source, including host routes

- **Overhead** Any additional memory involved in allocating the routes for the particular route source other than the memory specified under *Memory*.

- **Memory** The number of bytes allocated to maintain all the routes for the particular route source

 ## What command displays all route maps that have been configured?

The SHOW ROUTE-MAP command displays all route maps configured, or only the one specified.

```
show route-map [map-name]
```

In this command, *map-name* is the name of a specific route-map.

What would be a sample output from the SHOW ROUTE-MAP command?

The following sample output is from the SHOW ROUTE-MAP command:

```
cs# show route-map
route-map foo, permit, sequence 10
Match clauses:
tag 1 2
Set clauses:
metric 5
route-map foo, permit, sequence 20
Match clauses:
tag 3 4
Set clauses:
metric 6
```

In this output:

● **route-map** Is the name of the route-map

● **permit** Indicates that the route is redistributed as controlled by the set actions

● **sequence** Is the number that indicates the position a new route map is to have in the list of route maps already configured with the same name

● **Match clauses tag** Indicates the conditions under which redistribution is allowed for the current route map

● **Set clauses metric** Indicates the particular redistribution actions to perform if the criteria enforced by the MATCH commands are met

How do I filter RIP updates received from other devices?

Use the DISTRIBUTE-LIST router configuration command to filter networks received in updates.

```
distribute-list access-list-number in [interface-name]
```

Use the NO form of this command to change or cancel the filter.

```
no distribute-list access-list-number in
  [interface-name]
```

In these commands:

● **access-list-number** Is the standard IP access list number. The list explicitly specifies which networks are to be received and which are to be suppressed.

● **In** Applies the access list to incoming routing updates

● **interface-name** Is the interface on which the access list should be applied to incoming updates. If no interface is specified, the access list will be applied to all incoming updates.

How does RIP maintain its routing information?

When a router learns about changes in the routes, it updates its routing table with the change and sends the entire routing table to its neighbors. Those routers incorporate the routing table into their own routing table, run the Bellman-Ford algorithm, and forward their updated routing tables. This process is not complete until all routers in the network converge. If there are no changes in the network, each router normally sends out its routing table to its neighbor every 60 seconds.

In the RIP routing table display, how do you determine which networks are discovered by the RIP routing protocol?

The networks discovered by the RIP routing protocol are preceded by the code letter R. The networks that are directly connected to the router, and have been configured with the NETWORK command, are preceded by the code letter C.

The following shows a routing table display that illustrates these codes.

```
Router# show ip route
Codes: C - connected, S - static, I - IGRP, R - RIP,
       M - mobile, D - DGP,
    J - EIGRP, EX - EIGRP external, O - OSPF,
       L1 - OSPF inter area
    E1 - OSPF external type 1,
       E2 - OSPF external type 2, E - EGP,
    1 - IS-IS, L1 - IS-IS level=1,
       L2 - IS-IS level=2, * - candidate default
Gateway of last resort not set
       172.16.0.0 255.255.255.0 is subnetted, 3 subnets
C      172.16.100.0 is directly connected via Ethernet0
R      172.16.101.0 120/I1 via 172.16.103.60, 00:00:14,
       Ethernet0
C      172.16.102.0 is directly connected via Loopback0
```

How do I filter networks from being advertised in updates?

You will use the DISTRIBUTE-LIST router configuration command to suppress networks from being advertised in updates.

```
distribute-list access-list-number out
  {interface-name | routing-process}
```

Use the NO form of this command to cancel this function.

```
no distribute-list access-list-number out
  {interface-name | routing-process}
```

In these commands:

● **access-list-number**   Is the standard IP access list number. The list explicitly specifies which networks are to be sent and which are to be suppressed in routing updates.

● **out**   Applies the access list to outgoing routing updates

- **interface-name** Is the name of a particular interface
- **routing-process** Is the name of a particular routing process, or *static* or *connected*

In the following example, only one network is to be advertised by a RIP routing process: network 192.1680.0.

```
access-list 1 permit 192.168.0.0
access-list 1 deny 0.0.0.0 255.255.255.255
router rip
network 192.168.0.0
distribute-list 1 out
```

 ### How do I create a default route?

Use the IP DEFAULT-NETWORK global configuration command to select a network as a candidate route for computing the gateway of last resort.

```
ip default-network network-number
```

Use the NO version of this command to remove the route.

```
no ip default-network network-number
```

 ### How do I generate a default route in RIP?

Use the DEFAULT-INFORMATION ORIGINATE router configuration command to generate a default route in RIP. The routing process will generate the default route if the ROUTE-MAP parameter is satisfied.

```
default-information originate [route-map mapname]
```

To disable this feature, use the NO form of this command.

```
no default-information originate
```

Does RIP version 1 support variable-length subnet masking?

No. RIPv1 can support only one subnet per network address, because routing updates do not have a Subnet Mask field.

What is an example of the route-map command?

The following example originates a default route (0.0.0.0/0) over a certain interface when 192.168.0.0/16 is present. This is called *conditional default origination*.

```
router rip
 version 2
 network 192.168.16.0
 default-information originate route-map condition
route-map condition permit 10
 match ip address 10
 set interface s1/0
access-list 10 permit 192.168.16.0 0.0.0.255
```

What is the format of a RIP update packet?

The fields of the RIP packet are as follows:

- **Command**   Indicates that the packet is a request or a response. The REQUEST command requests the responding system to send all or part of its routing table. Destinations for which a response is requested are listed later in the packet. The RESPONSE command represents a reply to a request or, more frequently, an unsolicited regular routing update. In the response packet, a responding system includes all or part of its routing table. Regular routing update messages include the entire routing table.

- **Version number**   Specifies the RIP version being implemented. With the potential for many RIP implementations in an internetwork, this field can be used to signal different, potentially incompatible, implementations.

- **Address family identifier**   Follows a 16-bit field of all zeros, and specifies the particular address family being used. On the Internet this address family is typically IP (value = 2), but other network types may also be represented.

● **Address**   Follows another 16-bit field of zeros. In Internet RIP implementations, this field typically contains an IP address.

● **Metric**   Follows two more 32-bit fields of zeros, and specifies the hop count. The hop count indicates how many internetwork hops (routers) must be traversed before the destination can be reached.

Up to 25 occurrences of the Address Family Identifier field through the Metric field are permitted in any single IP RIP packet. In other words, up to 25 destinations may be listed in any single RIP packet. Multiple RIP packets are used to convey information from larger routing tables.

Like other routing protocols, RIP uses certain timers to regulate its performance. The RIP Routing Update timer is generally set to 30 seconds, ensuring that each router will send a complete copy of its routing table to all neighbors every 30 seconds. The Route Invalid timer determines how much time must expire without a router having heard about a particular route before that route is considered invalid. When a route is marked invalid, neighbors are notified of this fact. This notification must occur prior to expiration of the Route Flush timer. When the Route Flush timer expires, the route is removed from the routing table. Typical initial values for these timers are 90 seconds for the Route Invalid timer and 270 seconds for the Route Flush timer.

How do you know on which network the updates are being sent?

The originating network number is displayed in parentheses following the sending update notice.

Are updates sent on all networks regardless of hop count?

No, networks exceeding the 15 hop count metric are flagged as inaccessible.

RIPV2

How do I enable RIPv2 authentication?

The two supported modes of authentication on an interface for which RIP authentication is enabled are plain text authentication and MD5 authentication. The default authentication in every RIP version 2 packet is plain text authentication. You should enter the following commands in interface configuration mode. To enable RIP authentication, use

```
ip rip authentication key-chain name-of-chain
```

To configure the interface to use MD5 digest authentication (or let it default to plain text authentication), use

```
ip rip authentication mode {text | md5}
```

 Note: *Do not use plain text authentication in RIP packets for security purposes, because the unencrypted authentication key is sent in every RIP version 2 packet. Use plain text authentication when security is not an issue—for example, to ensure that misconfigured hosts do not participate in routing.*

How do I disable route summarization under RIPv2?

RIPv2 supports automatic route summarization by default. The software summarizes subprefixes to the classful network boundary when crossing classful network boundaries. If you have disconnected subnets, disable automatic route summarization to advertise the subnets. When route summarization is disabled, the software transmits subnet and host routing information across classful network boundaries. To disable automatic summarization, enter the following command in router configuration mode:

```
no auto-summary
```

What are the differences between the RIPv1 and RIPv2 update packets?

The RIPv2 update packet format is shown here:

```
0 1 2 3 4 5 6 7 0 1 2 3 4 5 6 7 0 1 2 3 4 5 6 7 0 1 2 3 4 5 6 7
+-+-+-+-+-+-+-+-+-+-+-+-+-+-+-+-+-+-+-+-+-+-+-+-+-+-+-+-+-+-+-+-+
| Command (1)    | Version (1)    |         Routing domain      |
+----------------+----------------+-----------------------------+
| Address Family Identifier (2)   |        Route Tag (2)        |
+---------------------------------+-----------------------------+
|                            IP Address (4)                     |
+--------------------------------------------------------------+
|                            Subnet Mask (4)                    |
+--------------------------------------------------------------+
|                            Next Hop (4)                       |
+--------------------------------------------------------------+
|                            Metric (4)                         |
+--------------------------------------------------------------+
```

The fields Command, Address Family Identifier (AFI), IP Address, and Metric all have the same meanings as in RIP 1. The Version field specifies version number 2 for RIP datagrams that use authentication or carry information in any of the newly defined fields.

In RIP 2 there is an optional authentication mechanism. When in use, this option uses an entire RIP entry, and leaves space to at most 24 RIP entries in the remainder of the packet. The most widespread authentication type is simple password; it is type 2.

The Routing Domain field enables some routing domains to interwork upon the same physical infrastructure, while logically ignoring each other, making it possible to implement various kinds of policies simply. There is a default routing domain, which is assigned the value 0.

The Route Tag (RT) field exists as a support for EGPs. This field is expected to carry autonomous system numbers for EGP and BGP. RIP systems that receive an RIP entry, which contains a non-zero RT value, must re-advertise that value.

The Subnet Mask field contains the subnet mask, which is applied to the IP address to yield the non-host portion of the address. If this field is zero, then no subnet mask is included for this entry.

Next Hop is the immediate next-hop IP address to which packets to the destination specified by this route entry should be forwarded. The purpose of the Next Hop field is to eliminate packets being routed through extra hops in the system. It is particularly useful when RIP is not being run on all of the routers on a network.

Multicasting is an optional feature in RIP 2, using IP address 224.0.0.9. This feature reduces unnecessary load on those hosts that are not listening to RIP 2. The IP multicast address is used for periodic broadcasts. In order to maintain backward compatibility, the use of the multicast address is configurable.

Note: *RIP 2 is totally backward compatible with RIP 1. Its applications support fine-tuning to be RIP 1 emulation, RIP 1 compatible, or fully RIP 2.*

How do I configure static routes?

Static routes are operator- or administrator-defined routes that cause packets moving between a source and a destination to take a specified path. Static routes can be important if the router cannot build a route to a particular destination. They are useful for specifying a gateway of last resort to which all unroutable packets will be sent.

To configure static routes, enter the following command in global configuration mode:

```
ip route prefix mask {address | interface}
  [distance] [tag tag] [permanent]
```

The router remembers static routes until you remove them (using the NO form of the IP ROUTE global configuration command). However, you can override static routes with dynamic routing information through prudent assignment of administrative distance values. Each dynamic routing protocol has a default administrative distance, as shown in Table 5-1. If you would like a static route to be overridden by information from a dynamic routing protocol, simply ensure that the administrative distance of the static route is higher than that of the dynamic protocol.

Route Source	Default Distance
Connected interface	0
Static route	1
Enhanced IGRP summary route	5
External BGP	20
Internal Enhanced IGRP	90
IGRP	100
OSPF	110
IS-IS	115
RIP	120
EGP	140
Internal BGP	200
Unknown	255

Table 5-1   Dynamic Routing Protocol Default Administrative Distances

Static routes that point to an interface will be advertised via RIP, IGRP, and other dynamic routing protocols, regardless of whether REDISTRIBUTE STATIC commands were specified for those routing protocols. This is because static routes that point to an interface are considered in the routing table to be connected and hence lose their static nature. However, if you define a static route to an interface that is not one of the networks defined in a NETWORK command, no dynamic routing protocols will advertise the route unless a REDISTRIBUTE STATIC command is specified for these protocols.

When an interface goes down, all static routes through that interface are removed from the IP routing table. Also, when the software can no longer find a valid next hop for the address specified as the forwarding router's address in a static route, the static route is removed from the IP routing table.

How do I manage authentication keys?

When you manage authentication keys, you must:

1. Define a key chain.
2. Identify the keys that belong to the key chain.
3. Specify how long each key is valid.

Each key has its own key identifier (specified with the KEY NUMBER command), which is stored locally. The combination of the key identifier and the interface associated with the message uniquely identifies the authentication algorithm and MD5 authentication key in use.

Multiple keys with lifetimes can be configured, but only one authentication packet is sent, regardless of how many valid keys exist. The router examines the key numbers in order from lowest to highest, and uses the first valid key it encounters. Lifetimes allow for overlap during key changes. Note that the router must know the time. Manage authentication keys by entering the commands below in global configuration mode.
To identify a key chain, use

```
key chain name-of-chain
```

To identify the key number in key chain configuration mode, use

```
key number
```

To identify the key string in key chain configuration mode, use

```
key-string text
```

To specify the time period in which the key can be received, use

```
accept-lifetime start-time
{infinite | end-time | duration seconds}
```

To specify the time period in which the key can be sent, use

```
send-lifetime start-time
{infinite | end-time | duration seconds}
```

You can use the SHOW KEY CHAIN command to display key chain information.

 What is a variable-length subnet mask?

Variable-length subnet masks provide the capacity to include more than one subnet within a network, and the capability to subnet an already subnetted network address.

 What would be a simple configuration example of key management?

The following example configures a key chain called *bushes*. In this example, the software will always accept and send *grass* as a valid key. The key *walnut* will be accepted from 1:30 P.M. to 3:30 P.M. and be sent from 2:00 P.M. to 3:00 P.M. The overlap allows for migration of keys or discrepancies in the router's time. Likewise, the key *panel* immediately follows *walnut*, and there is a half-hour leeway on each side to handle time-of-day differences.

```
interface ethernet 0
   ip rip authentication key-chain bushes
   ip rip authentication mode md5
router rip
   network 172.19.0.0
   version 2
key chain bushes
   key 1
      key-string grass
   key 2
      key-string walnut
      accept-lifetime 13:30:00 Jan 25 1996
       duration 7200
      send-lifetime 14:00:00 Jan 25 1996 duration 3600
   key 3
      key-string panel
      accept-lifetime 14:30:00 Jan 25 1996
       duration 7200
      send-lifetime 15:00:00 Jan 25 1996 duration 3600
```

 What would be a sample configuration of a key chain?

The following example configures a key chain called *simpson*:

```
key chain simpson
 key 1
  key-string oj
 key 2
  key-string bart
  accept-lifetime 00:00:00 Dec 5 1995
   23:59:59 Dec 5 1995
  send-lifetime 06:00:00 Dec 5 1995
   18:00:00 Dec 5 1995
```

What command sets automatic summarization to its default behavior?

Use the AUTO-SUMMARY router configuration command to restore the default behavior of automatic summarization of subnet routes into network-level routes.

```
auto-summary
```

To disable this feature and transmit subprefix routing information across classful network boundaries, use the NO form of this command.

```
no auto-summary
```

Note: *Route summarization reduces the amount of routing information in the routing tables. RIP version 1 always uses automatic summarization. If you are using RIP version 2, you can turn off automatic summarization by specifying NO AUTO-SUMMARY.*

Tip: *If you must perform routing between disconnected subnets, disable automatic summarization. When automatic summarization is off, subnets are advertised.*

TRIGGERED RIP

What is triggered RIP?

The triggered extensions to RIP are particularly appropriate for WANs where the cost—financial or packet overhead—would

make periodic transmission of routing (or service-advertising) updates unacceptable. For example:

- Connection-oriented public data networks (X.25 packet-switched networks or ISDN)
- Point-to-point links supporting PPP link-quality monitoring or echo request to determine link failure

A triggered RIP implementation runs standard RIP on LANs, allowing them to interoperate transparently with implementations adhering to the original specifications.

Can triggered RIP support multiple paths?

For devices using standard RIP, only one path between networks is maintained in the routing table. If a device finds two paths to the same network, the path with the lower metric is stored; or, if they have the same metric, one of the paths is chosen. When a device is using triggered RIP, all paths between networks are stored, and secondary paths can be used if the primary path should fail.

Can RIP be configured to send triggered updates?

You configure RIP to generate an update on a specified interface each time it recalculates a route's metric. Such an update is called a triggered update. A triggered update contains only the routes that have changed. (RIP also sends full updates at regular intervals on interfaces configured for triggered updating.)

What are some of the problems with triggered updates?

Triggered updates would be sufficient if we could guarantee that the wave of updates would reach every appropriate router immediately, but there are two main problems:

- Packets containing the update message can be dropped or corrupted by some link in the network
- The triggered updates do not happen instantaneously. It is possible that a router that has not yet received the

triggered update will issue a regular update at just the wrong time, causing the bad route to be reinserted in a neighbor that had already received the triggered update.

 Note: *Coupling triggered updates with holddown is designed to get around these problems. The holddown rule states when a route is removed, new routes to the destination will not be accepted for a set period of time to allow the triggered update to propagate throughout the network.*

COMPATIBILITY

 ### Can IGRP and RIP run at the same time?

Yes, you can run IGRP and RIP at the same time. However, there are significant issues that will cause concern, such as topology changes. IGRP information will override the RIP information because of IGRP's administrative distance. IGRP and RIP have different update timers, and because they require different amounts of time to propagate routing updates, one part of the network will end up believing IGRP routes and another part will end up believing RIP routes. This will result in routing loops.

Even though these loops do not exist for very long, the Time To Live (TTL) will quickly reach zero, and ICMP will send a "TTL exceeded" message. This message will cause most applications to stop attempting network connections.

Will the router validate the source IP address for updates?

To validate the source IP address of incoming routing updates for RIP and IGRP routing protocols, you must use the VALIDATE-UPDATE-SOURCE router configuration command.

```
validate-update-source
```

To disable this function, use the NO form of this command.

```
no validate-update-source
```

This command is only applicable to RIP and IGRP. The software ensures that the source IP address of incoming routing updates is on the same IP network as one of the addresses defined for the receiving interface. Disabling split-horizon on the incoming interface will also cause the system to perform this validation check. For unnumbered IP interfaces (interfaces configured as IP UNNUMBERED), no checking is performed.

 ### What would be an example of using the VALIDATE-UPDATE SOURCE command?

In the following example, a router is configured to not perform validation checks on the source IP address of incoming RIP updates:

```
router rip
network 192.168.0.0
no validate-update-source
```

 ### How do I use the DEBUG IP RIP command?

You would use the DEBUG IP RIP command to display information on RIP routing transactions.

```
debug ip rip
```

The NO form of this command disables debugging output.

```
[no] debug ip rip
```

You may also use the TERMINAL MONITOR command to set the ability to display DEBUG command output and system error messages to the current terminal.

```
terminal monitor
```

Use the TERMINAL NO MONITOR command to disable this feature.

```
terminal no monitor
```

Chapter 6

Configuring IS-IS

Answer Topics!

? Controlling hello packets

? Configuring administrative distance

? Redistributing routing information

? Duration of the validity of a hello packet

? NSAP-to-SNPA mapping

? Setting the CLNS MTU

? Configuring administrative distance for routes learned from CLNS

? Ignoring packets with internal checksum errors

? Filtering IS-IS neighbors

? Redistributing routing information from one domain to another

? Setting a tag value

Configuring IS-IS @ a Glance

IS-IS (Intermediate System-to-Intermediate System) is a link-state, hierarchical routing protocol based on the DECnet Phase V routing algorithm. IS-IS can operate over a variety of subnetworks, including broadcast LANs, WANs, and point-to-point links. IS-IS is a link-state protocol and is actually quite similar to OSPF in that it contains a Hello protocol to discover neighboring nodes, and uses a flooding protocol to propagate link information. IS-IS uses a sequence number for messages, but it is a simple incrementing counter. When the counter reaches the "ceiling," an IS-IS router has no option but to fake a failure and trigger a purge of all old information. However, this is not a problem since the sequence numbers used are 32 bits long, giving a very large sequence number space before a ceiling is reached. At least two technical problems exist, however: IS-IS uses a tiny metric (6 bits), severely limiting the information that can be conveyed with it; in addition, the link-state number is only an 8-bit value, limiting the number of records that a router can advertise to 256. A non-technical problem is that IS-IS is bound to OSI, and as such is much slower to evolve and to respond to change compared to OSPF.

This chapter discusses the IS-IS implementation and configuration commands. It is divided into the following sections:

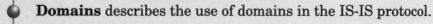

Domains describes the use of domains in the IS-IS protocol.

Messages defines some of the messages received by the IS-IS router.

Areas defines the parameters of networks and interfaces within the IS-IS area.

Link-State Update describes the commands used to modify/adjust the link-state parameters of IS-IS.

Metrics reviews the method of discovering new neighbors.

DOMAINS

 ## How do I specify the interface circuit type?

You can specify adjacency levels on a specified interface
(also called the *interface circuit type*). Enter the following
command in interface configuration mode:

```
isis circuit-type {level-1 | level-1-2 | level-2-only}
```

 ## How does the router know its system role type?

You must configure the router to act as a Level 1 (intra-area)
router, as both a Level 1 router and a Level 2 (inter-area)
router, or as an inter-area router only. Enter the following
command in router configuration mode:

```
is-type {level-1 | level-1-2 | level-2-only}
```

 Note: *It is highly recommended that you configure the type
of IS-IS router. If there is only one area, there is no need to
run two copies of the same algorithm. You have the option to
run L1-only or L2-only everywhere. If IS-IS is used for CLNS
routing, L1-only must be used everywhere. If IS-IS is used just
for IP routing, it is slightly preferred to run L2-only everywhere,
as this allows easy addition of other areas later.*

 ## Which command displays the IS-IS link-state database?

You display the IS-IS link-state database by entering the
following commands in EXEC mode:

```
show isis database [level-1] [l2] [detail] [lspid]
```

to display the IS-IS link-state database [level-2] [l1], and

```
show isis spf-log
```

to display how often and why the router has run a full SPF
(shortest path first) calculation.

What would be a sample configuration of IS-IS as an IP routing protocol?

The following example configuration shows how to configure three routers to run IS-IS as an IP routing protocol environment. Router 1 has Ethernet and serial interfaces; Router 2 has a serial and two Ethernet interfaces; and Router 3 has two Ethernet interfaces.
Configuration for Router 1:

```
router isis
  net 51.0001.0000.0000.000a.00
interface ethernet 0
  ip router isis
interface serial 0
  ip router isis
```

Configuration for Router 2:

```
router isis
  net 51.0001.0000.0000.000b.00
interface ethernet 0
  ip router isis
interface ethernet 1
  ip router isis
interface serial 0
  ip router isis
```

Configuration for Router 3:

```
router isis
  net 51.0001.0000.0000.000c.00
interface ethernet 1
  ip router isis
interface ethernet 2
  ip router isis
```

How do I create a default route?

Whenever you specifically configure redistribution of routes into an IS-IS routing domain, the router does not, by default, redistribute the default route into the IS-IS routing domain.

However, you can force the boundary router to redistribute the default route, or generate a default route into its L2 LSP. You can use a route map to conditionally advertise the default route, depending on the existence of another route in the router's routing table. To create a default route, enter the following command in router configuration mode:

```
default-information originate [route-map map-name]
```

Note: *You can use a route map to conditionally advertise the default route, depending on the existence of another route in the router's routing table.*

How do I enable IS-IS on the router?

IS-IS requires that you create an IS-IS routing process and assign it to specific interfaces. You can specify only one IS-IS process per router. Only one IS-IS process is allowed whether you run it in integrated mode, ISO CLNS only, or IP only. To enable IS-IS on the router, enter the following commands in global configuration mode. To enable IS-IS routing and specify an IS-IS process for IP, which places you in router configuration mode, use

```
router isis
```

To configure NETs for the routing process (you can specify a name for a NET as well as an address), use

```
net network-entity-title
```

To enter interface configuration mode, use

```
interface type number
```

To specify the interfaces that should be actively routing IS-IS, use

```
ip router isis [tag]
```

The following shows an example of a router configuration on which IS-IS is enabled.

```
version 11.0
service udp-small-servers
```

```
service tcp-small-servers
!
hostname Router
!
!
clns routing
!
interface Ethernet0
ip address 192.168.68.1 255.255.255.0
ip router isis
isis adjacency-filter temp match-all
!
interface Serial0
ip address 172.16.1.1 255.255.255.252
no fair-queue
```

How do I configure an IS-IS network entity?

To configure an IS-IS network entity title (NET) for the routing process, use the NET router configuration command.

```
net network-entity-title
```

To remove a NET, use the no form of this command.

```
no net network-entity-title
```

In these commands, *network-entity-title* is the NET that specifies the area address and the system ID for an IS-IS routing process. This argument can be either an address or a name.

Does IS-IS support redistribution?

You may use the REDISTRIBUTE router configuration command to redistribute routes from one routing domain into another routing domain.

```
redistribute router-name [tag] [route-map map-tag]
```

The NO REDISTRIBUTE command disables redistribution, or disables any of the specified keywords.

```
no redistribute router-name [tag] [route-map map-tag]
```

In these commands:

- **router-name**   Is the type of other routing protocol that is to be redistributed as a source of routes into the current routing protocol being configured. The keywords supported are iso-igrp, isis, and static [clns]. The keyword STATIC [clns] is used to redistribute CLNS prefix static routes. This causes the router to inject any static CLNS routes into the domain. The optional CLNS keyword is used when redistributing into IS-IS.

- **tag**   Is the meaningful name for a routing process which is optional

- **route-map map-tag**   A route map should be interrogated to filter the importation of routes from this source routing protocol to the current routing protocol. If not specified, all routes are redistributed. If this keyword is specified, but no route map tags are listed, no routes will be imported. The argument *map-tag* is the identifier of a configured route map.

 Note: *The CLNS (Connectionless Network Service) protocol is a standard for the network layer of the OSI model that does not require a circuit to be established before data is transmitted. The ISO IGRP is a dynamic distance vector routing protocol designed by Cisco for routing an autonomous system that contains large, arbitrarily complex networks with diverse bandwidth and delay characteristics. ISO IGRP supports three levels of routing: system routing, area routing, and interdomain routing.*

How would a sample configuration for redistribution for IS-IS look?

This sample configuration illustrates redistribution of ISO-IGRP routes of Florida and ISO-IGRP routes of Idaho into the IS-IS area tagged Texas:

```
router isis Texas
redistribute iso-igrp Florida
redistribute iso-igrp Idaho
```

This sample configuration illustrates redistribution of IS-IS routes of Russia and ISO-IGRP routes of Cuba into the ISO-IGRP area tagged USA:

```
router iso-igrp USA
redistribute isis Russia
redistribute iso-igrp Cuba
```

Under what conditions would I assign a static address under IS-IS?

You would use the CLNS NET global configuration command to assign a static address for a router. If the router is configured to support ISO CLNS, but is not configured to dynamically route CLNS packets using ISO IGRP or IS-IS, use this command to assign an address to the router.

```
clns net {net-address | name}
```

Use the NO form of this command to remove any previously configured NET or network service access point (NSAP) address.

```
no clns net {net-address | name}
```

In this command, *name* is the CLNS host name to be associated with this interface.

Note: *Addresses in the ISO network architecture are called NSAP addresses and network entity titles. Each node in an OSI network has one or more NETs. In addition, each node has many NSAP addresses. Each NSAP address differs from one of the NETs for that node in only the last byte. This byte is called the N-selector. Its function is similar to the port number in other protocol suites. Cisco's implementation supports all NSAP address formats that are defined by ISO 8348/Ad2; however, we provide ISO IGRP or IS-IS dynamic routing only for NSAP addresses that conform to the address constraints defined in the ISO standard for IS-IS (ISO 10589).*

 How do I assign an NSAP address or name to the router?

Use the CLNS NET INTERFACE configuration command to assign an NSAP address or name to a router interface. If the router is configured to support ISO CLNS, but is not configured to dynamically route CLNS packets using an ISO IGRP or IS-IS, use this command to assign an address to the router.

```
clns net {nsap-address | name}
```

Use the NO form of this command to remove any previously configured NSAP address.

```
no clns net {nsap-address | name}
```

In this command,

● **nsap-address**   Is the specific NSAP address

● **name**   Is the name to be associated with this interface

MESSAGES

How do I interpret the output from the SHOW ISIS SPF-LOG display?

The following is an actual display output from the SHOW ISIS SPF-LOG command:

```
show isis spf-log
Level 1 SPF log
            Last trigger
When    Duration Nodes Count       LSP          Triggers
00:15:46  3124   40    1      milles.00-00      TLVCODE
00:15:24  3216   41    5      milles.00-00      TLVCODE NEWLSP
00:15:19  3096   41    1      deurze.00-00      TLVCODE
00:14:54  3004   41    2      milles.00-00      ATTACHFLAG LSPHEADER
00:14:49  3384   41    1      milles.00-01      TLVCODE
00:14:23  2932   41    3      milles.00-00      TLVCODE
00:05:18  3140   41    1                        PERIODIC
00:03:54  3144   41    1      milles.01-00      TLVCODE
```

```
00:03:49   2908   41   1        milles.01-00        TLVCODE
00:03:28   3148   41   3        bakel.00-00         TLVCODETLVCONTENT
00:03:15   3054   41   1        milles.00-00        TLVCODE
00:02:53   2958   41   1        mortel.00-00        TLVCODE
00:02:48   3632   41   2        milles.00-00        NEWADJ  TLVCODE
00:02:23   2988   41   1        milles.00-01        TLVCODE
00:02:18   3016   41   1        gemert.00-00        TLVCODE
00:02:14   2932   41   1        bakel.00-00         TLVCONTENT
00:02:09   2988   41   2        bakel.00-00         TLVCONTENT
00:01:54   3228   41   1        milles.00-00        TLVCODE
00:01:38   3120   41   3        rips.03-00          TLVCONTENT
```

In this output:

● **When**   Represents how long ago (hh:mm:ss) a full SPF calculation occurred. The last 20 occurrences are logged.

● **Duration**   Is the number of milliseconds it took to complete this SPF run. Elapsed time is wall clock time, not CPU time.

● **Nodes**   Are the number of routers and pseudonodes (LANs) that make up the topology calculated in this SPF run

● **Count**   Is the number of events that triggered this SPF run. When there is a topology change, often multiple LSPs are received in a short time. A router waits five seconds before running a full SPF run, so it can include all new information. This count denotes the number of events (such as receiving new LSPs) that occurred while the router was waiting its five seconds before running full SPF.

● **LSP**   Link-state packets. Whenever a full SPF calculation is triggered by the arrival of a new LSP, the router stores the LSP ID. The LSP ID can give a clue as to the source of routing instability in an area. If multiple LSPs are causing an SPF run, only the LSP ID of the last received LSP is remembered.

● **Triggers**   A list of all reasons that triggered a full SPF calculation. Possible triggers are described in Table 6-1.

Trigger	Explanation
PERIODIC	Typically, every 15 minutes a router runs a periodic full SPF calculation
NEWSYSID	A new system ID (via NET) was configured on this router
NEWAREA	A new area (via NET) was configured on this router
NEWLEVEL	A new level (via IS-TYPE) was configured on this router
RTCLEARED	A CLEAR CLNS ROUTE command was issued on this router
NEWMETRIC	A new metric was configured on an interface of this router
IPBACKUP	An IP route disappeared, which was not learned via IS-IS, but via another protocol with better administrative distance. IS-IS will run a full SPF to install an IS-IS route for the disappeared IP prefix.
IPQUERY	A CLEAR IP ROUTE command was issued on this router
ATTACHFLAG	This router is now attached to the L2 backbone, or it has just lost contact to the L2 backbone
ADMINDIST	Another administrative distance was configured for the IS-IS process on this router
AREASET	Set of learned area-addresses in this area changed
NEWADJ	This router has created a new adjacency to another router
DBCHANGED	A CLEAR ISIS * command was issued on this router
BACKUPOVFL	An IP prefix disappeared. The router knows there is another way to reach that prefix, but has not stored that backup route. The only way to find the alternative route is to run a full SPF run.
NEWLSP	A new router or pseudonode appeared in the topology
LSPEXPIRED	Some LSP in the LSDB has expired
LSPHEADER	ATT/P/OL bits or is-type in an LSP header changed
TLVCODE	TLV code mismatch, indicating that different TLVs are included in the newest version of an LSP
TLVCONTENT	TLV contents changed. This normally indicates that an adjacency somewhere in the area has come up or gone down. Look at the "Last trigger LSP" to get an indication of where the instability may have occurred.

Table 6-1 Possible Triggers of an SPF Calculation

How do I cause the router to create a message when neighbors change state?

Use the LOG-ADJACENCY-CHANGES router configuration command to cause IS-IS to generate a log message when an IS-IS adjacency changes state (up or down).

```
log-adjacency-changes
```

Use the NO form of this command to disable this function.

```
no log-adjacency-changes
```

AREAS

What does an IS-IS NSAP address consist of?

An IS-IS NSAP address is divided into two parts: an area address and a system ID. Level 2 routing (routing between areas) uses the area address. Level 1 routing (routing within an area) uses the system ID address. The NSAP address is laid out as follows:

● The area address is the NSAP address, not including the system ID and N-selector

● The system ID is found between the area address and the N-selector byte

● The N-selector (S) is the last byte of the NSAP address

The IS-IS routing protocol interprets the bytes from the AFI up to (but not including) the System ID field in the domain specific part (DSP) as an *area identifier*. The system ID specifies the system, and the maximum address size is 20 bytes.

 What rules are mandatory for IS-IS addresses?

All IS-IS NSAP addresses must obey the following constraints:

- No two nodes can have addresses with the same NET—that is, addresses that match all but the N-selector (S) field in the DSP
- No two nodes residing within the same area can have addresses in which the system ID fields are the same
- ISO IGRP and IS-IS should not be configured for the same area. Do *not* specify an NSAP address where all bytes up to (but not including) the system ID are the same when enabling both ISO IGRP and IS-IS routing.
- A router can have one or more area addresses. Cisco's implementation of IS-IS requires at least eight bytes: one byte for area, six bytes for system ID, and one byte for N-selector.

 What does an IS-IS NSAP look like?

The following is an example of OSI network and GOSIP (Government OSI Profile) NSAP addresses using the ISO IGRP implementation. It is in the OSI network NSAP address format:

```
|  Domain  | Area | System ID  | S|
47.0004.004D.0003.0000.0C00.62E6.00
```

 How do I assign multiple area addresses to IS-IS areas?

IS-IS routing supports the assignment of multiple area addresses on the same router, which is called *multihoming*. Multihoming provides a mechanism for smoothly migrating network addresses, as follows:

- **Splitting up an area**   Nodes within a given area can accumulate to a point that they are difficult to manage, cause excessive traffic, or threaten to exceed the usable address space for an area. Multiple area addresses can be assigned so that you can smoothly partition a network into separate areas without disrupting service.

● **Merging areas**   Use transitional area addresses to merge as many as three separate areas into a single area that share a common area address

● **Transition to a different address**   You may need to change an area address for a particular group of nodes. Use multiple area addresses to allow incoming traffic intended for an old area address to continue being routed to associated nodes.

You must statically assign the multiple area addresses on the router (up to three area addresses on a router). The number of areas allowed in a domain is unlimited.

All the addresses share the same system ID. As an example, you can assign one address (*area1* plus system ID), and two additional addresses in different areas (*area2* plus system ID and *area3* plus system ID) where the system ID is the same.

Routers can dynamically learn about any adjacent router by informing each other of their area addresses. If two routers share at least one area address, the set of area addresses of the two routers is merged. The merged set cannot contain more than three addresses. If there are more than three, the three addresses with the lowest numerical values are kept, and all others are dropped.

Enter the following commands in global configuration mode:

```
router isis [tag]
```

which enables IS-IS routing and enters router configuration mode, and

```
net network-entity-title
```

which configures NETs for the routing process. The router can have up to three NETs.

The following example illustrates specifying a single NET:

```
router isis phillips
net 47.0004.004d.0001.0000.0c11.1111.00
```

 What command is used to display IS-IS router neighbors?

Use the SHOW CLNS IS-NEIGHBORS command to display IS-IS related information for IS-IS router adjacencies. Neighbor entries are sorted according to the area in which they are located.

```
show clns is-neighbors [interface-type unit] [detail]
```

In this command:

● **interface-type unit**   Is an optional parameter that specifies that information for a particular interface is to be displayed. For example, e0 specifies the first Ethernet interface; e1 specifies the second Ethernet interface. You must specify both the *interface-type* and *unit* number.

detail   Is an optional parameter. When specified, the areas associated with the intermediate systems are displayed. Otherwise, a summary display is provided.

 What would be a sample display from entering the SHOW CLNS IS-NEIGHBOR command?

A sample display is shown here:

```
Router# show clns is-neighbors
System Id          Interface  State  Type  Priority  Circuit Id        Format
0000.0C00.0C35     Ethernet1  Up     L1    64        0000.0C00.62E6.03  Phase V
0800.2B16.24EA     Ethernet0  Up     L1L2  64/64     0800.2B16.24EA.01  Phase V
0000.0C00.3E51     Serial1    Up     L2    0         04                 Phase V
0000.0C00.62E6     Ethernet1  Up     L1    64        0000.0C00.62E6.03  Phase V
```

In this output:

● **System Id**   Identifies the value of the system

● **Interface**   Is the interface on which the router was discovered

● **State**   Describes the adjacency state. *Up* and *init* are the states.

● **Type**   Specifies L1, L2, and L1L2 type adjacencies

● **Priority**   Indentifies the IS-IS priority that the respective neighbor is advertising. The highest-priority neighbor is elected the designated IS-IS router for the interface.

● **Circuit Id**   Shows the neighbor's idea of what the designated IS-IS router is for the interface

● **Format**   Indicates if the neighbor is a Phase V (OSI) adjacency or Phase IV (DECnet) adjacency

What is the command to show all destinations the router knows?

Use the SHOW CLNS ROUTE command to display all of the destinations to which a certain router knows how to route packets. The SHOW CLNS ROUTE command shows the IS-IS Level 2 routing table as well as static and ISO-IGRP learned prefix routes. The table stores IS-IS area addresses and prefix routes sorted by category. In the following command, *nsap* is the CLNS address:

```
show clns route [nsap]
```

What command enables IS-IS on an interface?

The CLNS ROUTER ISIS interface configuration command enables IS-IS routing for OSI on a specified interface.

```
clns router isis [tag]
```

Use the NO form of this command with the appropriate area tag to disable IS-IS routing for the system.

```
no clns router isis [tag]
```

In these commands, *tag* is a meaningful name for a routing process. If not specified, a null tag is assumed. It must be unique among all CLNS router processes for a given router. Use the same text for the argument *tag* as specified in the ROUTER ISIS global configuration command.

LINK-STATE UPDATE

 How do I set the overload bit—and under what conditions would it need to be set?

To configure the router to set the overload bit in its non-pseudonode LSPs, enter the following command in router configuration mode:

```
set-overload-bit
```

Under normal conditions, the setting of the overload bit is allowed only when a router runs into problems. As an example, when a router is experiencing a memory shortage, it might be that the link-state database is not complete, resulting in an incomplete or inaccurate routing table. Setting the overload bit in its LSPs tells other routers to ignore the unreliable router in their SPF calculations until the router has recovered from its problems. The result will be that other routers in the IS-IS area see no paths through this router. However, IP and CLNS prefixes directly connected to this router still will be reachable. This command can be useful when you want to connect a router to an ISIS network, but don't want real traffic flowing through it under any circumstances. Examples are:

- A test router in the lab, connected to a production network
- A router configured as an LSP flooding server (for example, on an NBMA network, in combination with the mesh-group feature)
- A router that is aggregating virtual circuits (VCs) used only for network management. In this case, the network management stations must be on a network directly connected to the router with the SET-OVERLOAD-BIT command configured.

What command do I use to summarize address ranges?

You can create aggregate addresses that are represented in the routing table by a summary address. This process is called *route summarization*. One summary address can include multiple groups of addresses for a given level, and routes learned from other routing protocols also can be summarized. The metric used to advertise the summary is the smallest metric of all the more specific routes. To create a summary of addresses for a given level, enter the following command in router configuration mode:

```
summary-address address mask
   {level-1 | level-1-2 | level-2}
```

How can I set the advertised hello interval?

You may specify the length of time (in seconds) between hello packets that the router sends on the interface by entering the following command in interface configuration mode:

```
isis hello-interval seconds {level-1 | level-2}
```

Note: *The hello interval can be configured independently for Level 1 and Level 2, except on serial point-to-point interfaces. (Because there is only a single type of hello packet sent on serial links, it is independent of Level 1 or Level 2.) Specify an optional level for X.25, SMDS, and Frame Relay multiaccess networks. X25, SMDS, ATM, and Frame Relay networks should be configured with point-to-point subinterfaces.*

How do I set the advertised CSNP interval?

CSNP stands for complete sequence number PDU. CSNPs are forwarded by the designated router to maintain database synchronization. You may configure the IS-IS CSNP interval

for the specific interface by entering the following command in interface configuration mode:

```
isis csnp-interval seconds {level-1 | level-2}
```

 Note: *This feature does not apply to serial point-to-point interfaces. It applies to WAN connections if the WAN is viewed as a multiaccess meshed network.*

 ## When should I modify the retransmission interval?

The setting of this parameter should be conservative, or else needless retransmission will result. The value you specify should be an integer greater than the expected round-trip delay between any two routers on the attached network. You may configure the number of seconds between retransmission of IS-IS LSPs for point-to-point links by entering the following command in interface configuration mode:

```
isis retransmit-interval seconds
```

 ## How do I set the LSP transmissions interval?

You can configure the delay between successive IS-IS link-state packet transmissions by entering the following command in interface configuration mode:

```
isis lsp-interval milliseconds
```

 ## Can I set or adjust the retransmission throttle interval?

You can configure the maximum rate at which IS-IS LSPs will be retransmitted on point-to-point links, in terms of the number of milliseconds between packets. This is different from the retransmission interval, which is the amount of time between successive retransmissions of the *same* LSP. To set the retransmission throttle interval, enter the following command in interface configuration mode:

```
isis retransmit-throttle-interval milliseconds
```

> **Tip:** *The retransmission throttle interval is typically not necessary, except in cases of very large networks with high point-to-point neighbor counts.*

How can I specify a designated router election?

You can configure the priority to use for designated router election. Priorities can be configured for Level 1 and Level 2 individually. To specify the designated router election, perform the following task in interface configuration mode:

```
isis priority value {level-1 | level-2}
```

How do I set the MTU of link-state IS-IS packets?

Use the LSP-MTU router configuration command to set the MTU size of IS-IS link-state packets.

```
lsp-mtu size
```

In this command, *size* is the maximum packet size in bytes. The size must be less than or equal to the smallest MTU of any link in the network. The default size is 1497 bytes. Use the NO form of this command to disable this function.

```
no lsp-mtu
```

METRICS

How do I configure IS-IS link-state metrics?

You may configure the default metric for Level 1 or Level 2 routing for a specified interface. Enter the following command in interface configuration mode:

```
isis metric default-metric {level-1 | level-2}
```

In this command, *default-metric* is the metric assigned to the link and used to calculate the cost from each router via the links in the network to other destinations. You can configure this metric for Level 1 or Level 2 routing. The range is from 0 to 63. The default value is 10.

 ## How can I set the hello multiplier?

You can adjust the number of IS-IS hello packets a neighbor must miss before the router should declare the adjacency as down, by entering the following command in interface configuration command:

```
isis hello-multiplier multiplier {level-1 | level-2}
```

The default value is 3.

 ## How do I assign a password for an interface?

You can assign different passwords for different routing levels. Specifying Level 1 or Level 2 configures the password for only Level 1 or Level 2 routing, respectively. If you do not specify a level, the default is Level 1. By default, authentication is disabled.

Enter the following commands in interface configuration mode:

```
isis password password {level-1 | level-2}
```

to configure the authentication password for a specified interface, and

```
domain-password password
```

to configure the routing domain authentication password.

What command do I use to determine which router is the next-hop router?

Use the WHICH-ROUTE command to know which next-hop router will be used, or if you have multiple processes running and want to troubleshoot your configuration. This command displays the routing table in which the specified CLNS destination is found.

```
which-route {nsap-address | clns-name}
```

In this command:

- **nsap-address** Is the CLNS destination network address
- **clns-name** Is the destination host name

What are some examples of using the WHICH-ROUTE command?

The following example shows that destination information for router *blue* is found in the IS-IS Level-1 routing table. The destination is on the local system.

```
blue# which-route blue
Route look-up for
 destination 39.0001.0000.0c00.bda8.00, GRAY
Found route in IS-IS level-1
 routing table - destination is local
```

The next example shows that destination information for NSAP address 49.0001.0000.0c00.bda8.00 is found in the ISO-IGRP Level-1 routing table. The destination is on the local system.

```
blue# which-route blue
Route look-up
 for destination 49.0001.0000.0c00.bda8.00
Found route in ISO-IGRP
 routing table - destination is local
```

The next example shows that destination information for router *black* is found in the IS-IS Level-1 routing table. The destination is not on the local system

```
blue# which-route black
Route look-up
 for destination 39.0001.0000.0c00.7f06.00, GREEN
Found route in IS-IS level-1 routing table
System
Id    SNPA           Interface State Holdtime Type Protocol
GREEN 0000.0c00.2d55 Ethernet0 Up     91         L1L2 IS-IS
Area Address(es): 39.0001
```

In these examples:

- **System ID** Is the six-byte value that identifies a system in an area. A name is displayed in this field if one has been assigned with the CLNS HOST global configuration command.

- **SNPA** Is the SNPA data-link address. (SNPA stands for subnetwork point of attachment.)

- **Interface**   Is the interface from which system information was learned

- **State**   Is the state of the ES or IS. Possible values are: *Init* (The system is an IS and is waiting for an IS-IS hello message. The neighbor to the IS-IS is not adjacent.) and *Up* (The ES or IS is reachable.)

- **Holdtime**   Indicates the number of seconds for which the information is valid

- **Protocol**   Indicates the protocol through which the adjacency was learned. Valid protocol sources are ES-IS, IS-IS, ISO-IGRP, and Static.

- **Type**   Indicates the adjacency type. Possible values are shown in Table 6-2.

How do I remove neighbor information from the database?

Use the CLEAR CLNS IS-NEIGHBORS command to remove intermediate system (IS) neighbor information from the adjacency database.

```
clear clns is-neighbors
```

Type	Value
ES	An end-system adjacency that is either discovered by the ES-IS protocol or statically configured
IS	A router adjacency that is either discovered by the IS-IS protocol or is statically configured
L1	A router adjacency for Level 1 routing only
L1L2	A router adjacency for Level 1 and Level 2 routing
L2	A router adjacency for Level 2 only

Table 6-2   Values of Adjacency Types

What command filters the establishment of neighbors?

Use the CLNS ADJACENCY-FILTER interface configuration command to filter the establishment of CLNS ES and IS adjacencies.

```
clns adjacency-filter {es | is} name
```

Use the NO form of this command to disable this filtering.

```
no clns adjacency-filter {es | is} name
```

In these commands:

- **es**   Indicates ES adjacencies are to be filtered
- **is**   Indicates IS adjacencies are to be filtered
- **name**   Is the name of the filter set or expression to apply

What command is used to adjust the rate at which ES and IS hellos are sent?

Use the CLNS CONFIGURATION-TIME global configuration command to specify the rate at which ES hellos and IS hellos are sent.

```
clns configuration-time seconds
```

In this command, *seconds* is the rate in seconds ES and IS hello packets are sent. Use the NO form of this command to restore the default value.

```
no clns configuration-time
```

What command allows IS hellos to ignore the N-selector byte?

Use the CLNS DEC-COMPATIBLE interface configuration command to allow IS hellos—sent and received—to ignore the N-selector byte.

```
clns dec-compatible
```

Use the NO form of this command to disable this feature.

```
no clns dec-compatible
```

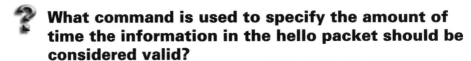 ## What command is used to specify the amount of time the information in the hello packet should be considered valid?

Use the CLNS HOLDING-TIME global configuration command to allow the sender of an ES hello or IS hello to specify the length of time you consider the information in the hello packets to be valid.

```
clns holding-time seconds
```

Use the NO form of this command to restore the default value (300 seconds).

```
no clns holding-time
```

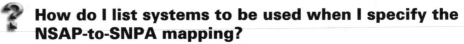 ## How do I list systems to be used when I specify the NSAP-to-SNPA mapping?

You can use the CLNS IS-NEIGHBOR interface configuration command to list all intermediate systems that will be used when you manually specify the NSAP-to-SNPA mapping.

```
clns is-neighbor nsap snpa
```

Use the NO form of this command to delete the specified IS neighbor.

```
no clns is-neighbor nsap
```

In these commands:

- **nsap** Indicates the NSAP of a specific intermediate system to enter as neighbor to a specific MAC address
- **snpa** Is a data-link (MAC) address

How do I set the CLNS MTU?

Use the CLNS MTU interface configuration command to set the maximum transmission unit (MTU) packet size for the interface.

```
clns mtu bytes
```

In this command, *bytes* is the maximum packet size in bytes. The minimum value is 512; the default and maximum packet sizes depend on the interface type. Use the NO form of this command to restore the default and maximum packet size.

```
no clns mtu
```

How do I configure administrative distance for routes learned from CLNS?

Use the DISTANCE router configuration command to configure the administrative distance for routes learned from CLNS.

```
distance value [clns]
```

Use the NO form of this command to restore the administrative distance to the default.

```
no distance value [clns]
```

In these commands:

- **value** Is the administrative distance, indicating the trustworthiness of a routing information source. This argument has a numerical value between 0 and 255. A higher relative value indicates a lower trustworthiness rating. Preference is given to routes with smaller values. The default, if unspecified, is 110.
- **clns** Indicates CLNS-derived routes for IS-IS

 What command allows the router to ignore packets with internal checksum errors?

Use the IGNORE-LSP-ERRORS router configuration command to allow the router to ignore IS-IS link-state packets that are received with internal checksum errors, rather than purging the link-state packets.

```
ignore-lsp-errors
```

Use the NO form of this command to disable this function.

```
no ignore-lsp-errors
```

 What command filters IS-IS neighbors?

The ISIS ADJACENCY-FILTER interface configuration command is used to filter the establishment of IS-IS adjacencies.

```
isis adjacency-filter name [match-all]
```

Use the NO form of this command to disable filtering of the establishment of IS-IS adjacencies.

```
no isis adjacency-filter name [match-all]
```

In these commands, MATCH-ALL determines that all NSAP addresses must match the filter in order to accept the adjacency. By default only one address need match the filter in order for the adjacency to be accepted.

 How do I redistribute routing information from one domain to another?

Use the REDISTRIBUTE router configuration command to redistribute routing information from one domain into another routing domain.

```
redistribute protocol [tag] [route-map map-tag]
redistribute static [clns | ip]
```

Use the NO form of this command to disable redistribution, or to disable any of the specified keywords.

```
no redistribute protocol [tag] [route-map map-tag]
no redistribute static [clns | ip]
```

In these commands:

- **protocol** Indicates the type of other routing protocol that is to be redistributed as a source of routes into the current routing protocol being configured. The keywords supported are iso-igrp, isis, and static.
- **tag** Is a meaningful name for a routing process
- **route-map map-tag** The route map should be interrogated to filter the importation of routes from this source routing protocol to the current routing protocol. If not specified, all routes are redistributed. If this keyword is specified, but no route map tags are listed, no routes will be imported. The argument *map-tag* is the identifier of a configured route map.
- **static** The keyword STATIC is used to redistribute static routes. When used without the optional keywords, this causes the Cisco IOS software to inject any OSI static routes into an OSI domain.
- **clns** The keyword CLNS is used when redistributing OSI static routes into an IS-IS domain
- **ip** keyword IP is used when redistributing IP into an IS-IS domain

How do I set a tag value?

Use the SET TAG ROUTE-MAP configuration command to set a tag value to associate with the redistributed routes.

```
set tag tag-value
```

Use the NO form of this command to disable redistributing routes with the specific tag.

```
no set tag tag-value
```

In these commands, *tag-value* indicates the tag value to associate with the redistributed route. If not specified, the default action is to forward the tag in the source routing protocol onto the new destination protocol.

Chapter 7

Configuring BGP

Answer Topics!

Configuring BGP @ a Glance

The primary function of a BGP system is to exchange network reachability information with other BGP systems, including information about the list of autonomous system paths. This information can be used to construct a graph of autonomous system connectivity from which routing loops can be pruned, and with which autonomous system-level policy decisions can be enforced. BGP version 4 supports classless interdomain routing (CIDR), which lets you reduce the size of your routing tables by creating aggregate routes, resulting in supernets. CIDR eliminates the concept of network classes within BGP and supports the advertising of IP prefixes. OSPF, Enhanced IGRP, ISIS-IP, and RIP can carry CIDR routes.

 BGP Support examines the commands used to configure and support the basic components of BGP.

 BGP IP Routing Support examines the commands used to modify BGP parameters and the commands used to redistribute routing information.

 ISPs and BGP reviews whether BGP is necessary to connect to an ISP.

 Monitor and Maintain BGP reviews the commands used to monitor and maintain BGP.

BGP SUPPORT

How do I enable the BGP routing protocol?

Use the ROUTER BGP command to activate the BGP protocol and identify the local autonomous system.

```
router bgp autonomous-system
```

Use the NETWORK command to permit BGP to advertise a network if it is present in the IP routing table.

```
network network-number
```

Note: *The NETWORK command is used to inject IGP routes into the BGP table. The network-mask portion of the command allows supernetting and subnetting. A maximum of 200 entries of the command is accepted. Alternatively, you could use the REDISTRIBUTE command to achieve the same result.*

How do I configure neighbors in BGP?

To configure BGP neighbors, enter the following command in router configuration mode:

```
neighbor {ip-address | peer-group-name}
 remote-as number
```

In this command:

- **ip address** Identifies the peer router
- **autonomous system** Identifies the autonomous system of the peer router. If this is the same as the local autonomous system, the session will be internal. If the autonomous systems are different, then the session will be external.

In the following example, a BGP router is assigned to autonomous system 123, and two networks are listed as originating in the autonomous system. Then the addresses of three remote routers (and their autonomous systems) are listed. The router being configured will share information about networks 131.108.0.0 and 192.31.7.0 with the neighbor routers as long as an exact match exists in the IP forwarding table. The first router listed is in a different autonomous system; the second NEIGHBOR command specifies an internal neighbor (with the same autonomous system number) at address 131.108.234.2; and the third NEIGHBOR command specifies a neighbor on a different autonomous system.

```
router bgp 123
network 121.108.0.0
network 192.31.7.0
neighbor 121.148.600.1 remote-as 167
neighbor 121.108.175.2 remote-as 123
neighbor 150.136.64.19 remote-as 99
```

How do I configure the BGP version?

By default, BGP sessions begin using BGP version 4, and negotiate downward to earlier versions if necessary. To prevent negotiation and force the BGP version used to communicate with a neighbor, enter the following command in router configuration mode:

```
neighbor {ip-address | peer-group-name} version value
```

In this command, *version* specifies the BGP version to use when communicating with a neighbor.

What are the types of BGP sessions?

BGP supports two types of sessions between and router and its neighbors. *External BGP* (EBGP) occurs between routers in two different autonomous systems. These routers are usually adjacent to one another, sharing the same media and a subnet. *Internal BGP* (IBGP) occurs between routers in the same autonomous system and is used to coordinate and synchronize routing policy within the autonomous system. Neighbors may be located anywhere in the autonomous system, even several hops away.

How are BGP sessions carried through the network?

BGP sessions are carried by the Transmission Control Protocol (TCP), a reliable support mechanism. BGP uses TCP port 179 for establishing its connection.

 ## What are the characteristics of BGP?

From RFC 1654, BGP Operations:

"The initial data flow of BGP is the entire BGP routing table. Incremental updates are sent as the routing table changes. BGP does not require periodic refresh of the entire BGP routing table. Therefore a BGP speaker must retain the current version of the entire BGP routing tables of all of its peers for the duration of the connection. KeepAlive messages are sent in response to errors or special conditions. If a connection encounters an error condition, a notification message is sent and the connection is closed."

 ## How do I configure BGP administrative weights?

An administrative weight is a number that you can assign to a path so that you can control the path selection process. The administrative weight is local to the router. A weight can be a number from 0 to 65535. Paths that the router originates have weight 32768 by default; other paths have weight 0. If you have particular neighbors that you want to prefer for most of your traffic, you can assign a higher weight to all routes learned from that neighbor. Enter the following command in router configuration mode to configure BGP administrative weights:

```
neighbor {ip-address | peer-group-name} weight weight
```

You may also assign weights based on autonomous system path access lists. A given weight becomes the weight of the route if the autonomous system path is accepted by the access list. Any number of weight filters is allowed. To assign weights based on autonomous system path access lists, enter the following command in global configuration mode:

```
neighbor ip-address filter-list
  access-list-number weight weight
```

 ## How do I configure BGP route filtering by neighbors?

If you want to restrict the routing information that the router learns or advertises, you can filter BGP routing updates to and from particular neighbors. To do this, define an access list and apply it to the updates. Distribute list filters are applied to network numbers and not autonomous system paths. To filter BGP routing updates, use the following command in router configuration mode:

```
router bgp xxx
neighbor {ip-address | peer-group-name}
 distribute-list access-list-number | name {in | out}
```

In this command, *xxx* is the BGP autonomous system number.

How do I configure BGP path filtering by neighbors?

In addition to filtering routing updates based on network numbers, you can specify an access list filter on both incoming and outbound updates based on the BGP autonomous system paths. (Each filter is an access list based on regular expressions.) To do this, define an autonomous system path access list and apply it to updates to and from particular neighbors. To configure BGP path filtering, enter the following command in global configuration mode:

```
router bgp xxx
neighbor {ip-address | peer-group-name}
 filter-list access-list-number
 {in | out | weight weight}
```

The following example demonstrates BGP path filtering by neighbor. The routes that pass AS path access list 1 will get weight 100. Only the routes that pass AS path access list 2 will be sent to 193.1.12.10. Similarly, only routes passing access list 3 will be accepted from 193.1.12.10.

```
router bgp 200
neighbor 193.1.12.10 remote-as 100
neighbor 193.1.12.10 filter-list 1 weight 100
neighbor 193.1.12.10 filter-list 2 out
neighbor 193.1.12.10 filter-list 3 in
ip as-path access-list 1 permit _109_
ip as-path access-list 2 permit _200$
ip as-path access-list 2 permit ^100$
ip as-path access-list 3 deny _690$
ip as-path access-list 3 permit .*
```

 How do I minimize the size of the routing table?

Classless interdomain routing (CIDR) enables you to create aggregate routes (or supernets) to minimize the size of routing tables. You can configure aggregate routes in BGP either by redistributing an aggregate route into BGP or by using the conditional aggregation feature described in the following task table. An aggregate address will be added to the BGP table if there is at least one more specific entry in the BGP table. To create an aggregate address in the routing table, enter one or more of the following commands in router configuration mode:

To create an aggregate entry in the BGP routing table,

```
aggregate-address address mask
```

To generate an aggregate with AS-SET,

```
aggregate-address address mask as-set
```

To advertise summary addresses only,

```
aggregate-address address-mask summary-only
```

To suppress selected, more specific routes,

```
aggregate-address address mask suppress-map map-name
```

To generate an aggregate based on conditions specified by the route map,

```
aggregate-address address mask advertise-map map-name
```

To generate an aggregate with attributes specified in the route map,

```
aggregate-address address mask attribute-map map-name
```

The following examples show how you can use aggregate routes in BGP, either by redistributing an aggregate route into BGP, or by using the conditional aggregate routing feature.

In the first example, the REDISTRIBUTE STATIC command is used to redistribute aggregate route 192.*.*.*:

```
ip route 192.0.0.0 255.0.0.0 null 0
router bgp 300
redistribute static
```

The next configuration creates an aggregate entry in the BGP routing table when there is at least one specific route that falls into the specified range. The aggregate route will be advertised as coming from your autonomous system, and has the atomic aggregate attribute set to show that information might be missing. (By default, atomic aggregate is set unless you use the AS-SET keyword in the AGGREGATE-ADDRESS command.)

```
router bgp 300
aggregate-address 192.0.0.0 255.0.0.0
```

The next example creates an aggregate entry using the same rules as in the preceding example, but the path advertised for this route will be an AS_SET consisting of all elements contained in all paths that are being summarized:

```
router bgp 300
aggregate-address 192.0.0.0 255.0.0.0 as-set
```

The next example not only creates the aggregate route for 192.*.*.*, but will also suppress advertisements of more specific routes to all neighbors:

```
router bgp 300
aggregate-address 192.0.0.0 255.0.0.0 summary-only
```

BGP IP ROUTING SUPPORT

 ### How does the use of the NETWORK command differ between IGP and BGP routing?

In most IGP configurations, the NETWORK command selects the interfaces that will participate in the routing process. In

BGP, the NETWORK command declares the route eligible for advertisement if the route is already present in the IP forwarding table.

How do I remove entries from the BGP routing table?

Use the CLEAR IP BGP command to remove entries and reset BGP sessions.

```
clear ip bgp {* | address}
```

In this command:

● ***** Clears all BGP peering sessions and starts rebuilding the BGP routing table

● **address** Identifies a specific peering session to be reset

Note: *Use the CLEAR IP BGP command after every configuration change to ensure that the change is activated, and that peer routers are informed.*

Can BGP routes be redistributed into the IP routing table?

Since BGP deals primarily with autonomous system pathing rather than routing decisions, BGP must work with an IGP (Interior Gateway Protocol) in order to advertise routes into an autonomous system. BGP does this automatically.

Can the best path selection be changed?

You may change the best path selection process by setting the network weight. Weight is a parameter that affects the best path selection process. To set the absolute weight for a network, enter the following command in router configuration mode:

```
network address mask weight weight
[route-map map-name]
```

What is BGP soft reconfiguration and how do I configure it?

When changes are made to a BGP peering session from either the network provider or the customer, the changes are not

implemented until the peering is reset. When a BGP peering session is reset, the routing tables from both the customer and the provider are exchanged. This can cause interruptions in service. Soft reconfiguration was developed to prevent these interruptions. Changes to routing policies can be made and activated without the need for clearing the peering session. Another advantage soft reconfiguration has is that is can be done on a per-neighbor basis, thus reducing the possibility of interruption to other peering sessions.

There are two types of soft reconfiguration. An update generated by the customer toward the provider is called inbound soft configuration. An update that is generated by the provider toward the customer is called outbound soft configuration. Both inbound and outbound soft configurations can be activated without resetting the BGP peering session. Care should be taken when generating a new set of inbound updates. When a new policy is sent during outbound policy reconfiguration, a new inbound policy of the neighbor can also take effect. When this occurs, the local BGP speaker should store all the received updates without modification, regardless of whether they are accepted or denied by the current inbound policy. This action is memory intensive and should be avoided if at all possible. Outbound soft reconfigurations do not have any memory overhead. An outbound reconfiguration policy can be activated in the other side of the BGP session to make the new inbound policy take effect.

To configure BGP soft configuration, enter the following command in router configuration mode:

```
Router bgp xxxx
neighbor {ip-address | peer-group-name}
 soft-reconfiguration inbound
```

In this command, *xxxx* is the BGP autonomous system number.

 How are route maps used to modify updates?

Route maps are used to set various route filters and attributes on a per-neighbor basis. Route maps can be set for both inbound and outbound updates. When activated, a route map can either allow or send both routes to certain IP address blocks, or send

or allow certain autonomous systems. Route maps can be used to set metrics on routes accepted or sent to the neighbor to establish preferred routes. Autonomous system path matching requires the AS-PATH ACCESS-LIST command. To configure and activate route maps use the following command in router configuration mode:

```
neighbor {ip-address | peer-group-name}
 route-map route-map-name {in | out}
```

The following example shows how you can use route maps to modify incoming data from a neighbor. Any route received from 192.168.1.1 that matches the filter parameters set in autonomous system access list 100 will have its weight set to 200 and its local preference set to 250, and it will be accepted.

```
router bgp 100
neighbor 192.168.1.1 route-map fix-weight in
neighbor 192.168.1.1 remote-as 1
route-map fix-weight permit 10
match as-path 100
set local-preference 250
set weight 200
ip as-path access-list 200 permit ^690$
ip as-path access-list 200 permit ^1800
```

What are communities and how are they configured?

Distribution of routing information can be controlled within BGP. Route information distribution is based on the following attributes:

- IP address
- AS path
- Communities

The Communities attribute is used to apply a routing policy to a group of BGP peers. This simplifies a router configuration by reducing the number of access lists and/or route maps that are active in a router. A community is a group of BGP peers that share some common attribute. BGP peers can belong to several communities. The Communities

attribute is an optional, transitive, global attribute in the numerical range from 1 to 4,294,967,200. Along with the Internet community, there are several communities that are predefined within the IOS software. They are as follows:

- **internet**   Advertise this route to the Internet community. All routers belong to it.
- **no-export**   Do not advertise this route to EBGP peers
- **no-advertise**   Do not advertise this route to any peer (internal or external)

You can determine through the use of communities what route information to allow or distribute to other BGP peers. A BGP router can set, append, or modify the community of a route when you learn, advertise, or redistribute. Aggregated routes have Communities attributes that contain communities from all the initial routes.

Community lists can be used to set groups of communities used in a match clause of a route map. A series of community lists can be created similar to an access list. Attributes are checked until a match is found. When an attribute is matched, the test is concluded. To create a community list, enter the following command in global configuration mode:

```
ip community-list community-list-number
 {permit | deny} community-number
```

The Communities attribute is not sent to BGP peers, by default. To send the Communities attribute to a BGP peer, use the following command in router configuration mode:

```
neighbor {ip-address | peer-group-name} send-community
```

This command specifies that the Communities attribute be sent to the neighbor at this IP address or peer group.

 What is a routing domain confederation and how is it configured?

One way to reduce the IBGP mesh is to divide an autonomous system into multiple autonomous systems and group them into

a single confederation. To the outside world, the confederation looks like a single autonomous system. Each autonomous system is fully meshed within itself, and has a few connections to other autonomous systems in the same confederation. Even though the peers in different autonomous systems have EBGP sessions, they exchange routing information as if they were IBGP peers. Specifically, the next-hop, MED, and local preference information is preserved. This enables us to retain a single Interior Gateway Protocol for all of the autonomous systems. To configure a BGP confederation, you must specify a confederation identifier.

To configure a BGP confederation identifier, enter the following command in router configuration mode:

```
bgp confederation identifier autonomous-system
```

In order to treat the neighbors from other autonomous systems within the confederation as special EBGP peers, enter the following command in router configuration mode:

```
bgp confederation peers
  autonomous-system [autonomous-system]
```

 ## What would be a sample configuration of peers in a confederation?

The following sample configuration is from several peers in a confederation. The confederation consists of three internal autonomous systems with autonomous system numbers 4001, 4002, and 4003. To the BGP speakers outside the confederation, the confederation looks like a normal autonomous system with autonomous system number 324 (specified via the BGP CONFEDERATION IDENTIFIER command). In a BGP speaker in autonomous system 4001, the BGP CONFEDERATION PEERS command marks the peers from autonomous systems 4002 and 4003 as special EBGP peers. Hence, peers 192.168.232.55 and 192.168.232.56 will get the local-preference, next-hop, and MED unmodified in the updates. The router at 143.61.79.1 is a normal EBGP

speaker, and the updates received by it from this peer will be just like a normal EBGP update from a peer in autonomous system 324.

```
router bgp 4001
bgp confederation identifier 324
bgp confederation peers 4002 4003
neighbor 192.168.232.55 remote-as 4002
neighbor 192.168.232.56 remote-as 4003
neighbor 143.61.79.1 remote-as 565
```

How do I disable automatic summarization of network numbers?

In BGP version 3, when a subnet is redistributed from an IGP into BGP, only the network route is injected into the BGP table. By default, this automatic summarization is enabled. To disable automatic network number summarization, enter the following command in router configuration mode:

```
no auto-summary
```

What are peer groups?

Often, in a BGP speaker, many neighbors are configured with the same update policies—for example, the same outbound route maps, distribute lists, filter lists, and update source. Neighbors with the same update policies can be grouped into peer groups to simplify configuration and, more importantly, to make updating more efficient. When you have many peers, this approach is highly recommended.

How are peer groups configured?

There are three steps in configuring a BGP peer group:

1. Create the peer group. To create a BGP peer group, enter the following command in router configuration mode:

   ```
   neighbor peer-group-name peer-group
   ```

2. Assign options to the peer group. After you create a peer group, you configure the peer group with NEIGHBOR commands. By default, members of the peer group inherit all the configuration options of the peer group. Members can also be configured to override the options that do not affect outbound updates. Peer group members will always inherit the following:

> REMOTE-AS (if configured)
> VERSION
> UPDATE-SOURCE
> OUT-ROUTE-MAP
> OUT-FILTER-LIST
> OUT-DIST-LIST
> MINIMUM-ADVERTISEMENT-INTERVAL
> NEXT-HOP-SELF

All the peer group members will inherit changes made to the peer group. Here is how you would specify a BGP neighbor using the peer group name:

```
neighbor {ip-address | peer-group-name}
  remote-as number
```

3. Make neighbors members of the peer group. To configure a BGP neighbor to be a member of that BGP peer group, enter the following command in router configuration mode, using the same peer group name:

```
neighbor ip-address peer-group peer-group-name
```

 Note: *There is a limitation on EBGP peer groups. Because all members of a peer group receive identical copies of an update, all the members (peering addresses) must be in the same logical IP subnet (LIS), so that the update is not invalidated or dropped.*

What other options are supported using peer groups?

The following options are supported using peer groups. Associate a description with a neighbor:

```
neighbor {ip-address | peer-group-name}
  description text
```

Allow a BGP speaker (the local router) to send the default route 0.0.0.0 to a neighbor for use as a default route:

```
neighbor {ip-address | peer-group-name}
 default-originate [route-map map-name]
```

Specify that the Communities attribute be sent to the neighbor at this IP address:

```
neighbor {ip-address | peer-group-name} send-community
```

Allow internal BGP sessions to use any operational interface for TCP connections:

```
neighbor {ip-address | peer-group-name}
 update-source interface
```

Allow BGP sessions, even when the neighbor is not on a directly connected segment:

```
neighbor {ip-address | peer-group-name} ebgp-multihop
```

Set the minimum interval between sending BGP routing updates:

```
neighbor {ip-address | peer-group-name}
 advertisement-interval seconds
```

Limit the number of prefixes allowed from a neighbor:

```
neighbor {ip-address | peer-group-name}
 maximum-prefix maximum [threshold] [warning-only]
```

Invoke MD5 authentication on a TCP connection to a BGP peer:

```
neighbor {ip-address | peer-group-name}
 password string
```

Specify a weight for all routes from a neighbor:

```
neighbor {ip-address | peer-group-name} weight weight
```

Filter BGP routing updates to/from neighbors, as specified in an access list:

```
neighbor {ip-address | peer-group-name}
 distribute-list {access-list-number | name}
 {in | out}
```

Establish a BGP filter:

```
neighbor {ip-address | peer-group-name}
 filter-list access-list-number
 {in | out | weight weight}
```

Disable next-hop processing on the BGP updates to a neighbor:

```
neighbor {ip-address | peer-group-name} next-hop-self
```

Specify the BGP version to use when communicating with a neighbor:

```
neighbor {ip-address | peer-group-name} version value
```

Apply a route map to incoming or outgoing routes:

```
neighbor {ip-address | peer-group-name}
 route-map map-name {in | out}
```

Configure the software to start storing received updates:

```
neighbor {ip-address | peer-group-name}
 soft-reconfiguration inbound
```

What would be a sample configuration of configuring an Internal BGP peer group?

In the following example, the peer group named *internal* configures the members of the peer group to be IBGP neighbors. By definition, this is an IBGP peer group because the ROUTER BGP command and the NEIGHBOR REMOTE-AS command indicate the same autonomous system (in this case, AS 300). All the peer group members use loopback 0 as the update source and use set-med as the outbound route map. The example also shows that, except for the neighbor at address 192.168.232.55, all the neighbors have filter-list 2 as the inbound filter list.

```
router bgp 300
neighbor internal peer-group
neighbor internal remote-as 300
neighbor internal update-source loopback 0
neighbor internal route-map set-med out
```

```
neighbor internal filter-list 1 out
neighbor internal filter-list 2 in
neighbor 192.168.232.53 peer-group internal
neighbor 192.168.232.54 peer-group internal
neighbor 192.168.232.55 peer-group internal
neighbor 192.168.232.55 filter-list 3 in
```

What would be an example of configuring an External BGP peer group?

In the following example, the peer group *external-peers* is defined without the NEIGHBOR REMOTE-AS command. This is what makes it an EBGP peer group. Each member of the peer group is configured with its respective autonomous system number separately. Thus, the peer group consists of members from autonomous systems 400, 500, and 600. All the peer group members have set-metric route map as an outbound route map and filter-list 93 as an outbound filter list. Except for neighbor 192.168.232.110, all have 106 as the inbound filter list.

```
router bgp 300
neighbor external-peers peer-group
neighbor external-peers route-map set-metric out
neighbor external-peers filter-list 93 out
neighbor external-peers filter-list 106 in
neighbor 192.168.232.90 remote-as 400
neighbor 192.168.232.90 peer-group external-peers
neighbor 192.168.232.100 remote-as 500
neighbor 192.168.232.100 peer-group external-peers
neighbor 192.168.232.110 remote-as 600
neighbor 192.168.232.110 peer-group external-peers
neighbor 192.168.232.110 filter-list 600 in
```

What is synchronization and why is it important?

Anytime your autonomous system passes traffic through it from another autonomous system to a third autonomous system, it is very important that your autonomous system be consistent about the routes that it advertises. For example, if your BGP were to advertise a route before all routers in your network had learned about the route through your IGP, your autonomous system could receive traffic that some routers

cannot yet route. To prevent this from happening, BGP must wait until the IGP has propagated routing information across your autonomous system. This causes BGP to be synchronized with the IGP. Synchronization is enabled by default. In some cases, you do not need synchronization. If you will not be passing traffic from a different autonomous system through your autonomous system, or if all routers in your autonomous system will be running BGP, you can disable synchronization. Disabling this feature can allow you to carry fewer routes in your IGP and allow BGP to converge more quickly. To disable synchronization, enter the following command in router configuration mode:

```
no synchronization
```

 ## What is a backdoor route and how is it configured?

A backdoor network is treated as a local network, except that it is not advertised. You can indicate which networks are reachable by using a backdoor route that the border router should use. To configure backdoor routes, enter the following command in router configuration mode:

```
network address backdoor
```

 ## Can I modify the BGP administrative distance parameters?

Administrative distance is a measure of the preference of different routing protocols. BGP uses three different administrative distances: external, internal, and local. Routes learned through External BGP are given the external distance, routes learned with Internal BGP are given the internal distance, and routes that are part of this autonomous system are given the local distance. To assign a BGP administrative distance, enter the following command in router configuration mode:

```
distance bgp external-distance internal-distance
local-distance
```

> ***Note:*** *Changing the administrative distance of BGP routes is considered dangerous and generally is not recommended. The external distance should be lower than any other dynamic routing protocol, and the internal and local distances should be higher than any other dynamic routing protocol.*

How do I adjust BGP timers?

BGP uses certain timers to control periodic activities such as the sending of keepalive messages, and the interval the Cisco IOS software waits after not receiving a keepalive message before declaring a peer dead. You can adjust these timers. When a connection is started, BGP will negotiate the holdtime with the neighbor. The smaller of the two holdtimes will be chosen. The keepalive timer is then set based on the negotiated holdtime and the configured keepalive time. To adjust BGP timers, enter the following command in router configuration mode:

```
timers bgp keepalive holdtime
```

How do I change the local path preference value?

You can define a particular path as more preferable or less preferable than other paths by changing the default local preference value of 100. To assign a different default local preference value, enter the following command in router configuration mode:

```
bgp default local-preference value
```

> ***Note:*** *You can use route maps to change the default local preference of specific paths.*

Can Network 0.0.0.0 be redistributed using BGP?

By default, you are not allowed to redistribute network 0.0.0.0. To permit the redistribution of network 0.0.0.0, enter the following command in router configuration mode:

```
default-information originate
```

 ### Can I select the path based on MEDs from other autonomous systems?

The MED is one of the parameters considered when selecting the best path among many alternative paths. The path with a lower MED is preferred over a path with a higher MED. By default, during the best-path selection process, MED comparison is done only among paths from the same autonomous system. You can allow comparison of MEDs among paths regardless of the autonomous system from which the paths are received. To do so, perform the following task in router configuration mode:

```
bgp always-compare-med
```

 ### What is route dampening?

Route dampening is a BGP feature designed to minimize the propagation of flapping routes across an internetwork. A route is considered to be *flapping* when it is repeatedly available, then unavailable, then available, then unavailable, and so on. For example, consider a network with three BGP autonomous systems: AS 1, AS 2, and AS 3. Suppose the route to network A in AS 1 flaps (it becomes unavailable). Under circumstances without route dampening, AS 1's EBGP neighbor to AS 2 sends a withdraw message to AS 2. The border router in AS 2, in turn, propagates the withdraw to AS 3. When the route to network A reappears, AS 1 sends an advertisement to AS 2, which sends it to AS 3. If the route to network A repeatedly becomes unavailable, then available, many withdrawals and advertisements are sent. This is a problem in an internetwork connected to the Internet, because a route flap in the Internet backbone usually involves many routes.

 ### How do I minimize flapping in my network?

This is how the route dampening feature minimizes the flapping problem: Suppose again that the route to network A flaps. The router in AS 2 (where route dampening is enabled)

assigns network A a penalty of 1000 and moves it to "history" state. The router in AS 2 continues to advertise the status of the route to neighbors. The penalties are cumulative. When the route flaps so often that the penalty exceeds a configurable suppress limit, the router stops advertising the route to network A, regardless of how many times it flaps. Thus, the route is dampened. The penalty placed on network A is decayed until the reuse limit is reached, whereupon the route is once again advertised. At half of the reuse limit, the dampening information for the route to network A is removed.

What is the terminology used when discussing route dampening?

The following terms are used when describing route dampening:

- **Flap**   A route is available, then unavailable, or vice versa
- **History state**   After a route flaps once, it is assigned a penalty and put into "history state," meaning the router does not have the best path, based on historical information
- **Penalty**   Each time a route flaps, the router configured for route dampening in another AS assigns the route a penalty of 1000. Penalties are cumulative. The penalty for the route is stored in the BGP routing table until the penalty exceeds the suppress limit. At that point, the route state changes from "history" to "damp."
- **Damp state**   In this state, the route has flapped so often that the router will not advertise this route to BGP neighbors
- **Suppress limit**   A route is suppressed when its penalty exceeds this limit. The default value is 2000.
- **Half-life**   Once the route has been assigned a penalty, the penalty is decreased by half after the half-life period (which is 15 minutes by default). The process of reducing the penalty happens every 5 seconds.
- **Reuse limit**   As the penalty for a flapping route decreases and falls below this reuse limit, the route is unsuppressed. That is, the route is added back to the BGP

table and once again used for forwarding. The default reuse limit is 750. The process of unsuppressing routes occurs at 10-second increments. Every 10 seconds, the router finds out which routes are now unsuppressed and advertises them to the world.

● **Maximum suppress limit** This value is the maximum amount of time a route can be suppressed. The default value is four times the half-life.

 Note: *The routes external to an AS learned via IBGP are not dampened. This policy prevents the IBGP peers from having a higher penalty for routes external to the AS.*

 ### How do I enable route dampening?

To enable BGP route dampening, enter the following command in global configuration mode:

```
bgp dampening
```

To change the default values of various dampening factors, enter the following command in global configuration mode:

```
bgp dampening half-life reuse suppress max-suppress
  [route-map map]
```

ISPS AND BGP

 ### Is BGP necessary to connect to an ISP?

No. You may use static and default routes, as well as BGP to connect to an ISP. The only time BGP would be required is when the local policy is different than the ISP policy.

What is a floating route?

A floating route is a statically configured route that can be overridden by dynamically learned routing information. It can be used to create a "path of last resort" that is used only when

no dynamic information is available. Establish a floating static route by using an administrative distance larger than the default distance used by the dynamic routing protocol.

What would be a RIP static route example?

In the following example, the route 0.0.0.0 is a default route in the IP routing table. If there is no matching route for the destination IP address in the routing table, then the 0.0.0.0 will match the address and cause the packet to be routed out interface serial 0. Router A has this configuration:

```
ip route 0.0.0.0 S0
router rip
network 12.0.0.0
```

What would be an OSPF static route example?

To propagate a default route into the OSPF autonomous system, use the DEFAULT-INFORMATION ORIGINATE ALWAYS command. The ALWAYS keyword causes the default route always to be advertised, whether or not the router has a default route, ensuring that the default route will get advertised. Using the example from the preceding question, router A would have this configuration:

```
ip route 0.0.0.0 0.0.0.0 S0
router ospf 222
network 12.0.0.0 0.225.255.225 area 1
default-information originate always
```

MONITOR AND MAINTAIN BGP

How do I reset EBGP connections immediately upon a link failure?

By default, when a link between external neighbors goes down, the BGP session will not be reset immediately. If you want the EBGP session to be reset as soon as an interface

goes down, enter the following command in router configuration mode:

```
bgp fast-external-fallover
```

How do I modify parameters while updating the IP routing table?

By default, when a BGP route is put into the IP routing table, the MED is converted to an IP route metric, the BGP next hop is used as the next hop for the IP route, and the tag is not set. However, you can use a route map to perform mapping. To modify metric and tag information when the IP routing table is updated with BGP learned routes, enter the following command in router configuration mode:

```
table-map route-map name
```

What command enables the monitoring and maintaining of BGP route dampening?

You can monitor the flaps of all the paths that are flapping. The statistics will be deleted once the route is not suppressed and is stable for at least one half-life. To display flap statistics, enter the following commands in EXEC mode. To display BGP flap statistics for all paths:

```
show ip bgp flap-statistics
```

To display BGP flap statistics for all paths that match the regular expression:

```
show ip bgp flap-statistics regexp regexp
```

To display BGP flap statistics for all paths that pass the filter:

```
show ip bgp flap-statistics filter-list list
```

To display BGP flap statistics for a single entry:

```
show ip bgp flap-statistics address mask
```

To display BGP flap statistics for more specific entries:

```
show ip bgp flap-statistics address mask longer-prefix
```

Once a route is dampened, you can display BGP route dampening information, including the time remaining before the dampened routes will be unsuppressed. To display the information, enter the following command in EXEC mode:

```
show ip bgp dampened-paths
```

? How do I clear BGP flap statistics?

To clear BGP flap statistics (thus making it less likely that the route will be dampened), enter the following commands in EXEC mode.
Clear BGP flap statistics for all routes:

```
clear ip bgp flap-statistics
```

Clear BGP flap statistics for all paths that match the regular expression:

```
clear ip bgp flap-statistics regexp regexp
```

Clear BGP flap statistics for all paths that pass the filter:

```
clear ip bgp flap-statistics filter-list list
```

Clear BGP flap statistics for a single entry:

```
clear ip bgp flap-statistics address mask
```

Clear BGP flap statistics for all paths from a neighbor:

```
clear ip bgp address flap-statistics
```

You can clear BGP route dampening information and unsuppress any suppressed routes by entering the following command in EXEC mode:

```
clear ip bgp dampening [address mask]
```

? How do I clear invalid cache, table, or database content?

You can remove all contents of a particular cache, table, or database. Clearing a cache, table, or database can become necessary when the contents of the particular structure have become, or are suspected to be, invalid. The following tasks

are associated with clearing caches, tables, and databases for
BGP. Enter these commands in EXEC mode.
Reset a particular BGP connection:

```
clear ip bgp address
```

Reset all BGP connections:

```
clear ip bgp *
```

Remove all members of a BGP peer group:

```
clear ip bgp peer-group tag
```

 ## How do I display BGP statistics?

You can display specific statistics such as the contents of
BGP routing tables, caches, and databases. Information
provided can be used to determine resource utilization and
solve network problems. You can also display information
about node reachability and discover the routing path your
device's packets are taking through the network. To display
various routing statistics, enter the following commands in
EXEC mode.
Display all BGP routes that contain subnet and supernet
network masks:

```
show ip bgp cidr-only
```

Display routes that belong to the specified communities:

```
show ip bgp community community-number [exact]
```

Display routes that are permitted by the community list:

```
show ip bgp community-list community-list-number
  [exact]
```

Display routes that are matched by the specified autonomous system path access list:

```
show ip bgp filter-list access-list-number
```

Display the routes with inconsistent originating autonomous systems:

```
show ip bgp inconsistent-as
```

Display the routes that match the specified regular expression entered on the command line:

```
show ip bgp regexp regular-expression
```

Display the contents of the BGP routing table:

```
show ip bgp [network] [network-mask] [subnets]
```

Display detailed information on the TCP and BGP connections to individual neighbors:

```
show ip bgp neighbors [address]
```

Display routes learned from a particular BGP neighbor:

```
show ip bgp neighbors [address]
  [received-routes | routes | advertised-routes | paths
  regular-expression | dampened-routes]
```

Display all BGP paths in the database:

```
show ip bgp paths
```

Display information about BGP peer groups:

```
show ip bgp peer-group [tag] [summary]
```

Display the status of all BGP connections:

```
show ip bgp summary
```

Chapter 8

Configuring EGP

Answer Topics!

Configuring EGP @ at Glance

As the first exterior gateway protocol to gain widespread acceptance in the Internet, EGP served a valuable purpose. EGP has three primary functions:

- Routers running EGP establish a set of neighbors. These neighbors are simply routers with which an EGP router wishes to share reachability information; there is no implication of geographic proximity.

- EGP routers poll their neighbors to see if they are alive.

- EGP routers send update messages containing information about the reachability of networks within their autonomous systems (AS).

Unfortunately, the weaknesses of EGP have become more apparent as the Internet has grown and matured. Because of these weaknesses, EGP has been phased out of the Internet, and has been replaced by other exterior gateway protocols such as the Border Gateway Protocol (BGP) and the Interdomain Routing Protocol (IDRP). Although EGP is a dynamic routing protocol, it uses a very simple design. It does not use metrics and therefore cannot make intelligent routing decisions. EGP routing updates contain network reachability information, which specifies that certain networks are reachable through certain routers.

This chapter is divided into three sections:

- **Autonomous Systems** reviews the commands necessary to enable the EGP process.

- **Neighbors** examines the configuration parameters of EGP.

- **Updates** reviews any updates to the EGP protocol.

AUTONOMOUS SYSTEMS

 ### How do I enable EGP routing?

To enable the EGP routing process, an AS number is required to identify the router. The network for which the EGP process will operate is also required. To enable the EGP routing process, use the following commands in router global configuration mode.
To define the autonomous system ID the router resides in, use:

```
autonomous-system local-as
```

To enable the EGP routing process, use:

```
router egp remote-as
```

To specify the network to be announced to EGP peers, use:

```
network network-number
```

 Note: *IP networks defined from the NETWORK configuration command that are learned by another routing protocol do not require the REDISTRIBUTE router configuration command. Interior gateway protocols such as IGRP require the use of the REDISTRIBUTE command.*

NEIGHBORS

 ### How do I configure EGP neighbor relationships?

Routers that are running the EGP routing process are not able to determine whether there are neighbor or peer routers to communicate with. The router is configured to define its neighbors and peers. This is accomplished through the use of the NEIGHBOR command in router configuration mode. To define the EGP neighbor or peer, use the NEIGHBOR command in router configuration mode:

```
neighbor ip-address
```

What is the neighbor acquisition process?

The neighbor acquisition process begins with two routers who must first become directly connected (neighbors) before they can exchange any routing information. One router sends a neighbor acquisition request to a potential neighbor with its hello interval and poll interval. The potential neighbor router responds with either a neighbor acquisition reply or neighbor acquisition refuse.

A router can stop being a neighbor by transmitting a neighbor cease message; the cease message is retransmitted until the receiver acknowledges with a neighbor cease acknowledgement.

 ## How is neighbor reachability determined?

To determine neighbor reachability, a router uses hello and I-heard-you (IHU) messages to check if a neighbor is reachable. These hello messages are transmitted once in the hello-time interval.

The router uses dual thresholds to identify reachability status:

- For a currently reachable neighbor, if fewer than x IHUs are received for the last x hellos, then the neighbor is unreachable

- For a currently unreachable neighbor, if more than x IHUs are received for the last x hellos, then the neighbor is reachable

Once determined reachable, the neighbors exchange the list of networks that can be reached through each neighbor. During this exchange, the router polls each neighbor every poll interval with a poll message. The polled router responds with a reachability message. The polling router retransmits if it doesn't receive the response in a reasonable amount of time, and declares the neighbor (and corresponding networks) unreachable after a set number of attempts. Unsolicited reachability messages are allowed for faster updates in reaction to changed topologies.

 ### How do I configure third-party EGP support?

EGP supports a third-party mechanism in which a router running the EGP routing process tells a neighbor or EGP peer that another router (the third party) can be used for certain network destinations. To invoke third-party router support in routing updates, use the following command in router configuration mode:

```
neighbor ip-address third-party third-party-ip-address
[internal | external]
```

Consider a router that is in AS 220. The router communicates with an EGP neighbor in AS 131 with address 192.168.6.5. Network 192.168.0.0 is advertised as originating within AS 220. Two additional routers with addresses 192.168.6.99 and 192.168.6.100 should be announced as third-party sources of routing information for networks that are accessible through those routers. The networks should also be considered as internal to AS 220. The commands used to define this topology are as follows:

```
autonomous-system 220
router egp 131
network 192.168.0.0
neighbor 192.168.6.5
neighbor 1192.168.6.5
   third-party 192.168.6.99 internal
neighbor 192.168.6.5
   third-party 192.168.6.100 internal
```

 ### What is the importance of a backdoor router and how is it configured?

To prevent a site from being isolated due to a router failure, EGP allows the use of backdoor or backup routers. The primary router resides in one AS and the backup router resides in another. The two routers announce the same network routes, but the backup router announces these routes with a higher metric than the primary router. Local networks are always announced with a metric of zero. Redistributed routes are usually announced with a metric specified by the user. If no metric is specified, redistributed routes have a metric of three by default. Redistributed networks are advertised with the same metric, and are learned from static or dynamic routes.

Consider a router that is in AS 220 communicating with an EGP neighbor in AS 113 with address 192.168.6.5. Network 192.168.0.0 is announced with a distance of 1, and networks learned by RIP are being advertised with a distance of 5. Access list 3 (not shown) determines which RIP-derived networks are allowed in outgoing EGP updates. The following router configuration commands are used to achieve this example:

```
autonomous-system 220
router egp 113
network 192.168.0.0
neighbor 192.168.6.5
redistribute rip
default-metric 5
distribute-list 3 out rip
```

 ## How do I configure default routes?

Network 0.0.0.0 can be announced as a default route. If the next hop for the default route can be advertised as a third party, it will be included as a third party. To enable the use of default EGP routes, enter the following command in router configuration mode:

```
default-information originate
```

What is a core gateway and how is it configured?

The EGP routing process expects to communicate with neighbors from a single autonomous system. Since the neighbors are in the same AS, the assumption is made that the neighbors all have consistent internal information. As a result of this assumption, when the EGP process is informed about a route from one of its neighbors, it will not send this information out to other neighbors. With core EGP, on the other hand, the assumption is that all neighbors are from different ASs and all have inconsistent information. This allows the EGP process to distribute routes to all the other neighbors (but not back to the originator). In this configuration

EGP becomes a central clearinghouse for information. The core gateway acts as a single, central manager of routing information. One core gateway process can be configured for each router. To invoke the core gateway process, enter the following commands in the order in which they appear in global configuration mode:

```
router egp 0
```

which allows a specific router to act as a peer with any reachable AS,

```
neighbor any [access-list-number]
```

which defines how an EGP process determines which neighbors will be treated as peers, or

```
neighbor any third-party ip-address
[internal | external]
```

which allows the specified address to be used as the next hop in EGP advertisements.

The following configuration examples show how an EGP core gateway can be configured. The first example shows an environment with three routers (designated C1, C2, and C3) attached to a public, packet-switched network. The routers are intended to route information using EGP. This configuration will be used on the core router; the other three routers cannot route traffic directly to each other via the network:

```
access-list 1 permit 10.0.0.0 0.255.255.255
! global access list assignment
router egp 0
neighbor any 1
```

The next configuration example allows an EGP process on any router on network 10.0.0.0 to act as a peer with the core router. All traffic in this configuration will flow through the core router. Third-party advertisements allow traffic to bypass the core router and go directly to the router that advertised reachability to the core.

```
access-list 2 permit 10.0.0.0 0.255.255.255
! global access list assignment
```

```
router egp 0
neighbor any 2
neighbor any third-party 10.1.1.1
```

 ***Note:*** *Split-horizon is performed only on a per-gateway basis. In other words, if an external router informs the router about a specific network, and that router is the best path, the router will not inform the originating external router about that path. Cisco routers can also perform per-gateway split-horizon on third-party updates.*

UPDATES

 ### How do I adjust EGP hello and poll time interval timers?

The EGP timers consist of a hello and a poll time interval timer. The hello timer sets the frequency (in seconds) with which the router sends hello messages to its peer. The poll timer sets how frequently updates are exchanged. To adjust EGP timers, enter the following command in router configuration mode:

```
timers egp hello polltime
```

What are some of the limitations of EGP?

Some of the limitations inherent in EGP are:

- It was designed for a tree-structured topology.
- It does not support policy routing.
- A misbehaved exterior gateway can inject false information into the network.
- It requires that the entire routing table be transmitted as a response to the poll.
- It needs a robust fragmentation and reassembly procedure.

Chapter 9

Configuring GDP

Answer Topics!

Configuring GDP @ a Glance

The Gateway Discovery Protocol (GDP) was developed by Cisco Systems to enable hosts to dynamically detect the arrival of routers on a directly connected network. Multiple routers may be present on a given network, and hosts may choose to use one or more of them to forward traffic. Hosts may detect and compensate for the failure of a router through the router's failure to regularly announce its availability.

GDP is a precursor to the more standardized and rigorous ICMP Router Discovery Protocol (IRDP). Unlike IRDP, GDP is based on the User Datagram Protocol (UDP) and binds by default to port 1997.

Topics to be covered in this chapter are:

- **GDP Syntax** provides information on the various parameters used in GDP configuration.

- **GDP Overview** discusses what Gateway Discovery Protocol is and how Cisco implements it.

- **Configuring GDP** shows how to invoke the GDP protocol process.

- **Network Security and GDP** covers determining whether your GDP network is secure.

GDP SYNTAX

What is the priority?

On a network with more than one possible gateway router, the priority number determines which device hosts should prefer. This setting is useful for configurations with primary and backup links or redundant gateways.

What is a good priority value?

The default priority value is 100. A good number for a backup router could be 90.

What if a host receives a low priority report first?

If a host detects and begins sending traffic to a lower priority router, that router should respond with ICMP redirects to build a table of the correct router to use for each destination.

What is the reporttime?

The reporttime parameter specifies the time in seconds between GDP report messages. This parameter should be set low enough that hosts can quickly discover when a device has failed though the absence of report packets, but not so low as to burden the network.

What is a typical value for reporttime?

The default reporttime value is five seconds. For configurations with many routers, it may be wise to lengthen the period such that the *average* network reporttime is once every five seconds. For example, in a network with three devices, set the reporttime parameter to 3 × 5 seconds (15 seconds).

What is the holdtime?

Holdtime specifies how long a host should regard a router as valid without receiving updated report announcements. This parameter obviously must be set longer than the reporttime,

but should not be set so long as to preclude hosts from quickly detecting new devices or failures.

On nonbroadcast media the holdtime specifies the number of seconds a host should wait before sending another query message.

 What is a typical value for holdtime?

The default holdtime is 15 seconds. Another good rule of thumb is to set the holdtime to three times the reporttime. This will allow for occasional UDP packet losses to congestion or other factors, and avoid unnecessary alarms from your hosts.

GDP OVERVIEW

 How is GDP related to IRDP?

Gateway Discovery Protocol was developed by Cisco to address specific customer needs at the time—allowing hosts to dynamically detect the presence of new routers, and compensating for router failures. GDP is not an industry standard, and has been all but supplanted by the more thorough and complex IRDP.

 How does it work?

GDP consists of two UDP messages: report and query. Report messages (UDP packets) are periodically broadcast by a router announcing its presence. Hosts may then detect the arrival or departure of routers by listening to their periodic broadcasts.

If a host wishes to query its environment (as it might when the machine is rebooted), it may broadcast a query packet onto its directly attached network. Each listening router will then respond with a report packet.

How does GDP avoid report/query flooding?

Routers may only announce themselves once per reporting period. This is set at startup with the reporttime parameter. Routers may not send unsolicited reports onto a nonbroadcast

network. Routers may only respond directly to query packets received on nonbroadcast attached interfaces (serial, X.25). For queries on a broadcast network (Ethernet), routers address their report messages directly to the querying host interface.

 ## When might I use GDP?

Some Cisco customers continue to implement GDP despite the invention of newer protocols that serve the same purposes. The most common reason is the inability of certain older-model Cisco routers to run newer protocols like the Hot Standby Routing Protocol. If your network still employs Cisco CGS or MGS routers, with versions of software earlier than IOS version 9.21, you might consider using GDP. Since GDP messages must be received and implemented on a host computer, you would only choose to implement GDP in an environment with Sun Solaris or other UNIX hosts capable of running the GDP daemon.

An alternate reason for configuring GDP might be preparation for Cisco's CCIE certification exam. Since the GDP has been carried into current versions of the IOS, it remains fair game for the CCIE lab.

 ## What problem does GDP solve?

Figure 9-1 shows a network topology where GDP might be employed. The routers NewYork and Frisco provide access for hosts H1 and H2 to a wide-area network. Many host operating systems allow only a single, default gateway address. Before these hosts attempt to communicate with a station off their own local network, they will send an Address Resolution Protocol (ARP) request for the MAC address of the default gateway. Subsequent traffic sent to a nonlocal host, such as H3, will be transmitted to the MAC address of the default gateway.

Since both routers are available, the choice of which router to configure as the default gateway becomes problematic. One possibility is to list either NewYork or Frisco as the default gateway for both hosts H1 and H2. The deficiency here is that

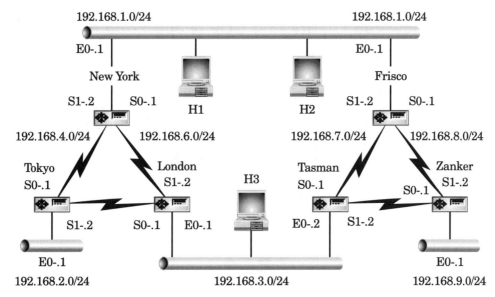

192.168.1.0/24   192.168.1.0/24

Figure 9-1   Sample network with GDP

if the chosen router fails, both hosts will be incapable of communicating off the local network until an administrator changes their default gateway setting, or until the chosen router is repaired or replaced. Another problem is that during normal operation, the router not chosen as the default gateway is idle.

An alternate solution would be to configure one of the routers, say Frisco, as the default gateway for host H1, and the other router, NewYork, as the default gateway for H2. Now we don't incur the economic penalty of having an idle router, but our network is still subject to disruption when one router or the other is unavailable.

GDP solves this problem by advertising the presence of both routers to properly configured host operating systems. The host can choose the "best" router from the available advertisements and forward nonlocal traffic through it. Should the preferred router fail, the host operating systems can choose a new default gateway from the alternate routers.

 ## How can I verify that GDP is operating properly?

The easiest way would be to observe the operation of GDP on host computers, paying particular attention to the router advertisement chosen for forwarding nonlocal traffic. If it is not possible to observe the hosts directly, we can always use the Cisco debug facility to see whether GDP advertisements are sent and received properly on the router interfaces. We will use the network topology of Figure 9-1 to test this capability.

In Figure 9-2, we configure router NewYork for GDP. The GDP service is initiated by the command:

```
NewYork(config-if)#ip gdp
```

If you wish to change the priority of a router from the default value of 100 to 200, use the following syntax:

```
NewYork(config-if)#ip gdp priority 200
```

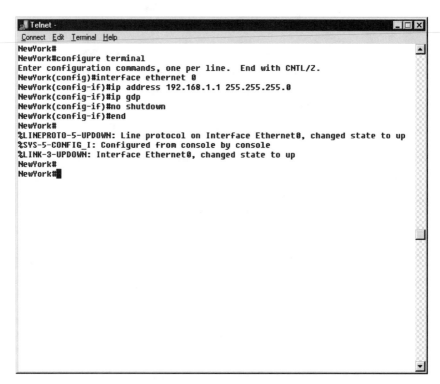

Figure 9-2 GDP configuration on router NewYork

You can choose a priority value in the range of 0–65535, with a larger integer considered by the hosts to be the preferable router. You can also modify the default 15-second period of time during which a client maintains information about an advertised gateway. The possible values for the holdtime parameter are 0–65535 seconds. Use the following command to change the period to 30 seconds:

```
NewYork(config-if)#ip gdp holdtime 30
```

We use similar syntax on router Frisco to configure GDP in Figure 9-3.

Note that we have configured IP address 192.168.1.2 on router Frisco and 192.168.1.1 on router NewYork. We will see these addresses in our debug messages. The IP addresses will be the mechanism we will use to distinguish the source of incoming GDP broadcasts. First though, let us look at an

Figure 9-3   GDP configuration on router Frisco

interface configuration for GDP. Figure 9-4 shows us that "Gateway Discovery is Enabled" on the Ethernet 0 interface. This is our indication that the IP GDP command has been issued in interface-specific configuration mode.

Now we are ready to examine the arrival and transmission of GDP packets using the IOS debug service. In Figure 9-5 you can see that NewYork sent a broadcast UDP packet at 03:50:22. The packet was sent on UDP port 1997 from NewYork's IP address to the local broadcast address 255.255.255.255. Two seconds later, a packet arrives on the Ethernet 0 interface, also sent to UDP port 1997. This second packet was likewise sent to the local broadcast address, but this one shows a source IP address of 192.168.1.2. Recall from Figure 9-3 that this is the Ethernet 0 interface of the Frisco router. These packets comprise the GDP report advertisements from both routers. The packets continue to arrive at four-second intervals.

Figure 9-4 GDP interface configuration

```
Telnet -                                                    _ □ ×
Connect  Edit  Terminal  Help
NewYork#
NewYork#debug ip packet detail
IP packet debugging is on (detailed)
NewYork#
Jan 18 03:50:22: IP: s=192.168.1.1 (local), d=255.255.255.255 (Ethernet0), len 4
0, sending broad/multicast
Jan 18 03:50:22:     UDP src=1997, dst=1997
Jan 18 03:50:24: IP: s=192.168.1.2 (Ethernet0), d=255.255.255.255, len 40, rcvd
2
Jan 18 03:50:24:     UDP src=1997, dst=1997
Jan 18 03:50:28: IP: s=192.168.1.1 (local), d=255.255.255.255 (Ethernet0), len 4
0, sending broad/multicast
Jan 18 03:50:28:     UDP src=1997, dst=1997
Jan 18 03:50:30: IP: s=192.168.1.2 (Ethernet0), d=255.255.255.255, len 40, rcvd
2
Jan 18 03:50:30:     UDP src=1997, dst=1997
Jan 18 03:50:34: IP: s=192.168.1.1 (local), d=255.255.255.255 (Ethernet0), len 4
0, sending broad/multicast
Jan 18 03:50:34:     UDP src=1997, dst=1997
Jan 18 03:50:36: IP: s=192.168.1.2 (Ethernet0), d=255.255.255.255, len 40, rcvd
2
Jan 18 03:50:36:     UDP src=1997, dst=1997
Jan 18 03:50:40: IP: s=192.168.1.1 (local), d=255.255.255.255 (Ethernet0), len 4
0, sending broad/multicast
Jan 18 03:50:40:     UDP src=1997, dst=1997█
```

Figure 9-5   Debugging GDP protocol exchanges

What alternatives to GDP should I consider?

In Chapter 10 of this book, we will consider the ICMP Router
Discovery Protocol (IRDP). This protocol is derived from
Cisco's GDP, but depends on ICMP messages rather than
UDP messages. Also in Chapter 10, we will look at two
technologies that, when combined in your network, provide
the functionality of GDP—namely the Dynamic Host
Configuration Protocol (DHCP) and Cisco's proprietary Hot
Standby Router Protocol (HSRP).

A final way to achieve the self-configuration and gateway
redundancy offered by GDP is to allow the host computers to
participate in the dynamic routing protocols implemented in
your network. If the hosts H1 and H2, shown in Figure 9-1,
all run a RIP routing daemon, for instance, they can hear RIP
routing updates from both Frisco and NewYork, and update
their local networks accordingly.

CONFIGURING GDP

❓ How do I configure my hosts to take advantage of GDP?

You must have GDP-compliant software on your hosts to take advantage of GDP. Check that your specific host supports GDP. Source code for the original GDPD daemon and the Sun IGMPD daemon can be found at ftp://ftp.cisco.com.

The goal of GDP is to enable hosts listening for GDP messages to learn and compensate when a router fails or when a new router arrives. One possible host action is to flush the host's ARP cache whenever an arrival or disappearance event occurs. Another is to update a host's routing table.

❓ What do the report messages look like?

Figure 9-6 shows the format of a GDP report message.

❓ What does the header information mean?

The headers in a GDP report message indicate the following:

- **Version**   The Version field is an eight-bit (one-byte) field describing the protocol version number. If an unrecognized or invalid version number is discovered, the GDP packet must be discarded. The GDP current version is 1.

- **Opcode**   The opcode specifies whether the message is a report or query message. An opcode 1 indicates a report; an opcode 2 is a query packet.

- **Count**   The count contains the number of address/ priority/holdtime occurrences in this particular message

- **Reserved**   This field must be set to zero

❓ How big is a typical report message?

A report packet for a router with a single interface is 12 bytes long. Each additional interface adds eight bytes to the message. Messages will typically announce a single interface with a 12-byte report message.

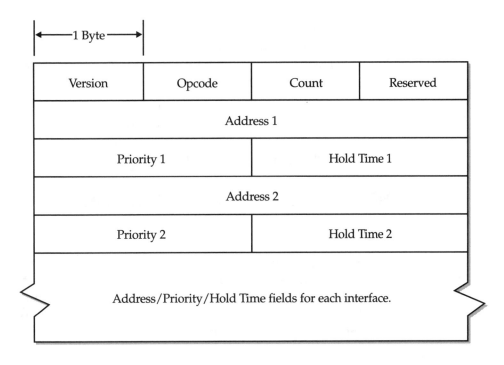

Figure 9-6   GDP report message format

What is the complete GDP syntax?

GDP is a very simple protocol with only three user-configurable parameters. To enable GDP on an interface use the IP GDP command. The complete command syntax is:

```
ip gdp [priority number | reporttime seconds |
 holdtime seconds]
```

Use the NO form of this command to disable GDP report messages.

```
no ip gdp
```

In this command:

- **priority *number***   (Optional) Specifies the GDP priority. A larger number indicates a higher preference. The default priority value is 100.

- **reporttime** *seconds* (Optional) Specifies the GDP reporting interval. The default reporttime is five seconds for broadcast media (Ethernet). GDP never preemptively reports onto nonbroadcast media (for example, direct serial links).

- **holdtime** *seconds* (Optional) Specifies the length of time this router's interface address should be used by a host without hearing new report messages. The default holdtime value is 15 seconds.

NETWORK SECURITY AND GDP

Is GDP safe?

Running GDP poses a small risk to the secure operation of your network and availability of your hosts. Most of the risks depend on the host configuration and GDP implementation. In designing a network architecture, one should carefully consider availability and security requirements when evaluating the network's exposure to risk. If the risk of malicious tampering is greater than the benefits of using GDP, clearly another fail-over and configuration solution should be employed.

Is GDP appropriate for my network?

In a public environment where your network may be directly attached to the Internet or have many users, it may be wise to statically configure your hosts.

What do the experts recommend?

By default the UDP-SMALL-SERVERS services are disabled in Cisco IOS version 11.2. UDP-SMALL-SERVERS includes UDP services for such common ports as ECHO, DISCARD, CHARGEN, TACACS, BOOTP, and GDP.

How do I tighten my security?

Because configurations are stored in NVRAM, if you're running Cisco IOS version 11.1 and upgrading to 11.2 or later, the TCP-SMALL-SERVERS and UDP-SMALL-SERVERS are not disabled automatically.

To disable these typically unnecessary services, use the NO form of the SERVICE command:

```
no service tcp-small-servers
```

The router will now generate ICMP-port-unreachable messages back to the sender for the ports in question.

```
no service udp-small-servers
```

The router will now silently discard UDP packets directed to the ports in question.

Once turned off, the "no" statements will disappear from the configurations in IOS 11.2 or greater, since that is now the default. Unfortunately, these statements are not held over and must be reinstated should you require an IOS version downgrade below 11.2.

Chapter 10

Configuring IRDP

Answer Topics!

Configuring IRDP @ a Glance

ICMP Router Discovery Protocol (IRDP), an extension of the Internet Control Message Protocol (ICMP), enables hosts to dynamically discover the IP address of default gateway routers. IRDP also enables hosts to automatically detect and correct for failed gateways in a multirouter environment.

IRDP is defined in RFC 1256 and provides for automatic host configuration of router addresses in analogous fashion to Dynamic Host Configuration Protocol (DHCP). IRDP is independent of any specific routing protocol; it consists of router-initiated broadcasts (router advertisements) and host-initiated query messages (router solicitations).

While IRDP does not provide for optimal discovery when multiple paths are present, if a host chooses a poor first-hop router for a particular destination, an ICMP redirect from the chosen device should identify a better candidate.

This chapter is divided into three sections:

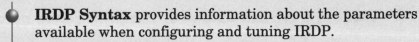 **IRDP Syntax** provides information about the parameters available when configuring and tuning IRDP.

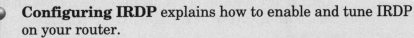 **Configuring IRDP** explains how to enable and tune IRDP on your router.

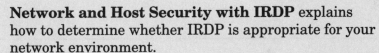 **Network and Host Security with IRDP** explains how to determine whether IRDP is appropriate for your network environment.

IRDP SYNTAX

What is the preference number?

On a diverse network with multiple routers, the network administrator can configure address preference levels to encourage or discourage the use of particular devices as default routers.

A typical configuration example is the case of a primary and backup link, as illustrated in Figure 10-1.

In this scenario the network administrator will want a more heavily weighted primary link (a link assigned a higher preference number). Values for this configuration could be:

P1: 1
P2: 1
S1: 0
S2: 0

What is a typical value for the preference number?

The preference number is defaulted to zero, with a valid range from -231 to 231. Higher numbers indicate higher

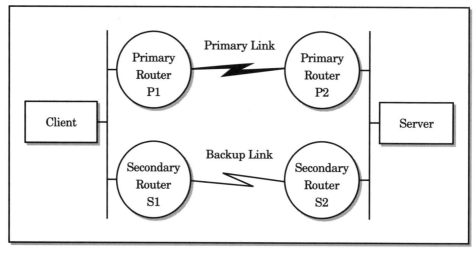

Figure 10-1   Sample configuration with primary and backup links

preference. Unless your configuration is complex, preference number values of 0, 1, 2, and -1 are typical.

Curiously, the specification allows a full, 32-bit, signed, two's-complement integer. The minimum value (0x80000000) is reserved, which means that the address is not to be used as a dynamically assigned default router address.

Can I ignore this parameter when I set up my network?

Yes. IRDP-aware hosts will attach to the first discovered router regardless of preference. If another router is discovered with equal or less preference, that host will not change its configuration.

However, when setting up a network, it's usually best to exercise some control over the goings-on. This principal is especially relevant in a configuration with slow, expensive, or unreliable links.

What is the maxadvertinterval?

Each router with IRDP enabled periodically multicasts (or broadcasts) a router advertisement from each of its (multicast) interfaces, announcing the IP addresses of that interface. The maxadvertinterval parameter specifies the time in seconds between router advertisements.

What is a typical value for maxadvertinterval?

The default value is 600 seconds (10 minutes). Typical times range from 7 to 10 minutes (420 to 600 seconds).

Valid times for maxadvertinterval range from 4 to 1800 seconds.

Can I ignore this parameter when I set up my network?

Yes. The default value of 10 minutes will suffice for most networks. For slow or lossy links between IRDP hosts and routers, you may want to shorten this interval to 3–5 minutes to prevent sending traffic to a failed or nonresponding router—in other words, to avoid creating a black hole.

 ### What is the minadvertinterval?

The minadvertinterval value specifies the minimum time allowed between sending unsolicited multicast router advertisements.

What is a typical value for minadvertinterval?

The minadvertinterval is typically set to 75 percent of the maxadvertinterval. It must be greater than three seconds, and cannot be longer than the maxadvertinterval value.

Can I ignore this parameter when I set up my network?

Yes. When the maxadvertinterval is set, the minadvertinterval is automatically calculated and reset to 75 percent of the maxadvertinterval.

What is the multicast flag?

The multicast flag instructs the router to send IRDP announcements to the all-systems multicast address (224.0.0.1) on a specified interface. This is in contrast to broadcast, where IRDP router advertisements are IP-broadcast onto a subnet with the local broadcast address of 255.255.255.255. Also, it should be noted that a multicast IRDP announcement has the IP TTL set to 1 to prevent flooding of IRDP into other networks.

Should I use multicast announcements?

The answer depends on your network, its intended use, and WAN connectivity. Multicast announcements (specifically, IRDP router advertisements) should not be announced to the world. They may help, however, in a private, multisegmented environment. Do not use multicast announcements if the hosts are on the same subnet as the access router.

 ### What is holdtime?

The holdtime parameter specifies in seconds the period for which router advertisements remain valid. If a router advertisement has not been received by a host before the holdtime expires, the host will seek to reestablish a valid default router by issuing a router solicitation message or attaching to the sender of the next valid router advertisement message received.

What is a typical value for holdtime?

The default holdtime is automatically calculated and set to three times the maxadvertinterval value. It must be greater than maxadvertinterval, but cannot be greater than 9000 seconds.

Is holdtime important?

Yes. Because the default values for holdtime and maxadvertinterval can be quite long, they may not be suitable for "black hole" detection. Referring to Figure 10-1, the server should detect and compensate for a failure of, say, router P2 by listening for P2's regular router advertisements. The server computer would then start using the secondary router S2 when such messages stopped appearing. If the holdtime and maxadvertinterval values are set very large, host detection and correction times may prove unacceptably long and result in temporary losses of service.

What are proxy advertisements?

A router can proxy-advertise other routers that use IRDP. That is, one device can announce to listening hosts another device's interface information as available to carry traffic. The command is:

```
ip irdp address address [number]
```

Should I use proxy advertisements?

Proxy advertisements can be a bad idea. The command is statically initiated and does not compensate for nonexistent or failed interfaces. It's best not to use proxy advertisements unless you know what you're doing and really need to do so.

CONFIGURING IRDP

 ### How do I make IRDP work on my router?

Configuring IRDP can be as simple as enabling the protocol on a specific interface:

```
ip irdp
```

With this command, the default parameter values are automatically used. If this is not desired, add more detail to the command by specifying the parameter and value.

To send IRDP advertisements to the multicast address on an interface:

```
ip irdp multicast
```

To set the IRDP holdtime parameter:

```
ip irdp holdtime seconds
```

To set the IRDP maximum and minimum interval between advertisements:

```
ip irdp maxadvertinterval seconds
ip irdp minadvertinterval seconds
```

To set the IRDP preference number:

```
ip irdp preference number
```

To set a proxy advertisement:

```
ip irdp address address [number]
```

Any combination of these parameters can be set in your configuration. The following configuration would enable IRDP, set the preference to 10, set multicast on, set holdtime to 180 seconds, set maxadvertinterval to 60 seconds and minadvertinterval to 50 seconds, and proxy-advertise the interface 10.128.0.1 with a preference of 5.

```
ip irdp
ip irdp multicast
ip irdp holdtime 180
ip irdp maxadvertinterval 60
```

```
ip irdp minadvertinterval 50
ip irdp preference 10
ip irdp address 10.128.0.1 5
```

What do the experts recommend?

In an ever changing and more connected network environment, it may be wise to not use IRDP unless absolutely necessary. Carefully consider your network, host, service level, and security requirements; then implement a network architecture to meet those requirements.

IRDP works well for a closed network, but presents unique and often unnecessary risks when working in an open, public, or semi-public environment.

Examples where IRDP may add value include private and closed data networks with primary and backup circuits. IRDP should probably not be used in an Internet-related environment.

What do IRDP messages look like?

Figure 10-2 illustrates the IRDP message structure. Note that the minimum IRDP message size is 16 bytes, with eight bytes additional per interface. Also note that this does not include the ICMP packet header.

By contrast, Figure 10-3 shows the relatively simple ICMP message broadcast by hosts.

What are the field definitions?

In the IRDP message structure, the fields are defined as follows:

● **Router Interface Address** Specifies the router's IP address, from which the message was sent

● **Type** For IRDP router advertisements the type field is set to 9. The type is set to 10 for IRDP router solicitations broadcast by hosts.

● **Code** For both IRDP advertisements and solicitations, the code field is set to 0

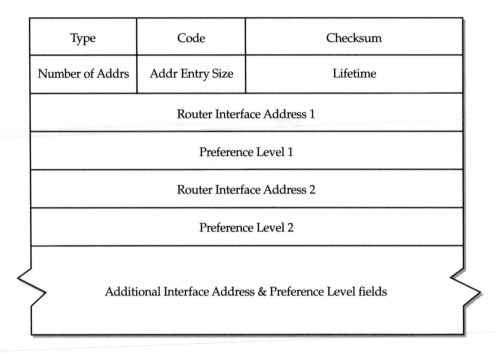

Type	Code	Checksum
Number of Addrs	Addr Entry Size	Lifetime
Router Interface Address 1		
Preference Level 1		
Router Interface Address 2		
Preference Level 2		
Additional Interface Address & Preference Level fields		

Figure 10-2 IRDP router advertisement message

● **Checksum** The checksum is calculated to be the one's complement of the one's complement sum of the ICMP message, starting with the ICMP type field. The checksum field is set to 0 when computing the checksum.

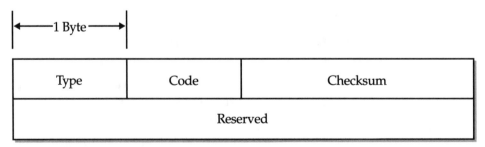

|←———1 Byte———→|

Type	Code	Checksum
Reserved		

Figure 10-3 IRDP router solicitation message

- **Number of Addrs**   Indicates the number of interface addresses contained in the message
- **Addr Entry Size**   Specifies the number of 32-bit words of information contained in each interface address (typically two)

What is the complete IRDP syntax?

To enable IRDP processing on an interface, use the IP IRDP interface configuration command. The complete IRDP syntax is as follows:

```
ip irdp [multicast | holdtime seconds |
maxadvertinterval seconds | minadvertinterval
seconds | preference number | address address [number]]
```

In this command:

- **multicast holdtime** *seconds*   (Optional) Specifies the time in seconds that router advertisements are held valid. The default value is three times the maxadvertinterval value. It must be greater than maxadvertinterval and less than 9000 seconds.

- **maxadvertinterval** *seconds*   (Optional) Specifies the maximum time interval between router advertisements. The default is 600 seconds.

- **minadvertinterval** *seconds*   (Optional) Specifies the minimum time interval between router advertisements. The default is 75 percent of the maxadvertinterval. Automatically defaults to three-quarters of maxadvertinterval when that value is changed.

- **preference** *number*   (Optional) Specifies the router's preference value. Values range from -231 to 231, with the default set to 0. A higher number indicates increased preference level.

- **address** *address* [*number*]   (Optional) Specifies an IP address (*address*) for this router to proxy-advertise. Also specifies that address' optional preference value (*number*, which defaults to 0).

To disable IRDP routing, use the NO form of this command.

```
no ip irdp
```

Figure 10-4 shows the IOS context-sensitive Help facility display for IRDP.

NETWORK AND HOST SECURITY WITH IRDP

 ## How do routers validate IRDP messages?

Routers silently discard any router solicitation messages sourced from their own address. Routers also silently discard messages with invalid checksums, messages with ICMP codes not set to zero, and messages with ICMP lengths of eight

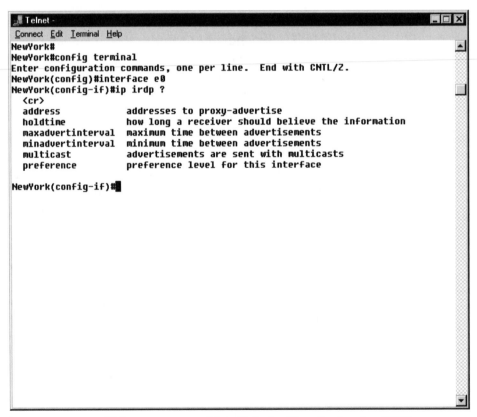

Figure 10-4 IOS context-sensitive Help facility display for IRDP

octets or greater. The contents of the ICMP Reserved field, and of any octets beyond the first eight, are ignored.

It should be noted that a router's validating IRDP messages does not necessarily enhance network security, but rather serves to prevent random bit errors from causing trouble. There are no provisions for host or router validation or authentication included in the IRDP protocol.

Is IRDP safe?

Unfortunately, the answer to this depends entirely on your network and its exposure to the outside world. Use of IRDP, like DHCP and GDP, requires a degree of trust in the user's network and common sense when connecting to the outside world.

Can my network be compromised if I use IRDP?

Yes, but only from within—assuming that basic firewall policies are installed between the private network and the public Internet.

As an extension of ICMP, IRDP does make it possible for any system attached to an IRDP link to masquerade as a default router for hosts on that link. Furthermore, any traffic sent to such an imposter is vulnerable to eavesdropping, denial of forwarding service ("black holes"), or session interception through modification, insertion, deletion, or alteration of packets.

Unfortunately, on most multicast or broadcast links where IRDP is suited, these risks are already present to any system already on the specific network.

In environments where these threats are unacceptable, dynamic router discovery should not be used. In these instances, static routes to the default gateway should be configured on hosts. Cisco's Hot Standby Router Protocol (HSRP) may prove a more attractive option as a recovery mechanism for link and network device failures.

When should I use IRDP?

IRDP is intended to ease network administration tasks and help implement redundancy in routed networks. The protocol must be implemented on host computers attached to a

network, and one or more routers directly connected to the same segment. The goal of IRDP is to allow a host to learn the address of a gateway by listening to network traffic. In this way, IRDP allows certain hosts to configure themselves for operation in an internetwork environment in a manner analogous to Dynamic Host Configuration Protocol. IRDP is admittedly less flexible than DHCP, but in many environments both protocols are implemented concurrently in order to provide service to the widest possible range of hosts.

You would implement IRDP in your network when multiple routers are present on the same segment, and hosts attached to the segment are capable of implementing IRDP. Figure 10-1 shows a typical environment. The client on the left would hear IRDP broadcasts from both routers and choose the one with the best precedence as its path to nonlocal addresses.

What popular host operating systems implement IRDP?

You can use IRDP with HPUX, Solaris, and some versions of LINUX. IRDP is not supported in Microsoft operating systems.

Must IRDP hosts be rebooted to change routers when the primary router fails?

No. An IRDP router advertises a parameter called the holdtime to the clients on its networks. A client retains the gateway address learned through IRDP for the holdtime. Before the holdtime expires, the client must refresh its gateway information by hearing another IRDP advertisement.

How can I verify that IRDP is working on my routers?

Let us configure IRDP in the network shown in Figure 10-5. First, we will configure IRDP between routers NewYork and Frisco. In this example, both routers are configured to send IRDP broadcasts from their E0 interfaces.

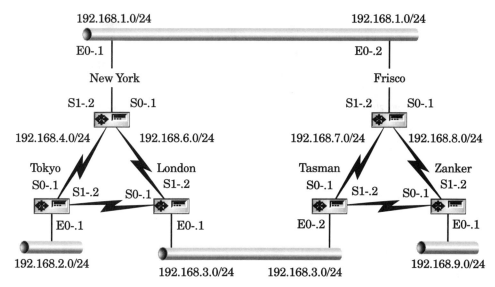

Figure 10-5   IRDP example topology

Begin by logging into router NewYork and entering privileged EXEC mode. Then, following the example shown in Figure 10-6, enable the router interface and start IRDP with the command:

```
NewYork(config-if)#ip irdp
```

Use similar commands on router Frisco, as shown in Figure 10-7. Notice that in both Figure 10-6 and Figure 10-7, we have issued a SHOW command to see the configuration of IRDP on the routers' Ethernet interfaces. We can see that the default IRDP parameters are set: broadcasts sent approximately every ten minutes (600 seconds), and advertisements good for three times that interval or 30 minutes (1800 seconds).

Another mechanism exists that will help us verify that IRDP is in fact working as we expect it. We can configure the DEBUG service to report all IP packets that arrive on, or are transmitted from an interface. In Figure 10-8, we turn on packet debugging with the command:

```
NewYork#debug ip packet
```

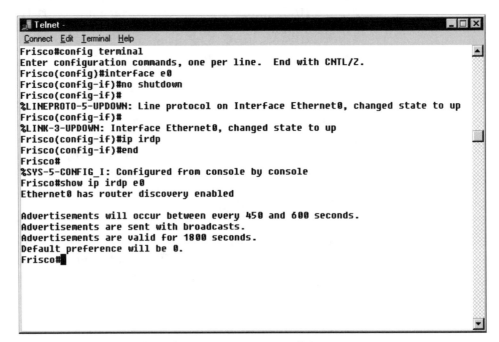

```
Telnet -                                                              _ □ ×
Connect  Edit  Terminal  Help
NewYork#config terminal
Enter configuration commands, one per line.  End with CNTL/Z.
NewYork(config)#interface e0
NewYork(config-if)#no shut
NewYork(config-if)#
%LINEPROTO-5-UPDOWN: Line protocol on Interface Ethernet0, changed state to up
NewYork(config-if)#
%LINK-3-UPDOWN: Interface Ethernet0, changed state to up
NewYork(config-if)#ip irdp
NewYork(config-if)#end
NewYork#
%SYS-5-CONFIG_I: Configured from console by console
NewYork#show ip irdp e0
Ethernet0 has router discovery enabled

Advertisements will occur between every 450 and 600 seconds.
Advertisements are sent with broadcasts.
Advertisements are valid for 1800 seconds.
Default preference will be 0.
NewYork#
```

Figure 10-6 IRDP configuration on router NewYork

```
Telnet -                                                              _ □ ×
Connect  Edit  Terminal  Help
Frisco#config terminal
Enter configuration commands, one per line.  End with CNTL/Z.
Frisco(config)#interface e0
Frisco(config-if)#no shutdown
Frisco(config-if)#
%LINEPROTO-5-UPDOWN: Line protocol on Interface Ethernet0, changed state to up
Frisco(config-if)#
%LINK-3-UPDOWN: Interface Ethernet0, changed state to up
Frisco(config-if)#ip irdp
Frisco(config-if)#end
Frisco#
%SYS-5-CONFIG_I: Configured from console by console
Frisco#show ip irdp e0
Ethernet0 has router discovery enabled

Advertisements will occur between every 450 and 600 seconds.
Advertisements are sent with broadcasts.
Advertisements are valid for 1800 seconds.
Default preference will be 0.
Frisco#
```

Figure 10-7 IRDP configuration on router Frisco

```
Telnet -                                                                    _ □ ×
Connect  Edit  Terminal  Help
NewYork#
NewYork#config terminal
Enter configuration commands, one per line.  End with CNTL/Z.
NewYork(config)#service timestamps debug datetime local
NewYork(config)#end
NewYork#
%SYS-5-CONFIG_I: Configured from console by console
NewYork#debug ip packet detail
IP packet debugging is on (detailed)
NewYork#
NewYork#
Jan 14 09:17:33: IP: s=192.168.1.2 (Ethernet0), d=255.255.255.255, len 36, rcvd
2
Jan 14 09:17:33:     ICMP type=9, code=0
Jan 14 09:17:50: IP: s=192.168.1.2 (Ethernet0), d=255.255.255.255, len 36, rcvd
2
Jan 14 09:17:50:     ICMP type=9, code=0
Jan 14 09:18:07: IP: s=192.168.1.2 (Ethernet0), d=255.255.255.255, len 36, rcvd
2
Jan 14 09:18:07:     ICMP type=9, code=0
NewYork#
Jan 14 09:26:38: IP: s=192.168.1.2 (Ethernet0), d=255.255.255.255, len 36, rcvd
2
Jan 14 09:26:38:     ICMP type=9, code=0
NewYork#
Jan 14 09:34:47: IP: s=192.168.1.2 (Ethernet0), d=255.255.255.255, len 36, rcvd
2
Jan 14 09:34:47:     ICMP type=9, code=0
```

Figure 10-8   Verifying IRDP with packet debugging

In order to keep track of when IRDP advertisements arrive, we have also configured the router to report the arrival time of each IRDP packet using the timestamp service.

For the sake of simplicity, we will look only at IRDP advertisements arriving on NewYork's E0 interface. When the Ethernet interface on Frisco is initialized, IOS quickly sends three IRDP advertisements at 17-second intervals. We see these arriving in Figure 10-8 at 09:17:33 and 09:17:50 and 09:18:17. We identify these packets as IRDP advertisements by looking at the ICMP type and code reported by DEBUG. We can tell that these advertisements were sent by router Frisco, by noting that the source address contained in the packet header is 192.168.1.2. Notice that the packets reported by DEBUG are ICMP type 9, and code 0.

After the initial string of packets arrives, the Frisco router is silent for approximately eight minutes. Recall from Figure 10-6 and Figure 10-7 that the default interval may vary from 450 seconds to 600 seconds. In this case, Frisco sends its next advertisement after about eight minutes. The final advertisement shown arrives some eight minutes and nine seconds later.

When should I use multicast IRDP advertisements?

The advertisements in the following example are sent to the broadcast address on the Ethernet connecting Frisco and NewYork. This might negatively impact a production network in that all hosts attached to this Ethernet segment must devote CPU cycles to process the broadcast. Even hosts whose operating systems are incapable of implementing the gateway information contained in the IRDP advertisement are obliged to receive the Ethernet frame into memory and decode its protocol type and ICMP message type, before they can discard the traffic and move on to other tasks. In many production environments, control of broadcast traffic on Ethernet or other shared media networks is an important consideration.

Consider the example network shown in Figure 10-9. In this diagram, we have connected several low-end workstations running operating systems that are incapable of responding to IRDP advertisements, and one server that is IRDP capable.

If we choose to send broadcast IRDP messages from both routers for the benefit of the HPUX server, each of the workstations will waste resources in receiving and discarding the traffic. To avoid this situation, we will configure IRDP multicasting on both NewYork and Frisco as shown in Figure 10-10 and Figure 10-11.

Now when we use the IOS debug service to monitor IP traffic on router NewYork, as shown in Figure 10-12, you can see that the destination address that receives the IRDP advertisement is 224.0.0.1, the "All Multicast Stations" group

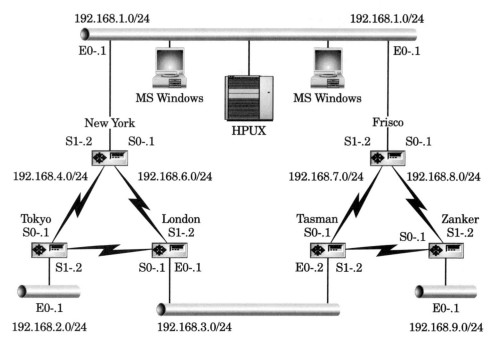

Figure 10-9 Multicast IRDP environment

address. Only multicast-capable stations will receive this traffic and hand it to ICMP for processing.

One cautionary note is in order here: While many PC operating systems will not recognize or process IRDP advertisements, it is entirely possible for them to recognize and respond to traffic sent to the "All Multicast Station" group address. For instance, the Microsoft NetShow application implements the Internet Group Management Protocol (IGMP) on Microsoft Win32 operating systems. If the low-end hosts in Figure 10-9 implement IGMP, they will still waste CPU cycles when Frisco and NewYork send IRDP advertisements.

 What alternatives to IRDP should I consider?

Since IRDP really performs two functions for us, making our hosts somewhat self-configuring, and helping hosts recover

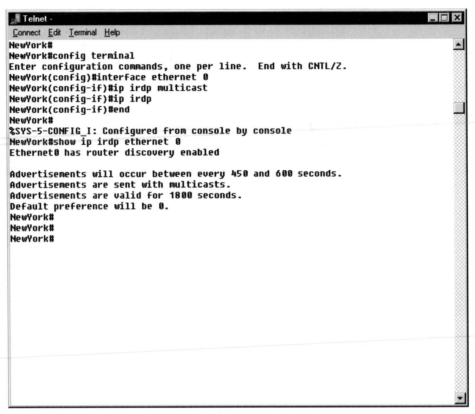

Figure 10-10 Multicast IRDP configuration on router NewYork

from router failures, we will consider two separate alternatives. First, to make hosts more self-configuring, you might wish to implement DHCP in your network. A host computer that implements DHCP is called a DHCP client. The client sends a link layer broadcast DHCP request to a device called the DHCP server. A properly configured server responds by offering to "lease" an IP address to the client. The client may hear responses from several DHCP servers, so it must select one lease and send a lease acknowledgment to one of them to accept the lease. The server that hears a lease acknowledgment returns an acknowledgment and the process is complete.

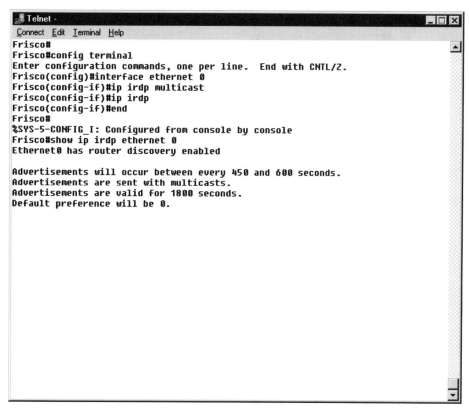

Figure 10-11 Multicast IRDP configuration on router Frisco

In order to make this process an alternative to IRDP, we want the DCHP server to send more than just an IP address. In fact, DHCP servers can be configured to offer a default gateway appropriate to the IP address offered in the lease. Thus, DHCP provides one alternative to the self-configuration functionality of IRDP. Figure 10-13 provides one example of a network configured with DHCP. Here the DHCP server lives on the same network segment as the client C1 requesting an IP address and default gateway information. Since the client sends a local broadcast as the first packet in the DHCP exchange, this situation requires no configuration on our routers. The DHCP client C2, on the other hand, cannot locally broadcast its request to the server. To allow fewer DHCP

```
 Telnet -                                                        _ □ ×
Connect  Edit  Terminal  Help
Frisco#
Frisco#
Frisco#
Frisco#debug ip packet detail
IP packet debugging is on (detailed)
Frisco#
Jan 17 08:17:29: IP: s=192.168.0.2 (local), d=224.0.0.1 (Ethernet0), len 36, sen
ding broad/multicast
Jan 17 08:17:29:     ICMP type=9, code=0
Frisco#
Frisco#
```

Figure 10-12   Multicast IRDP advertisement

servers, we need a way to permit one DHCP server to provide configuration information to the clients on many network segments. Cisco provides us a mechanism to implement such a solution.

In Figure 10-14, we configure router Tokyo to translate the local broadcast DHCP request from client C2 to a unicast with the destination address of our DHCP server. The following router interface command instructs the router software to listen for certain UDP broadcasts and translate them into unicast packets to the address 10.32.0.2:

```
Tokyo(config-if)#ip helper-address 10.32.0.2
```

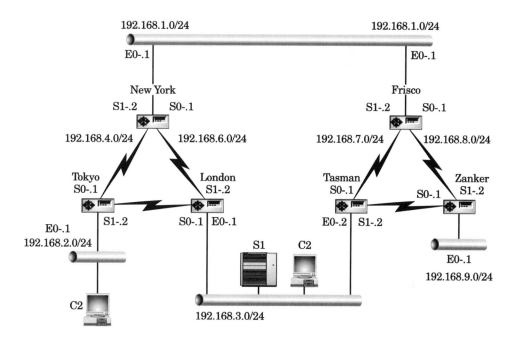

192.168.1.0/24   192.168.1.0/24

E0-.1   E0-.1

New York   Frisco

S1-.2   S0-.1   S1-.2   S0-.1

192.168.4.0/24   192.168.6.0/24   192.168.7.0/24   192.168.8.0/24

Tokyo   London   Tasman   Zanker

S0-.1   S1-.2   S0-.1   S0-.1   S1-.2

E0-.1   S1-.2   S0-.1   E0-.1   E0-.2   S1-.2

192.168.2.0/24

S1   C2

E0-.1

192.168.9.0/24

C2

192.168.3.0/24

Figure 10-13   DHCP environment

The DHCP client C2 sends its initial request as a UDP broadcast on port 68. When router Tokyo hears the broadcast on its Ethernet 0 interface, it replaces the 255.255.255.255 local broadcast destination address with 10.32.0.2, and forwards the packet through the internetwork. When our DHCP server receives the request, it formulates a unicast reply on UDP port 67, which offers a lease to C2. We can verify our configuration with the command:

```
Tolyo#show ip interface Ethernet 0
```

In Figure 10-14, the display shows us that, "Helper Address is 10.32.0.2."

The second function of IRDP, providing redundant gateways in case one fails, can be achieved by implementing Cisco's Hot-Standby Router Protocol. In an HSRP

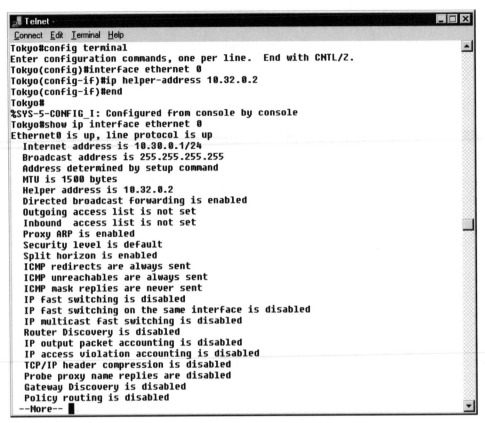

Figure 10-14 IP helper-address configuration

environment such as that shown in Figure 10-15, the two hot-standby routers, Frisco and NewYork, are capable of receiving traffic sent to a virtual router address. One of the two routers will be the active router for the purposes of receiving and retransmitting traffic sent to the virtual address. Both active and standby routers send a multicast hello to IP address 224.0.0.2 in order to advertise that they are still up and responding. If the primary router fails to send the hello packet on schedule, the backup router will assume the active role and begin responding at the virtual IP address. Since the hello packets are sent every three seconds by default, traffic continues to flow to and from hosts with minimal disruption.

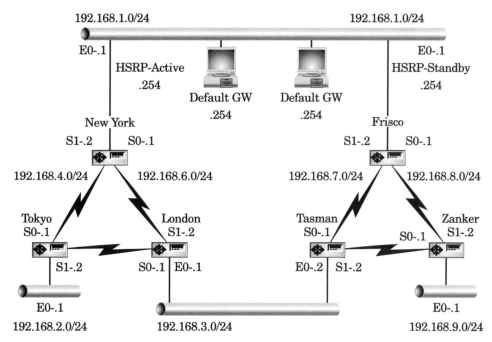

Figure 10-15 HSRP environment

Configuring HSRP is somewhat more complicated than setting up IRDP, but the payoff is the speed with which the network heals after a router failure. In the case of HSRP, routing should be disrupted no more than five seconds, whereas with IRDP, hosts may hold onto a failed gateway address for as long as 30 minutes. Figure 10-16 shows the steps for configuring HSRP on router NewYork. We are using a single virtual IP address, but many Cisco router models allow you multiple virtual IPs, to enable HSRP to work in VLAN environments.

HSRP is implemented with the STANDBY commands, as follows:

```
NewYork(config-if)#standby ip 192.168.1.254
NewYork(config-if)#standby priority 110
NewYork(config-if)#standby preempt
```

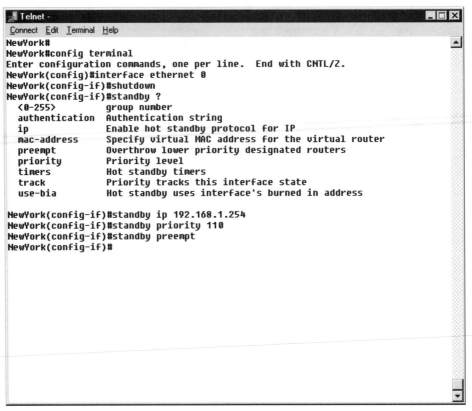

```
Telnet -                                                    _ □ ✕
Connect  Edit  Terminal  Help
NewYork#
NewYork#config terminal
Enter configuration commands, one per line.  End with CNTL/Z.
NewYork(config)#interface ethernet 0
NewYork(config-if)#shutdown
NewYork(config-if)#standby ?
  <0-255>        group number
  authentication Authentication string
  ip             Enable hot standby protocol for IP
  mac-address    Specify virtual MAC address for the virtual router
  preempt        Overthrow lower priority designated routers
  priority       Priority level
  timers         Hot standby timers
  track          Priority tracks this interface state
  use-bia        Hot standby uses interface's burned in address

NewYork(config-if)#standby ip 192.168.1.254
NewYork(config-if)#standby priority 110
NewYork(config-if)#standby preempt
NewYork(config-if)#
```

Figure 10-16 HSRP configuration on router NewYork

The default priority for an HSRP standby router is 100, so using priority 110 ensures that NewYork will be the active router implementing the virtual IP address 192.168.1.254. You can see from the IOS Help display in Figure 10-16 that there are a number of parameters for tuning HSRP performance. If you are configuring HSRP in a WAN or switched-network environment, you should take these into consideration.

Configuration of the backup router is slightly different. In Figure 10-17, we set up HSRP for router Frisco. Notice the command:

```
Frisco(config-if)#standby preempt
```

Figure 10-17 HSRP configuration on router Frisco

Since we configure Frisco with a lower-than-default priority, it will become the standby router for IP address 192.168.1.254. The PREEMPT syntax informs Frisco that it is allowed to take over the shared virtual IP address 192.168.1.254, should NewYork fail to send the multicast hello message.

We can observe HSRP in action using the IOS DEBUG facility. Here we examine DEBUG output from Frisco as its interface is enabled, but while NewYork is disabled.

```
Frisco(config-if)#no shut
Frisco(config-if)#
%LINEPROTO-5-UPDOWN: Line protocol on Interface
 Ethernet0, changed state to up
Jan 17 08:38:15: IP: s=192.168.0.2 (local),
```

```
 d=224.0.0.1 (Ethernet0), len 36,
 sending broad/multicast
Jan 17 08:38:15:      ICMP type=9, code=0
%LINK-3-UPDOWN: Interface Ethernet0, changed state
 to up Jan 17 08:38:25: IP: s=192.168.0.2 (local),
 d=224.0.0.2 (Ethernet0), len 48,
 sending broad/multicast
Jan 17 08:38:25:      UDP src=1985, dst=1985
Jan 17 08:38:28: IP: s=192.168.0.2 (local),
 d=224.0.0.2 (Ethernet0), len 48,
 sending broad/multicast
Jan 17 08:38:28:      UDP src=1985, dst=1985
Jan 17 08:38:31: IP: s=192.168.0.2 (local),
 d=224.0.0.2 (Ethernet0), len 48,
 sending broad/multicast
Jan 17 08:38:31:      UDP src=1985, dst=1985
Jan 17 08:38:32: IP: s=192.168.0.2 (local),
 d=224.0.0.1 (Ethernet0), len 36,
 sending broad/multicast
Jan 17 08:38:32:      ICMP type=9, code=0
%STANDBY-6-STATECHANGE: Standby: 0:
 Ethernet0 state Speak        -> Standby
%STANDBY-6-STATECHANGE: Standby: 0:
 Ethernet0 state Standby      -> Active
Jan 17 08:38:34: IP: s=192.168.0.2 (local),
 d=224.0.0.2 (Ethernet0), len 48,
 sending broad/multicast
Jan 17 08:38:34:      UDP src=1985, dst=1985
Jan 17 08:38:37: IP: s=192.168.0.2 (local),
 d=224.0.0.2 (Ethernet0), len 48,
 sending broad/multicast
Jan 17 08:38:37:      UDP src=1985, dst=1985
Jan 17 08:38:40: IP: s=192.168.0.2 (local),
 d=224.0.0.2 (Ethernet0), len 48,
 sending broad/multicast
Jan 17 08:38:40:      UDP src=1985, dst=1985
Jan 17 08:38:43: IP: s=192.168.0.2 (local),
 d=224.0.0.2 (Ethernet0), len 48,
 sending broad/multicast
Jan 17 08:38:43:      UDP src=1985, dst=1985
Jan 17 08:38:46: IP: s=192.168.0.2 (local),
 d=224.0.0.2 (Ethernet0), len 48,
 sending broad/multicast
```

```
Jan 17 08:38:46:      UDP src=1985, dst=1985
Jan 17 08:38:49: IP: s=192.168.0.2 (local),
  d=224.0.0.1 (Ethernet0), len 36,
  sending broad/multicast
Jan 17 08:38:49:      ICMP type=9, code=0
Jan 17 08:38:49: IP: s=192.168.0.2 (local),
  d=224.0.0.2 (Ethernet0), len 48,
  sending broad/multicast
Jan 17 08:38:49:      UDP src=1985, dst=1985
Jan 17 08:38:52: IP: s=192.168.0.2 (local),
  d=224.0.0.2 (Ethernet0), len 48,
  sending broad/multicast
Jan 17 08:38:52:      UDP src=1985, dst=1985
Jan 17 08:38:55: IP: s=192.168.0.2 (local),
  d=224.0.0.2 (Ethernet0), len 48,
  sending broad/multicast
Jan 17 08:38:55:      UDP src=1985, dst=1985
Jan 17 08:38:58: IP: s=192.168.0.2 (local),
  d=224.0.0.2 (Ethernet0), len 48,
  sending broad/multicast
Jan 17 08:38:58:      UDP src=1985, dst=1985
```

In this DEBUG trace, we notice several interesting events. The first packet sent by Frisco carries a destination address of 224.0.0.1. This is our IRDP multicast advertisement. It turns out that many production networks employing both UNIX and Microsoft hosts use IRDP in parallel with other, more flexible tools. Next, the router sends a packet to 224.0.0.2, the HSRP multicast address. DEBUG informs us that these packets belong to the UDP protocol, and that they are sent to port 1985. After sending three advertisements and hearing no other router advertising HSRP at a higher priority, Frisco assumes the role of active router for IP address 192.168.1.254 and issues statechange messages to the console, informing us that its role has moved from "speak" to standby to active.

At this point, the hosts in Figure 10-15 can send traffic to the rest of our internetwork, using a default gateway at 192.168.1.254. Router Frisco hears the IP ARP from clients and responds as if we had configured its Ethernet interface with this address. When we enable router NewYork's Ethernet interface as shown in Figure 10-18, it quickly

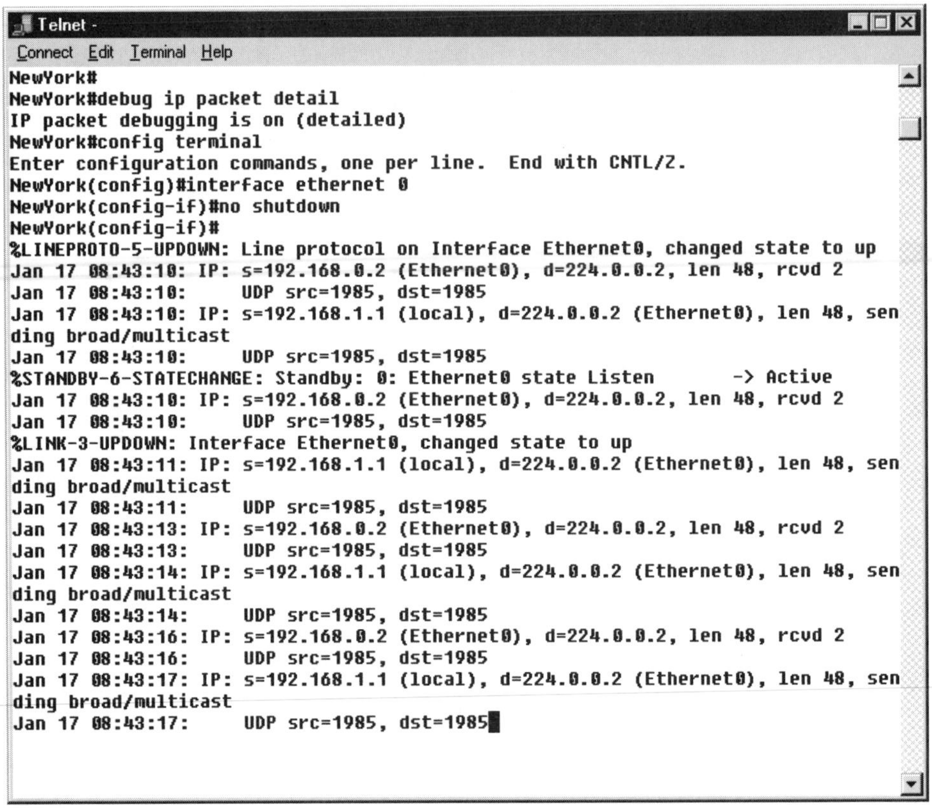

```
Telnet -                                                    _ □ ×
Connect  Edit  Terminal  Help
NewYork#
NewYork#debug ip packet detail
IP packet debugging is on (detailed)
NewYork#config terminal
Enter configuration commands, one per line.  End with CNTL/Z.
NewYork(config)#interface ethernet 0
NewYork(config-if)#no shutdown
NewYork(config-if)#
%LINEPROTO-5-UPDOWN: Line protocol on Interface Ethernet0, changed state to up
Jan 17 08:43:10: IP: s=192.168.0.2 (Ethernet0), d=224.0.0.2, len 48, rcvd 2
Jan 17 08:43:10:    UDP src=1985, dst=1985
Jan 17 08:43:10: IP: s=192.168.1.1 (local), d=224.0.0.2 (Ethernet0), len 48, sen
ding broad/multicast
Jan 17 08:43:10:    UDP src=1985, dst=1985
%STANDBY-6-STATECHANGE: Standby: 0: Ethernet0 state Listen      -> Active
Jan 17 08:43:10: IP: s=192.168.0.2 (Ethernet0), d=224.0.0.2, len 48, rcvd 2
Jan 17 08:43:10:    UDP src=1985, dst=1985
%LINK-3-UPDOWN: Interface Ethernet0, changed state to up
Jan 17 08:43:11: IP: s=192.168.1.1 (local), d=224.0.0.2 (Ethernet0), len 48, sen
ding broad/multicast
Jan 17 08:43:11:    UDP src=1985, dst=1985
Jan 17 08:43:13: IP: s=192.168.0.2 (Ethernet0), d=224.0.0.2, len 48, rcvd 2
Jan 17 08:43:13:    UDP src=1985, dst=1985
Jan 17 08:43:14: IP: s=192.168.1.1 (local), d=224.0.0.2 (Ethernet0), len 48, sen
ding broad/multicast
Jan 17 08:43:14:    UDP src=1985, dst=1985
Jan 17 08:43:16: IP: s=192.168.0.2 (Ethernet0), d=224.0.0.2, len 48, rcvd 2
Jan 17 08:43:16:    UDP src=1985, dst=1985
Jan 17 08:43:17: IP: s=192.168.1.1 (local), d=224.0.0.2 (Ethernet0), len 48, sen
ding broad/multicast
Jan 17 08:43:17:    UDP src=1985, dst=1985█
```

Figure 10-18   HSRP activity on router NewYork

becomes the active router for the address, based on its higher standby priority.

At this point, clients that had previously been speaking through router Frisco probably have an entry in their ARP cache for the IP address 192.168.1.254. If NewYork assumes the IP address from Frisco, but uses its own burned-in MAC address, the clients would have to wait for their ARP cache entries to time out before making use of the new path provided by NewYork. Typical ARP cache timeouts may be in the range of 1–20 minutes, depending on the host in question. To solve this problem, Cisco's HSRP implements not only a virtual IP address, but a virtual MAC address as well. When

NewYork assumes the active HSRP role, it uses the same virtual MAC address as Frisco. Care should be taken when implementing HSRP in switched or bridged environments, since a switch MAC database may not respond well to such apparent movement of MAC addresses.

Chapter 11

Configuring IP Multicast Routing

Answer Topics!

Configuring IP Multicast Routing @ a Glance

IP multicasting is a solution for the needs for users of both corporate intranets and the Internet. The first general use of IP multicast is the multicast backbone (MBONE). This network rides on the Internet and is used for audio and video broadcasts of events such as Internet Engineering Task Force (IETF) meetings, NASA space-shuttle launches, and even a Rolling Stones concert. The MBONE was developed to test and evaluate IP multicast transmission. IP multicast transmission is similar to IP unicast transmission. A *unicast* is a datagram transmission from a source host to a single destination. Examples of Unicast transmission are e-mail, Web-site browsing, and FTP. A *multicast* is a transmission of datagrams from a single source host to multiple destinations.

This chapter covers the following areas:

- **Internet Group Management Protocol (IGMP)** explores the concept of IP multicasting and IGMP on Cisco routers.

- **Protocol Independent Multicast (PIM)** examines Cisco's IP multicast routing protocol and how it is implemented on Cisco routers.

- **Distance Vector Multicast Routing Protocol (DVMRP)** examines how Cisco routers interpret and forward DVMRP packets.

- **Multicast Extension to OSPF (MOSPF)** explores Cisco's support of MOSPF and defines MOSPF.

- **PIM and DVMRP Interoperability** focuses on Cisco router operation in a combination PIM and DVMRP environment.

INTERNET GROUP MANAGEMENT PROTOCOL (IGMP)

What is IP multicasting?

IP multicasting is defined in Request for Comment (RFC) 1112 and RFC 2236 as packet transmission to a host group. A *host group* is a number of devices that share a single IP address. IP multicast transmission is the same as IP unicast; datagrams are sent with the same "best-effort" reliability. This means there is no guarantee that datagrams will be received intact and in order by all hosts in the group. There are three levels of host support:

Level	Description
0	No support for IP multicasting
1	Will send but not receive IP multicasts
2	Full support for IP multicasting

What is an example of IP multicasting?

The best-known example of IP multicasting is the multicast backbone (MBONE). This backbone is used for many-to-many communication, such as Internet teleconferences and video broadcasts.

What IP addresses are used for IP multicasting?

Currently, the address space that is reserved for IP multicasting is the Class D addresses in the range of 224.0.0.0 to 239.255.255.255. These addresses' high-order bits are defined as "1110".

What is the Internet Group Management Protocol (IGMP)?

Internet Group Management Protocol (IGMP) is a protocol used by IP hosts to report to neighboring multicast routers about any host groups they belong to. IGMP is part of the Internet Protocol, meaning that IGMP messages are encapsulated in IP datagrams. Hosts that are using IGMP must have the full TCP/IP protocol stack operating and must conform to level 2 of the IP multicasting specification.

 ## How do I configure IGMP on my Cisco router?

To configure IGMP on a Cisco router, you must enable IP multicasting. This will enable the router to act as a multicast router. To enable IP multicasting, use the following command in router configuration mode:

```
IP MULTICAST-ROUTING
```

 ## How can I tell which interfaces are running IGMP?

You can display the interfaces that are running IGMP by using the SHOW IP IGMP INTERFACE command from EXEC mode. This command displays each interface that is running IGMP, along with information on IGMP routing on the interface. Following is an example of the output from the SHOW IP IGMP INTERFACE command:

```
Router# show ip igmp interface
Ethernet0 is up, line protocol is up
Internet address is 176.16.1.6, subnet mask is 255.255.0.0
IGMP is enabled on interface
IGMP query interval is 60 seconds
Inbound IGMP access group is not set
Multicast routing is enabled on interface
Multicast TTL threshold is 0
Multicast designated router (DR) is 176.16.10.1
No multicast groups joined
Ethernet1 is up, line protocol is up
Internet address is 176.16.2.1, subnet mask is 255.255.0.0
IGMP is enabled on interface
IGMP query interval is 60 seconds
Inbound IGMP access group is not set
Multicast routing is enabled on interface
Multicast TTL threshold is 0
Multicast designated router (DR) is 192.168.68.1
Multicast groups joined: 225.2.2.2 226.2.2.2
```

❓ How do I display a list of available IP multicast routes?

You can display a list of IP multicast routes on a router by using the SHOW IP MROUTE command with the SUMMARY option. This command displays the available routes with information on the source router and multicast group. Following is an example of the SHOW IP MROUTE command:

```
Router# show ip mroute summary
IP Multicast Routing Table
Flags: D - Dense, S - Sparse, C - Connected, L - Local,
       P - Pruned R - RP-bit set, F - Register flag,
       T - SPT-bit set, J - Join SPT
Timers: Uptime/Expires
Interface state: Interface, Next-Hop, State/Mode
(*, 224.255.255.255), 2d16h/00:02:30, RP 172.16.10.1,
 flags: SJPC
(*, 224.2.127.253), 00:58:18/00:02:00, RP 172.16.10.1,
 flags: SJC
(*, 224.1.127.255), 00:58:21/00:02:03, RP 172.16.10.1,
 flags: SJC
(*, 224.2.127.254), 2d16h/00:00:00, RP 172.16.10.1,
 flags: SJCL
```

The information displayed in the output is as follows:

Field	Description
*, 224.255.255.255	Indicates the source router and multicast group. The asterisk (*) indicates all groups.
2d16h/00:02:30	The length of time the entry has been in the multicast routing table.
RP 172.16.10.1	The IP address of the router, identified as the Rendezvous Point (RP).
flags: SJC	Information about the entry. In this case, the flags are S: Sparse Mode; J: Shortest Path Tree bit has been set; and C: The Multicast group is directly connected.

What is CGMP?

CGMP stands for *Cisco Group Management Protocol*. This protocol was developed by Cisco to allow IP multicast routing capabilities to Cisco Catalyst switches. CGMP runs on both Cisco routers and Catalyst switches. The routers and switches communicate with each other to better manage multicast routing for IP as well as other protocols, such as Simple Multicast Routing Protocol (SMRP), to run more efficiently.

How do I enable CGMP on my Cisco router?

CGMP is enabled in interface configuration mode on interfaces that are connected to a Cisco Catalyst switch. Currently, only 802 media (such as Ethernet and Token Ring) and ATM interfaces support CGMP on Cisco routers. When activated, the router sends a CGMP Join message to advertise its existence to the Catalyst switch. To enable CGMP on a Cisco router interface (either 802 media or ATM) that is connected to a Cisco Catalyst switch, use the following command syntax:

```
IP CGMP
```

What is CGMP proxy?

CGMP proxy is used for the purpose of advertising non-CGMP-enabled routers by a router that is CGMP-enabled. This allows multicast packets to be routed to the non-CGMP-enabled routers that have both multicast servers and clients attached to them. To enable CGMP and CGMP proxy on a Cisco router, use the following command syntax in router interface configuration mode:

```
IP CGMP PROXY
```

This enables CGMP on 802 media or ATM interface, and declares the router to be a CGMP proxy router.

PROTOCOL INDEPENDENT MULTICAST (PIM)

 What is Protocol Independent Multicast (PIM)?

PIM is a multicast routing protocol that provides scalable interdomain multicast routing. This protocol is used for Internet multicast routing and is not to be dependent on any single unicast routing protocol, such as RIP or OSPF. PIM is a router-to-router routing protocol, as opposed to IGMP, which is a host-to-router protocol. There are two types of PIM: sparse mode and dense mode.

In sparse-mode PIM, a router takes the position that other multicast routers will not forward packets to the hosts in the group unless specifically requested to do so. When a new host joins a multicast group, routers send PIM Join messages to the nearest rendezvous point (RP). The RP adds the host to its table and then sends Join messages to the source. When this distribution tree is built, packets are forwarded to it.

Dense-mode PIM routers expect all other routers to forward multicast packets. If no neighbors or hosts are connected to a segment, Prune messages are sent to the source, telling it not to send multicast packet to this segment. This is what is called *source-based multicast trees*.

Another mode can be used on Cisco routers. *Sparse-dense mode* can be used when the interface is routing multicast traffic in both dense and sparse modes.

 How do I configure PIM on my Cisco router?

When PIM is enabled, IGMP is also activated on the same interface. Depending on which mode is used, the router's multicast routing table also starts to populate. In dense mode, all interfaces that are dense-mode are added to the multicast routing table. In sparse mode, interfaces are added to the multicast routing table when the router receives Join messages from either downstream or directly connected routers. To enable PIM on a Cisco router, use the following router interface configuration command:

```
IP PIM MODE
```

This enables PIM on an interface. *MODE* is defined as dense, sparse, or sparse-dense.

If PIM is used in sparse mode, you have to select one or more routers to be a Rendezvous Point (RP). Both senders and receivers of multicast packets to announce their presence and to learn about new senders use RPs. The IP address of the RP is configured in routers that are identified as leaf routers. *Leaf routers* are routers that are directly connected to either the sender or receiver of multicast packets. To set the IP address of the RP, use the following command in router configuration mode:

```
IP PIM RP-ADDRESS ADDRESS [ACCESS-LIST-NUMBER]
[OVERRIDE]
```

What is a Rendezvous Point?

A *Rendezvous Point (RP)* is a router that is used by multicast packet senders to advertise their existence and by multicast packet receivers to discover new senders. If you are configuring PIM in sparse mode, you must configure the leaf routers (routers that are directly attached to either multicast receivers or senders) with the IP address of the router that is designated as the RP. The leaf routers then learn about the existence of the RP and begin to forward packets.

How do I display which interfaces are configured for PIM?

You can display a list of interfaces that are configured for PIM by using the SHOW IP PIM INTERFACE command from EXEC mode. The command displays information on what interfaces are running PIM, the mode in which the interface is running PIM, and other information. Following is an example of the output of the SHOW IP PIN INTERFACE command:

```
Router# show ip pim interface
Address        Interface Mode Neighbor  Query     DR
                              Count     Interval
192.168.68.1 Ethernet0 Dense   2         30        192.168.68.5
192.168.50.1 Ethernet1 Dense   2         30        192.168.50.7
11.1.20.1    Tunnel0   Dense   1         30        0.0.0.0
```

The fields displayed provide the following information:

Field	Description
192.168.68.1	Address of the next-hop router
Ethernet0	Interface type configured to run PIM
Dense	Mode of PIM running on the interface
2	The number of devices that have been discovered to be PIM routers
30	Frequency in which PIM router query messages are sent (30 seconds is the default)
192.168.68.5	Address of the designated router

 ### How do I determine what PIM neighbors have been discovered?

You can display a list of PIM neighbors that have been discovered by using the SHOW IP PIM NEIGHBOR command from EXEC mode on the router. The IP address, interface, and other information are displayed for each neighbor found. Following is an example of the output from the command:

```
Router# show ip pim neighbor
PIM Neighbor Table
Neighbor Address  Interface  Uptime    Expires   Mode
192.168.37.2      Ethernet0  17:38:16  0:01:25   Dense
192.168.37.33     Ethernet0  17:33:20  0:01:05   Dense (DR)
10.2.45.19        Tunnel0    19:14:59  0:01:09   Dense
```

The fields that are displayed are as follows:

Field	Description
192.168.37.2	Neighbor discovered
Ethernet0	Interface from which the neighbor was discovered
17:38:16	Length of time that the neighbor has been available
0:01:25	Length of time before the host is removed from the routing table
Dense	The mode in which the interface is running

DISTANCE VECTOR MULTICAST ROUTING PROTOCOL (DVMRP)

 What is Distance Vector Multicast Routing Protocol (DVMRP)?

Distance Vector Multicast Routing Protocol (DVMRP) is defined in RFC 1075 as a routing protocol derived from Routing Information Protocol (RIP) for routing multicast packets through the Internet or an intranet. DVMRP differs from RIP in the way that routing tables are developed. Whereas RIP sends packets based on next-hop information, DVMRP builds delivery trees based on previous-hop back to the source. DVMRP is based on the mrouted program, which is a public-domain multicast routing protocol used by many vendors. Currently, DVMRP is the routing protocol used by the MBONE, although this protocol may change to PIM in the future.

 How does Cisco implement DVMRP?

Cisco does not implement full DVMRP. Cisco routers use PIM for routing multicast packets and implement DVMRP to forward and receive multicast packets from DVMRP hosts. DVMRP routes can be propagated into and through PIM clouds, but the information is used only by PIM. Cisco routers do not use DVRMP to route multicast packets.

MULTICAST EXTENSION TO OSPF (MOSPF)

 What is MOSPF?

Multicast Open Shortest Path First (MOSPF) protocol is defined in RFC 1584 as an extension to OSPF that allows the routing of IP multicast packets using the OSPF link-state database. This allows nonmulticast routers running OSPF to route multicast packets to routers that are running multicast protocols. Routers that are running IP multicast build their database of senders and receivers, whereas routers that are

nonmulticast but are running OSPF are able to send and receive multicast packets.

 Do Cisco routers support MOSPF?

Cisco routers do not support the Type 6 Link-State Announcement (LSA), which is for MSOPF. When an MOSPF packet is received on a Cisco router, a syslog entry is generated. Large numbers of syslog entries can be generated if the router receives a large amount of MOSPF packets. You can disable these syslog entries when the router receives OSPF Type 6 LSAs by using the following command in router configuration mode:

```
OSPF IGNORE LSA MOSPF
```

PIM AND DVMRP INTEROPERABILITY

 What does PIM and DVMRP interoperability mean?

Because Cisco routers do not implement the full DVRMP routing protocol, interoperability is needed to allow DVMRP multicast packets to be forwarded and received by Cisco routers. Routers that are running PIM can discover dynamically other routers that are running DVMRP. When DVMRP routers are discovered, the PIM router sends Report messages to the DVMRP routers with information on reachable sources via PIM routes. Directly connected subnets and networks are advertised by default. Multicast packets that are DVMRP-originated are forwarded and received to DVMRP hosts.

To enable DVMRP sources advertised and the metrics used when sending DVMRP messages, use the following command in router configuration mode:

```
IP DVMRP METRIC METRIC [LIST ACCESS-LIST-NUMBER]
    [[PROCESS-ID] [DVMRP]]
```

This sets the metric associated with a set of destinations for DVMRP reports.

> **Note:** *The mrouted protocol is a public-domain implementation of DVMRP. When Cisco routers are connected to DVMRP routers or operate with DVMRP routers over an MBONE tunnel, DVMRP advertisements produced by the Cisco IOS software can cause older versions of mrouted to corrupt their routing tables and those of their neighbors. To prevent this situation from occurring, take the following steps:*
>
> 1. *Routers connected to the MBONE should have an access list to limit the number of unicast routes that are advertised via DVMRP.*
>
> 2. *Use mrouted Version 3.8 or later. These versions implement a nonpruning version of DVMRP. The mrouted protocol is a public-domain implementation of DVMRP.*

 ## How can I tell whether there are any DVMRP routes in the IP routing table?

You can determine whether there are any DVMRP routes in the routing table by using the SHOW IP DVMRP ROUTE command from EXEC mode. The command displays the block advertised, the length of time that the route has been in the table, the amount of time left before the route expires, and the source of the route. Following is an example of the output from the SHOW IP DVMRP ROUTE command:

```
Router# show ip dvmrp route
DVMRP Routing Table - 1 entry
131.146.0.0/16 [100/11] uptime 10:55:50, expires 00:02:00
via 172.16.1.1, Ethernet0
```

Chapter 12

Monitoring the IP Network

Answer Topics!

Monitoring the IP Network @ a Glance

Today's corporate and service provider IP networks are getting larger. As a result, the need for monitoring grows as well. Network administrators, as well as network operation centers, need information to establish the overall health of the network. The need for up-to-date operational network health is more and more vital. The ability to monitor large IP networks is made easier on Cisco routers and switches through the use of software commands that are available from user prompts or from Simple Network Management Protocol (SNMP) applications such as Cisco Works and TrafficDirector.

This chapter covers the following areas:

- **Displaying IP Routing Tables** explores the various commands used to display IP routing tables on Cisco routers.

- **Displaying Neighbors** explores how to show neighbors that have been discovered in the various IP routing protocols supported on Cisco routers.

- **Displaying Statistics** explores how Cisco routers display statistics for the various IP routing protocols.

- **Parameters and Status** provides information on how to configure SNMP and verify connectivity; explores RMON and how Cisco uses RMON probes for IP monitoring.

DISPLAYING IP ROUTING TABLES

 How do I display the IP routing table on a Cisco router?

To display the IP routing table on a Cisco router, use the SHOW IP ROUTE command. This command displays all the routes that are available and the source of the route. The command syntax is as follows:

```
SHOW IP ROUTE [ADDRESS [MASK] [LONGER-PREFIXES]] |
     [PROTOCOL [PROCESS-ID]]
```

The following options are available with the SHOW IP ROUTE command:

 ADDRESS   Displays routing information for a specific address

● **MASK**   Displays the subnet mask used

● **LONGER-PREFIXES**   Pairs the address and subnet mask to display only matches to the address/mask

● **PROTOCOL**   Specifies routes based on a routing protocol or a keyword, such as connected or static

● **PROCESS-ID**   Specifies a process of a certain protocol

 What does the output of the SHOW IP ROUTE command display?

The output from the SHOW IP ROUTE command displays the following information:

```
Codes: C - Connected, S - Static, I - IGRP, R - RIP,
M - Mobile, B - BGP D - EIGRP, EX - EIGRP external,
O - OSPF, IA - OSPF inter area, E1 - OSPF external type 1,
E2 - OSPF external type 2, E - EGP, i - IS-IS,
L1 - IS-IS level 1, L2 - IS-IS level 2
```

The next section of the display shows the IP routes that have been discovered and the interface from which the route advertisement originates:

```
172.16.0.0 255.255.255.0 is subnetted, 3 subnets
C        172.16.100.0 is directly connected, Ethernet0
R        172.16.101.0 [120/1] via 172.16.100.60,
           00:00:14, Ethernet0
C        172.16.102.0 is directly connected, Loopback0
```

The information displayed in the output is as follows:

Field	Description
C	Route is directly connected
172.16.100.0	IP address block that is directly connected
Ethernet0	Interface to which the IP address block is connected

How do I display a summary of routes that are in the routing table of a Cisco router?

You can display a summary of routes that are in the routing table by using the SHOW IP ROUTE SUMMARY command. This command displays a table of the various routing protocols that have been configured in the router and the number of routes that have been discovered by the protocol. Following is an example of a route summary contained in the routing table of a Cisco router:

```
Router# show ip route summary
Route Source    Networks  Subnets  Overhead  Memory (bytes)
connected       0         3        126       360
static          1         2        126       360
bgp 100         100       12       878       91080
Total           101       15       1130      92160
```

The information shown in the display is as follows:

Field	Description
Route Source	The source protocol, static routes, or other sources
Networks	The number of network prefixes in the routing table
Subnets	The number of subnets in the routing table
Overhead	The amount of memory used in addition to the amount that is specified in the memory field
Memory	The amount of memory used to maintain the routes from the source protocol

 ## How do I display the IP routing table for certain IP address blocks?

You can display routing information by using the SHOW IP ROUTE command with optional information to display route information for certain IP address blocks. To display IP route information for certain blocks, use the SHOW IP ROUTE command, along with the IP address block specified, as shown here,

```
SHOW IP ROUTE [ADDRESS]
```

and in the following code example:

```
Router# Show ip route 172.16.0.0
Routing entry for 172.16.0.0 (mask 255.255.0.0)
Known via "static", distance 100, metric 10989
Last update from 172.16.35.1 on Ethernet0, 0:00:58 ago
Routing Descriptor Blocks: * 172.16.35.1, from
  172.16.35.1, 0:00:58 ago, via Ethernet0 Route metric
  is 10989, traffic share count is 1 Total delay is
  45130 microseconds, minimum bandwidth is 1544 Kbit
  Reliability 255/255, minimum MTU 1500 bytes
  Loading 2/255, Hops 4
Router#
```

 ## How do I display routing information for connected networks?

You can display routing information by using the SHOW IP ROUTE command with optional information that displays route information for IP networks that are directly connected to the router. To display IP route information for connected networks, use the SHOW IP ROUTE command, along with the option CONNECTED, as follows:

```
SHOW IP ROUTE CONNECTED
```

This shows directly connected routes that are current in the IP routing table.

An example of the output from SHOW IP ROUTE CONNECTED shows the following information:

```
Router# Show ip route connected
C       172.16.100.0 is directly connected, Ethernet0
C       172.16.102.0 is directly connected, Loopback0
Router#
```

 ## How do I display routing information for static routes?

You can display routing information by using the SHOW IP ROUTE command with optional information that displays route information for static routes. To display IP route information for static routes, use the SHOW IP ROUTE command along with the option STATIC, as follows:

```
SHOW IP ROUTE STATIC
```

An example of the output from SHOW IP ROUTE STATIC shows the following information:

```
Router# Show ip route static
S       172.16.100.0 is directly connected, Ethernet0
S       172.16.102.0 is directly connected, Ethernet1
```

 ## How do I display routing information for Border Gateway Protocol?

You can display routing information by using the SHOW IP ROUTE command with the option for Border Gateway Protocol information to display route information for BGP-routed networks. To display IP route information for BGP, use the SHOW IP ROUTE command with the option BGP, as follows:

```
SHOW IP ROUTE BGP
```

An example of the output from SHOW IP ROUTE BGP shows the following information:

```
Router#sh ip route bgp
B    206.51.253.0/24 [200/0] via 192.168.68.1, 4d22h
B    205.204.1.0/24 [200/15] via 192.168.68.1, 3w2d
B    204.17.221.0/24 [200/1] via 192.168.70.2, 3d18h
```

The information displayed in the output is as follows:

Field	Description
B	Route is BGP-originated
206.51.253.0/24	The IP block and subnet (displayed in summarized format) being announced
[200/0]	200 is the administrative distance of the source of the block being announced. 0 is the metric of the route
192.168.68.1	The source address from which the route is being announced
4d22h	The route has been valid for 4 days, 22 hours

DISPLAYING NEIGHBORS

 ## How do I display neighbor information for Border Gateway Protocol?

To display neighbor information for Border Gateway Protocol (BGP), use the SHOW IP BGP NEIGHBOR command. The command displays information such as the Autonomous System (AS) number, the IP address of the neighbor, and

additional information. To display neighbor information for BGP, use the SHOW IP BGP NEIGHBOR command:

```
SHOW IP BGP NEIGHBORS [ADDRESS] [RECEIVED-ROUTES | ROUTES |
    ADVERTISED-ROUTES | {PATHSREGULAR-EXPRESSION} |
    DAMPENED-ROUTES]
```

The options available for BGP NEIGHBOR commands are:

- **address**   Displays the address of the neighbor from which you are requesting information
- **received-routes**   Displays routes received from the specified neighbor
- **routes**   Displays routes that are received and accepted as a subset of the output from the **received-routes** keyword
- **advertised-routes**   Displays the routes that the router has advertised to a neighbor
- **paths regular-expression**   Regular expression used to match the paths received from a neighbor
- **dampened-routes**   Displays dampened routes to the neighbor at the specified IP address

 ## How do I display the routes that are being announced by a BGP neighbor?

You can display routes that are being advertised by a neighbor by using the SHOW IP BGP REGEXP command. This command displays a list of routes that are being advertised by a neighbor based on the neighbor's Autonomous System (AS) number. The routes include both valid and dampened routes. To display the routes being advertised by a BGP neighbor, use the SHOW IP BGP REGEXP command as follows:

```
SHOW IP BGP REGEXP [REGULAR EXPRESSION]
```

This displays routes being advertised by the AS that match the regular expression.

Following is an example of the output from the SHOW IP BGP REGEXP command, showing the matches for the AS that is entered:

```
Router# show ip bgp regexp 4003
BGP table version is 1359, local router ID is 192.168.68.5
Status codes: s suppressed, * valid, > best, i - internal
Origin codes: i - IGP, e - EGP, ? - incomplete
   Network       Next Hop        Metric  Weight  Path
                                 LocPrf
*  192.168.1.0  192.168.25.1             0       4003 ?
*  192.168.2.0  192.168.25.1             0       4003 ?
*  192.168.3.0  192.168.25.1             0       4003 ?
*  192.168.4.0  192.168.25.1             0       4003 ?
*  192.168.5.0  192.168.25.1             0       4003 ?
```

Field	Description
*	Valid route has been discovered
192.168.1.0	IP address block has been discovered
192.168.25.1	IP address of the router announcing the blocks
4003 ?	The block is being announced by AS 4003. The question mark (?) means that the path is incomplete.

 ## How do I display neighbor information for Enhanced Interior Gateway Protocol?

To display neighbor information for Enhanced Interior Gateway Protocol (EIGRP), use the SHOW IP EIGRP NEIGHBORS command. The command displays the Autonomous System (AS) number, the IP address of the neighbor, and additional information. To display neighbor information for EIGRP, use the SHOW IP EIGRP NEIGHBORS command as follows:

```
SHOW IP EIGRP NEIGHBORS [type number]
```

The options available for this command include:

- **type**   Interface type (Ethernet, serial, FDDI, and so on)
- **number**   Interface number

 ### How do I display neighbor information for Open Shortest Path First routing protocol?

To display neighbor information for Open Shortest Path First (OSPF), use the SHOW IP OSPF NEIGHBOR command. The command displays the Autonomous System (AS) number, the IP address of the neighbor, and additional information. To display neighbor information for OSPF, use the SHOW IP OSPF NEIGHBOR command as follows:

```
SHOW IP OSPF NEIGHBOR [type number] [neighbor-id] [DETAIL]
```

The options available for the SHOW IP OSPF NEIGHBOR command are as follows:

- **type**   Interface type (Ethernet, serial, FDDI, and so on)
- **number**   Interface number
- **neighbor-id**   Neighbor ID

Note: *If the DETAIL option is used with the SHOW IP OSPF NEIGHBOR command, all neighbors are displayed with routing detail for each neighbor.*

DISPLAYING STATISTICS

 ### What types of statistics are available?

Many types of statistics are available, ranging from the list of active routing protocols on the various interfaces, to the number of datagrams received and transmitted, to the number of IP packets that are rejected based on access lists. These statistics are available through Telnet/console access or configurable via SNMP.

 ## What methods of gathering statistics are available on Cisco routers?

Several methods are available for gathering and displaying statistics for IP traffic and protocol information. Statistics can be gathered from the router via the console port, through Telnet access, or through the HTTP interface. The use of SHOW commands is available from both USER and EXEC modes, although commands available to USER mode are more limited. Statistics can also be gathered through the use of Simple Network Management Protocol (SNMP)-based programs such as Remote Monitoring (RMON) probes and applications such as Cisco Works. These programs can gather statistics based on configurable traps and present them in a way that is understandable to the user. This data can be stored for future use to enable the user to determine long-term trends.

 ## What is Remote Monitoring (RMON)?

Remote Monitoring (RMON) is the gathering of information for network administrators to monitor, analyze, and troubleshoot LANs and interconnecting WANs. RMON information, as explained in RFC 1757, comes from the Management Information Base (MIB) as an extension of SNMP. RMON is accomplished via hardware devices or software commonly known as a probe, which is attached to the remote LAN or WAN interconnection. The probe, through a graphical user interface or GUI program, provides nine types of information, such as packets and bytes sent, dropped packets, host statistics, and other types of events. Cisco routers and switches contain the software within its operating system to support RMON.

 ## How can I determine whether RMON is running on my Cisco router?

You can determine whether RMON is running on a Cisco router by using the SHOW RMON command from the EXEC prompt. The output provides information on the number of

RMON packets the router has processed, whether RMON is running in promiscuous mode, and other information. RMON is enabled on Ethernet interfaces when SNMP has been enabled. You must have SNMP running to enable RMON. RMON runs in two modes: native and promiscuous. In native mode, the router monitors only packets destined for the Ethernet interface. In promiscuous mode, the router monitors all packets. Following is an example of the SHOW RMON command:

```
Router# show rmon
24678 packets input (4489 promiscuous), 0 drops
24678 packets processed, 0 on queue,
 queue utilization 15/64
```

The information displayed in the output is as follows:

Field	Description
24678 packets input	The amount of packets received on RMON-enabled interfaces.
4489 promiscuous	The number of packets seen by the router when the interface is in promiscuous mode.
0 drops	The number of RMON packets dropped due to buffer overflow.
24678 packets processed	The actual number of RMON processed packets.
0 on queue	The number of RMON packets waiting to be processed.
15/64	15 packets were queued for processing; this is the largest number of packets waiting to be processed. 64 packets is the size of the queue.

 What command displays RMON statistics?

The command SHOW RMON STATISTICS provides the user information that is contained in the router's RMON statistics table. The command displays the interfaces that RMON is running on, the number of octets and packets received, the number of broadcast and multicast packet received, the number of errors detected, and a breakdown of packet lengths

received. Following is an example of the output from the
SHOW RMON STATISTICS command:

```
Router# show rmon statistics
Interface 1 is active, and owned by config
 Monitors ifEntry.1.1 which has
 Received 59813689 octets, 156853 packets,
 1905 broadcast and 8267 multicast packets,
 0 undersized and 0 oversized packets,
 0 fragments and 0 jabbers,
 0 CRC alignment errors and 0 collisions.
 # of dropped packet events (due to lack of resources): 0
 # of packets received of length (in octets): 0
  64: 2876, 65-127: 13490, 128-255: 1276,
  256-511: 4213, 512-1023: 10987, 1024-1518:1256
```

The information displayed in the output is as follows:

Field	Description
Interface 1 is active, and owned by config	Index of the entry, state of the interface, and owner of the interface
Monitors ifEntry.1.1	Source of the data that is located in the etherStatsDataSource in RMON
Received 59813689 octets	Number of octets received
156853 packets	Number of packets received
1905 broadcast	Number of broadcast packets received
8267 multicast packets	Number of multicast packets received
0 undersized	Packets smaller than 64 octets
0 oversized	Packets longer than 1518 octets
0 fragments	Packets smaller than 64 octets that have some type of corruption (FCS errors)
0 jabbers	Packets larger than 1518 octets that have some type of corruption (FCS errors)
0 CRC alignment errors	Packets between 64 and 1518 octets that have some type of corruption (FCS errors)

Field	Description
0 collisions	Number of Ethernet collisions
# of dropped packet events (due to lack of resources): 0	Number of packets dropped due to a lack of resources
# of packets received of length (in octets): 64: 2876, 65-127: 13490, 128-255: 1276, 256-511: 4213, 512-1023: 10987, 1024-1518:1256	Divides the number of packets received into size categories

PARAMETERS AND STATUS

 How do I configure my Cisco router to work with an SNMP-based monitoring application such as Cisco Works?

To use an SNMP-based monitoring application (or agent), you must enable SNMP on the router. The relationship between the router and the agent is defined through the use of community strings. *Community strings* are similar to a password that the agent uses to gain access to the router. The most commonly used community string is PUBLIC. The PUBLIC string provides read-only access for the agent to begin monitoring. To configure a Cisco router for an SNMP-based application, and to allow that application to access and begin monitoring a network, use the following commands in router configuration mode:

Command	Description
SNMP-SERVER COMMUNITY PUBLIC	Enables SNMP and allows read-only access to hosts using the string PUBLIC
SNMP-SERVER HOST 192.168.68.3 PUBLIC	Defines host 192.168.68.3 as a host to send SNMP trap messages with the community string PUBLIC

 ### How do I verify that SNMP is running on my Cisco router?

To verify that SNMP is running, use the SHOW SNMP command from either the USER or EXEC prompt. This command provides information on SNMP communications on the router. Following is the output that is displayed:

```
Router# show snmp
Chassis: 01516789
48 SNMP packets input
    0 Bad SNMP version errors
    5 Unknown community name
    0 Illegal operation for community name supplied
    0 Encoding errors
    33 Number of requested variables
    0 Number of altered variables
    0 Get-request PDUs
    18 Get-next PDUs
    0 Set-request PDUs
89 SNMP packets output
    0 Too big errors (Maximum packet size 1500)
    0 No such name errors
    0 Bad values errors
    0 General errors
    35 Response PDUs
    24 Trap PDUs
SNMP logging: enabled
    Logging to 192.168.68.3, 0/10, 13 sent, 0 dropped.
```

What method do I use to verify connectivity from my network monitoring application to my routers?

This question has several answers, depending on the configuration of the software. Most, if not all, packages have the capability to poll routers to verify connectivity. The method of polling can vary from simple ping packets to SNMP GET queries. You can set traps within the software to provide a warning if connectivity to a router or the network is lost. Check your application's manuals for the directions for polling and traps for lost connectivity warnings.

Glossary

10Base2 Ethernet specification using 50-ohm thin coaxial cable and a signaling rate of 10-Mbps baseband.

10Base5 Ethernet specification using standard (thick) 50-ohm baseband coaxial cable and a signaling rate of 10-Mbps baseband.

10BaseFL Ethernet specification using fiber-optic cabling and a signaling rate of 10-Mbps baseband, and FOIRL.

10BaseT Ethernet specification using two pairs of twisted-pair cabling (Category 3, 4, or 5): one pair for transmitting data and the other for receiving data, and a signaling rate of 10-Mbps baseband.

10Broad36 Ethernet specification using broadband coaxial cable and a signaling rate of 10-Mbps.

100BaseFX Fast Ethernet specification using two strands of multimode fiber-optic cable per link and a signaling rate of 100-Mbps baseband. A 100BaseFXlink cannot exceed 400 meters in length.

100BaseT Fast Ethernet specification using UTP wiring and a signaling rate of 100-Mbps baseband. 100BaseT sends link pulses out on the wire when there is no data traffic present.

100BaseT4 Fast Ethernet specification using four pairs of Category 3, 4, or 5 UTP wiring and a signaling rate of100-Mbps baseband. The maximum length of a 100BaseT4 segment is 100 meters.

100BaseTX Fast Ethernet specification using two pairs of UTP or STP wiring and 100-Mbps baseband signaling. One pair of wires is used to receive data; the other is used to transmit. A 100BaseTX segment cannot exceed 100 meters in length.

100BaseX 100-Mbps baseband Fast Ethernet specification based on the IEEE 802.3 standard. 100BaseX refers to the 100BaseFX and 100BaseTX standards for Fast Ethernet over fiber-optic cabling.

AAL (ATM adaptation layer)   Service-dependent sublayer of the data-link layer. The function of the AAL is to accept data from different applications and present it to the ATM layer in 48-byte ATM segments.

AARP (AppleTalk Address Resolution Protocol) The protocol that maps a data-link address to an AppleTalk network address.

ABR (area border router)   Router located on the border of an OSPF area, which connects that area to the backbone network. An ABR would be a member of both the OSPF backbone and the attached area. It maintains routing tables describing both the backbone topology and the topology of the other area.

access list   A sequential list of statements in a router configuration that identify network traffic for various purposes, including traffic and route filtering.

acknowledgment   Notification sent from one network device to another to acknowledge that a message or group of messages has been received. Sometimes abbreviated ACK. Opposite of **NAK**.

active hub   A multiport device that repeats and amplifies LAN signals at the physical layer.

active monitor   A network device on a Token Ring that is responsible for managing ring operations. The active monitor ensures that tokens are not lost, or that frames do not circulate indefinitely on the ring.

address   A numbering convention used to identify a unique entity or location on a network.

address mapping   Technique that allows different protocols to operate together by associating addresses from one format with those of another.

address mask   A string of bits, which, when combined with an address, describes which portion of an address refers to the network or subnet and which part refers to the host. *See also* **subnet mask**.

address resolution   A technique for resolving differences between computer addressing schemes. Address resolution most often specifies a method for mapping network layer addresses to data-link layer addresses. *See also* **address mapping**.

Address Resolution Protocol   *See* **ARP**.

administrative distance   A rating of the preferability of a routing information source. Administrative distance is expressed as a value between 0 and 255. The higher the value, the lower the preference.

advertising   A process in which a router sends routing or service updates at frequent intervals so that other routers on the network can maintain lists of usable routes or services.

algorithm   A specific process for arriving at a solution to a problem.

AMI (alternate mark inversion)   The line-code type that is used on T1 and E1 circuits. In this code, zeros are represented by 01 during each bit cell, and ones are represented by 11 or 00, alternately, during each bit cell.

ANSI (American National Standards Institute)   An organization of representatives of corporate, government, and other entities that coordinates standards-related activities, approves U.S. national standards, and develops positions for the United States in international standards organizations.

AppleTalk   A suite of communications protocols developed by Apple Computer for allowing communication among their devices over a network.

application layer   Layer 7 of the OSI reference model. This layer provides services to end-user application processes such as electronic mail, file transfer, and terminal emulation.

ARP (Address Resolution Protocol)   Internet protocol used to map an IP address to a MAC address.

ASBR (autonomous system boundary router)   An ASBR is an ABR connecting an OSPF autonomous system to a non-OSPF network. ASBRs run two protocols: OSPF and another routing protocol. ASBRs must be located in a nonstub OSPF area.

asynchronous transmission   Describes digital signals that are transmitted without precise clocking or synchronization.

ATM (Asynchronous Transfer Mode)   An international standard for cell relay suitable for carrying multiple service types (such as voice, video, or data) in fixed-length (53-byte) cells. Fixed-length cells allow cell processing to occur in hardware, thereby reducing latency.

ATM adaptation layer   *See* **AAL**.

ATM Forum   International organization founded in 1991 by Cisco Systems, NET/ADAPTIVE, Northern Telecom, and Sprint to develop and promote standards-based implementation agreements for ATM technology.

AUI (attachment unit interface)   An interface between an MAU and a NIC (network interface card) described in the IEEE 802.3 specification. AUI often refers to the physical port to which an AUI cable attaches.

autonomous system   A group of networks under a common administration that share in a common routing strategy. Sometimes abbreviated AS.

B8ZS (binary 8-zero substitution)   The line-code type that used on T1 and E1 circuits. With B8ZS, a special code is substituted whenever eight consecutive zeros are sent over

the link. This code is then interpreted at the remote end of the connection.

backoff   The retransmission delay used by contention-based MAC protocols such as Ethernet, after a network node determines that the physical medium is already in use.

bandwidth   The difference between the highest and lowest frequencies available for network signals. The term may also describe the throughput capacity of a network link or segment.

baseband   A network technology in which a single carrier frequency is used. Ethernet is a common example of a baseband network technology.

baud   Unit of signaling speed equal to the number of separate signal elements transmitted in one second. Baud is synonymous with bits per second (bps), as long as each signal element represents exactly one bit.

B channel (bearer channel)   An ISDN term meaning a full-duplex, 64-kbps channel used to send user data.

bearer channel   *See* **B channel**.

BECN   backward explicit congestion notification. A Frame Relay network facility that allows switches in the network to advise DTE devices of congestion. The BECN bit is set in frames traveling in the opposite direction of frames encountering a congested path.

best-effort delivery   Describes a network system that does not use a system of acknowledgment to guarantee reliable delivery of information.

BGP (Border Gateway Protocol)   An interdomain path-vector routing protocol. BGP exchanges reachability information with other BGP systems. It is defined by RFC 1163.

binary   A numbering system in which there are only two digits, ones and zeros.

BNC connector   Standard connector used to connect coaxial cable to an MAU or line card.

BOOTP (Bootstrap Protocol)   Part of the TCP/IP suite of protocols, used by a network node to determine the IP address of its Ethernet interfaces, in order to boot from a network server.

bps   Bits per second.

BRI (Basic Rate Interface)   ISDN interface consisting of two B channels and one D channel for circuit-switched communication. ISDN BRI can carry voice, video, and data.

bridge   Device that connects and forwards packets between two network segments that use the same data-link communications protocol. Bridges operate at the data link layer of the OSI reference model. A bridge will filter, forward, or flood an incoming frame based on the MAC address of the frame.

broadband   A data transmission system that multiplexes multiple independent signals onto one cable. Also, in telecommunications, any channel with a bandwidth greater than 4 KHz. In LAN terminology, a coaxial cable using analog signaling.

broadcast   Data packet addressed to all nodes on a network. Broadcasts are identified by a broadcast address that matches all addresses on the network.

broadcast address   Special address reserved for sending a message to all stations. At the data-link layer, a broadcast address is a MAC destination address of all 1s.

broadcast domain   The group of all devices that will receive the same broadcast frame originating from any device within the group. Because routers do not forward broadcast frames, broadcast domains are typically bounded by routers.

buffer   A memory storage area used for handling data in transit. Buffers are used in internetworking to compensate

for differences in processing speed between network devices or signaling rates of segments. Bursts of packets can be stored in buffers until they can be handled by slower devices.

bus   Common physical path composed of wires or other media, across which signals are sent from one part of a computer to another.

bus topology   A topology used in LANs. Transmissions from network stations propagate the length of the medium and are then received by all other stations.

byte   A series of consecutive binary digits that are operated upon as a unit, usually eight bits.

cable   Transmission medium of copper wire or optical fiber wrapped in a protective cover.

cable range   A range of network numbers on an extended AppleTalk network. The cable range value can be a single network number or a contiguous sequence of several network numbers. Nodes assign addresses within the cable range values provided.

CAM   Content-addressable memory.

carrier   Electromagnetic wave or alternating current of a single frequency, suitable for modulation by another, data-bearing signal.

Carrier Detect   *See* **CD**.

carrier sense multiple access with collision detection *See* **CSMA/CD**.

Category 5 cabling   One of five grades of UTP cabling described in the EIA/TIA-586 standard. Category 5 cabling can transmit data at speeds up to 100 Mbps.

CCITT (Consultative Committee for International Telegraphy and Telephony)   International organization responsible for the development of communications standards. Now called the ITU-T. *See* **ITU-T**.

CD (Carrier Detect)   Signal that indicates whether an interface is active.

CDDI (Copper Distributed Data Interface)   The implementation of FDDI protocols over STP and UTP cabling. CDDI transmits over distances of approximately 100 meters, providing data rates of 100 Mbps. CDDI uses a dual-ring architecture to provide redundancy.

cell   The basic data unit for ATM switching and multiplexing. A cell consists of a five-byte header and 48 bytes of payload. Cells contain fields in their headers that identify the data stream to which they belong.

CHAP (Challenge Handshake Authentication Protocol) Security feature used with PPP encapsulation, which prevents unauthorized access by identifying the remote end. The router or access server determines whether that user is allowed access.

checksum   Method for checking the integrity of transmitted data. A checksum is an integer value computed from a sequence of octets taken through a series of arithmetic operations. The value is recomputed at the receiving end and compared for verification.

CIDR (classless interdomain routing)   Technique supported by BGP4 and based on route aggregation. CIDR allows routers to group routes together in order to cut down on the quantity of routing information carried by the core routers. With CIDR, several IP networks appear to networks outside the group as a single, larger entity. With CIDR, IP addresses and their subnet masks are written as four octets, separated by periods, followed by a forward slash and a two-digit number that represents the subnet mask.

CIR (committed information rate)   The rate at which a Frame Relay network agrees to transfer information under normal conditions, averaged over a minimum increment of time. CIR, measured in bits per second, is one of the key negotiated tariff metrics.

circuit switching   A system in which a dedicated physical path must exist between sender and receiver for the entire duration of a call. Used heavily in telephone networks.

client   Node or software program, or front-end device, that requests services from a server.

CLNS (Connectionless Network Service)   An OSI network layer service, for which no circuit need be established before data can be transmitted. Routing of messages to their destinations is independent of other messages.

collision   In Ethernet, the result of two nodes transmitting simultaneously. The frames from each device cause an increase in voltage when they meet on the physical media, and are damaged.

congestion   Traffic in excess of network capacity.

connectionless   Term used to describe data transfer without the prior existence of a circuit.

console   A DTE device, usually consisting of a keyboard and display unit, through which users interact with a host.

contention   Access method in which network devices compete for permission to access the physical medium. Compare with **circuit switching** and **token passing**.

cost   A value, typically based on media bandwidth or other measures, that is assigned by a network administrator and used by routing protocols to compare various paths through an internetwork environment. Cost values are used to determine the most favorable path to a particular destination—the lower the cost, the better the path.

count to infinity   A condition in which routers continuously increment the hop count to particular networks. Often occurs in routing algorithms that are slow to converge. Usually, an arbitrary hop count ceiling is imposed to limit the extent of this problem.

CPE (customer premises equipment) Terminating equipment, such as terminals, telephones, and modems, installed at customer sites and connected to the telephone company network.

CRC (cyclic redundancy check) An error-checking technique in which the receiving device performs a calculation on the frame contents and compares the calculated number to a value stored in the frame by the sending node.

CSMA/CD (carrier sense multiple access collision detect) Media-access mechanism used by Ethernet and IEEE 802.3. Devices use CSMA/CD to check the channel for a carrier before transmitting data. If no carrier is sensed, the device transmits. If two devices transmit at the same time, the collision is detected by all colliding devices. Collisions delay retransmissions from those devices for a randomly chosen length of time.

CSU (channel service unit) Digital interface device that connects end-user equipment to the local digital telephone loop. Often referred to together with DSU, as CSU/DSU.

datagram Logical unit of information sent as a network layer unit over a transmission medium without prior establishment of a circuit.

data-link layer Layer 2 of the OSI reference model. This layer provides reliable transit of data across a physical link. The data link layer is concerned with physical addressing, network topology, access to the network medium, error detection, sequential delivery of frames, and flow control. The data link layer is divided into two sublayers: the MAC sublayer and the LLC sublayer.

DCE (data circuit-terminating equipment) The devices and connections of a communications network that represent the network end of the user-to-network interface. The DCE provides a physical connection to the network and provides a

clocking signal used to synchronize transmission between DCE and DTE devices. Modems and interface cards are examples of DCE devices.

D channel   Data channel. Full-duplex, 16-kbps (BRI) or 64-kbps (PRI) ISDN channel.

DDR (dial-on-demand routing)   Technique whereby a router can automatically initiate and close a circuit-switched session as transmitting stations demand. The router spoofs keepalives so that end stations treat the session as active. DDR permits routing over ISDN or telephone lines using an external ISDN terminal adapter or modem.

DECnet   Group of communications products (including a protocol suite) developed and supported by Digital Equipment Corporation. DECnet/OSI (also calledDECnet Phase V) is the most recent iteration and supports both OSI protocols and proprietary Digital protocols. Phase IV Prime supports inherent MAC addresses that allow DECnet nodes to coexist with systems running other protocols that have MAC address restrictions. *See also* **DNA**.

dedicated line   Communications line that is indefinitely reserved for transmissions, rather than switched as transmission is required. *See also* **leased line**.

de facto standard   A standard that exists because of its widespread use.

default route   A routing table entry that is used to direct packets when there is no explicit route present in the routing table.

de jure standard   Standard that exists because of its development or approval by an official standards body.

delay   The time between the initiation of a transaction by a sender and the first response received by the sender. Also, the time required to move a packet from source to destination over a network path.

demarc   The demarcation point between telephone carrier equipment and CPE.

demultiplexing   The separating of multiple streams of data that have been multiplexed into a common physical signal for transmission, back into multiple output streams. Opposite of multiplexing.

destination address   Address of a network device to receive data.

DHCP (Dynamic Host Configuration Protocol)   Provides a mechanism for allocating IP addresses dynamically so that addresses can be reassigned instead of belonging to only one host.

discovery mode   Method by which an AppleTalk router acquires information about an attached network from an operational router and then uses this information to configure its own addressing information.

distance vector routing algorithm   Class of routing algorithms that use the number of hops in a route to find a shortest path to a destination network. Distance vector routing algorithms call for each router to send its entire routing table in each update to each of its neighbors. Also called Bellman-Ford routing algorithm.

DLCI (data-link connection identifier)   A value that specifies a virtual circuit in a Frame Relay network.

DNA (Digital Network Architecture)   Network architecture that was developed by Digital Equipment Corporation. DECnet is the collective term for the products that comprise DNA (including communications protocols).

DNIC (Data Network Identification Code)   Part of an X.121 address. DNICs are divided into two parts: the first specifying the country in which the addressed PSN is located and the second specifying the PSN itself. *See also* **X.121**.

DNS (Domain Name System)   System used in the Internet for translating names of network nodes into addresses.

DSP (domain specific part)   Part of an ATM address. A DSP is comprised of an area identifier, a station identifier, and a selector byte.

DTE (data terminal equipment)   Device at the user end of a user-network interface that serves as a data source, destination, or both. DTE connects to a data network through a DCE device (for example, a modem) and typically uses clocking signals generated by the DCE. DTE includes such devices as computers, routers, and multiplexers.

DUAL (Diffusing Update Algorithm)   Convergence algorithm used in EIGRP. DUAL provides constant loop-free operation throughout a route computation by allowing routers involved in a topology change to synchronize at the same time, without involving routers that are unaffected by the change.

DVMRP (Distance Vector Multicast Routing Protocol) DVMRP is an internetwork gateway protocol that implements a typical dense mode IP multicast scheme. Using IGMP, DVMRP exchanges routing datagrams with its neighbors.

dynamic routing   Routing that adjusts automatically to changes in network topology or traffic patterns.

E1   Wide-area digital transmission scheme used in Europe that carries data at a rate of 2.048 Mbps.

EIA/TIA-232   Common physical layer interface standard, developed by EIA and TIA, that supports unbalanced circuits at signal speeds of up to 64 kbps. Formerly known as RS-232.

encapsulation   The process of attaching a particular protocol header to a unit of data prior to transmission on the network. For example, a frame of Ethernet data is given a specific Ethernet header before network transit.

end point   Device at which a virtual circuit or virtual path begins or ends.

enterprise network   A privately maintained network connecting most major points in a company or other organization. Usually spans a large geographic area and supports multiple protocols and services.

entity   Generally, an individual, manageable network device. Sometimes called an alias.

error control   Technique for detecting and correcting errors in data transmissions.

Ethernet   Baseband LAN specification invented by Xerox Corporation and developed jointly by Xerox, Intel, and Digital Equipment Corporation. Ethernet networks use the CSMA/CD method of media access control and run over a variety of cable types at 10 Mbps. Ethernet is similar to the IEEE 802.3 series of standards.

EtherTalk   Apple Computer's data-link product that allows an AppleTalk network to be connected by Ethernet cable.

explorer packet   Generated by an end station trying to find its way through a SRB network. Gathers a hop-by-hop description of a path through the network by being marked (updated) by each bridge that it traverses, thereby creating a complete topological map.

Fast Ethernet   Any of a number of 100-Mbps Ethernet specifications. Fast Ethernet offers a speed increase ten times that of the 10BaseT Ethernet specification, while preserving such qualities as frame format, MAC mechanisms, and MTU. Such similarities allow the use of existing 10BaseT applications and network management tools on Fast Ethernet networks. Based on an extension to the IEEE 802.3 specification. Compare with **Ethernet**. *See also* **100BaseFX; 100BaseT; 100BaseT4; 100BaseTX; 100BaseX; IEEE 802.3**.

FDDI (Fiber Distributed Data Interface)   LAN standard, defined by ANSI X3T9.5, specifying a 100-Mbps token-passing network using fiber-optic cable, with transmission distances of up to 2 km. FDDI uses a dual-ring architecture to provide redundancy. Compare with **CDDI**.

FECN (forward explicit congestion notification)   A facility in a Frame Relay network to inform DTE receiving the frame that congestion was experienced in the path from source to destination. DTE receiving frames with the FECN bit set can request that higher-level protocols take flow-control action as appropriate.

file transfer   Category of popular network applications that features movement of files from one network device to another.

filter   Generally, a process or device that screens network traffic for certain characteristics, such as source address, destination address, or protocol, and determines whether to forward or discard that traffic or routes based on the established criteria.

firewall   Router or other computer designated as a buffer between public networks and a private network. A firewall router uses access lists and other methods to ensure the security of the private network.

Flash memory   Nonvolatile storage that can be electrically erased and reprogrammed as necessary.

flash update   Routing update sent asynchronously when a change in the network topology occurs.

flat addressing   A system of addressing that does not incorporate a hierarchy to determine location.

flooding   Traffic-passing technique used by switches and bridges in which traffic received on an interface is sent out all of the interfaces of that device except the interface on which the information was originally received.

flow control   Technique for ensuring that a transmitting device, such as a modem, does not overwhelm a receiving device with data. When the buffers on the receiving device are full, a message is sent to the sending device to suspend transmission until it has processed the data in the buffers.

forwarding   The process of sending a frame or packet toward its destination.

fragment   Piece of a larger packet that has been broken down to smaller units.

fragmentation   Process of breaking a packet into smaller units when transmitting over a network medium that is unable to support a transmission unit the original size of the packet.

frame   Logical grouping of information sent as a data-link layer unit over a transmission medium. Sometimes refers to the header and trailer, used for synchronization and error control, which surround the user data contained in the unit. The terms cell, datagram, message, packet, and segment are also used to describe logical information groupings at various layers of the OSI reference model and in various technology circles.

Frame Relay   Industry-standard, switched data-link layer protocol that handles multiple virtual circuits over a single physical interface. Frame Relay is more efficient than X.25, for which it is generally considered a replacement.

frequency   Number of cycles, measured in hertz, of an alternating current signal per unit of time.

FTP (File Transfer Protocol)   An application protocol, part of the TCP/IP protocol stack, used for transferring files between hosts on a network.

full duplex   Capability for simultaneous data transmission and receipt of data between two devices.

full mesh   A network topology in which each network node has either a physical circuit or a virtual circuit connecting it to every other network node.

gateway   In the IP community, an older term referring to a routing device. Today, the term router is used to describe devices that perform this function, and gateway refers to a

special-purpose device that performs an application layer conversion of information from one protocol stack to another.

GB Gigabyte. Approximately 1,000,000,000 bytes.

GBps Gigabytes per second.

Gb Gigabit. Approximately 1,000,000,000 bits.

Gbps Gigabits per second.

GNS (Get Nearest Server) Request packet sent by a client on an IPX network to locate the nearest active server of a particular type. An IPX network client issues a GNS request to solicit either a direct response from a connected server or a response from a router that tells it where on the internetwork the service can be located. GNS is part of the IPX SAP.

half duplex Capability for data transmission in only one direction at a time between a sending station and a receiving station.

handshake Sequence of messages exchanged between two or more network devices to ensure transmission synchronization.

hardware address *See* **MAC address**.

HDLC (High-Level Data Link Control) Bit-oriented synchronous data-link layer protocol developed by ISO and derived from SDLC. HDLC specifies a data encapsulation method for synchronous serial links and includes frame characters and checksums in its headers.

header Control information placed before data when encapsulating that data for network transmission.

hello packet Multicast packet that is used by routers for neighbor discovery and recovery. Hello packets also indicate that a client is still operating on the network.

Hello protocol   Protocol used by OSPF and other routing protocols for establishing and maintaining neighbor relationships.

hierarchical addressing   A scheme of addressing that uses a logical hierarchy to determine location. For example, IP addresses consist of network numbers, subnet numbers, and host numbers, which IP routing algorithms use to route the packet to the appropriate location.

holddown   State of a routing table entry in which routers will neither advertise the route nor accept advertisements about the route for a specific length of time (known as the holddown period).

hop   Term describing the passage of a data packet between two network nodes (for example, between two routers). *See also* **hop count**.

hop count   Routing metric used to measure the distance between a source and a destination. RIP uses hop count as its metric.

host   A computer system on a network. Similar to the term node except that host usually implies a computer system, whereas node can refer to any networked system, including routers.

host number   Part of an IP address that designates which node is being addressed. Also called a host address.

hub   A term used to describe a device that serves as the center of a star topology network; or, an Ethernet multiport repeater, sometimes referred to as a concentrator.

ICMP (Internet Control Message Protocol)   A network layer Internet protocol that provides reports of errors and other information about IP packet processing. ICMP is documented in RFC 792.

IEEE (Institute of Electrical and Electronics Engineers) A professional organization among whose activities are the development of communications and networking standards. IEEE LAN standards are the most common LAN standards today.

IEEE 802.3 IEEE LAN protocol for the implementation of the physical layer and the MAC sublayer of the data-link layer. IEEE 802.3 uses CSMA/CD access at various speeds over various physical media.

IEEE 802.5 IEEE LAN protocol for the implementation of the physical layer and MAC sublayer of the data-link layer. Similar to Token Ring, IEEE 802.5 uses token passing access over STP cabling.

IGP (Interior Gateway Protocol) A generic term for an Internet routing protocol used to exchange routing information within an autonomous system. Examples of common Internet IGPs include IGRP, OSPF, and RIP.

interface A connection between two systems or devices; or in routing terminology, a network connection.

Internet Term used to refer to the global internetwork that evolved from the ARPANET, that now connects tens of thousands of networks worldwide.

Internet protocol Any protocol that is part of the TCP/IP protocol stack. *See* **TCP/IP**.

internetwork Collection of networks interconnected by routers and other devices that functions (generally) as a single network.

internetworking General term used to refer to the industry that has arisen around the problem of connecting networks together. The term may be used to refer to products, procedures, and technologies.

Inverse ARP (Inverse Address Resolution Protocol)
Method of building dynamic address mappings in a Frame
Relay network. Allows a device to discover the network
address of a device associated with a virtual circuit.

IP (Internet Protocol)   Network layer protocol in the
TCP/IP stack offering a connectionless datagram service. IP
provides features for addressing, type-of-service specification,
fragmentation and reassembly, and security. Documented in
RFC 791.

IP address   A 32-bit address assigned to hosts using the
TCP/IP suite of protocols. An IP address is written as four
octets separated by dots (dotted decimal format). Each
address consists of a network number, an optional
subnetwork number, and a host number. The network and
subnetwork numbers together are used for routing, while the
host number is used to address an individual host within the
network or subnetwork. A subnet mask is often used with the
address to extract network and subnetwork information from
the IP address.

IPX (Internetwork Packet Exchange)   NetWare
network layer (Layer 3) protocol used for transferring data
from servers to workstations. IPX is similar to IP in that it
is a connectionless datagram service.

IPXCP (IPX Control Protocol)   The protocol that
establishes and configures IPX over PPP.

IPXWAN   A protocol that negotiates end-to-end options for
new links on startup. When a link comes up, the first IPX
packets sent across are IPXWAN packets negotiating the
options for the link. When the IPXWAN options have been
successfully determined, normal IPX transmission begins, and
no more IPXWAN packets are sent. Defined by RFC 1362.

ISDN (Integrated Services Digital Network)
Communication protocol, offered by telephone companies,
that permits telephone networks to carry data, voice, and
other source traffic.

ITU-T (International Telecommunication Union Telecommunication Standardization Sector)
International body dedicated to the development of worldwide standards for telecommunications technologies. ITU-T is the successor to CCITT.

KB   Kilobyte. Approximately 1,000 bytes.

Kb   Kilobit. Approximately 1,000 bits.

KBps   Kilobytes per second.

Kbps   Kilobits per second.

keepalive interval   Period of time between keepalive messages sent by a network device.

keepalive message   Message sent by one network device to inform another network device that it is still active.

LAN (local-area network)   High-speed, low-error data network covering a relatively small geographic area. LANs connect workstations, peripherals, terminals, and other devices in a single building or other geographically limited area. LAN standards specify cabling and signaling at the physical and data-link layers of the OSI model. Ethernet, FDDI, and Token Ring are the most widely used LAN technologies.

LANE (LAN emulation)   Technology that allows an ATM network to function as a LAN backbone. In this situation LANE provides multicast and broadcast support, address mapping (MAC-to-ATM), and virtual circuit management.

LAPB (Link Access Procedure, Balanced)   The data-link layer protocol in the X.25 protocol stack. LAPB is a bit-oriented protocol derived from HDLC.

LAPD (Link Access Procedure on the D channel)
ISDN data link layer protocol for the D channel. LAPD was derived from the LAPB protocol and is designed to satisfy the signaling requirements of ISDN basic access. Defined by ITU-T Recommendations Q.920 and Q.921.

latency   The amount of time elapsed between the time a device requests access to a network and the time it is allowed to transmit; or, amount of time between the point at which a device receives a frame and the time that frame is forwarded out the destination port.

LCP (Link Control Protocol)   A protocol used with PPP, which establishes, configures, and tests data-link connections.

leased line   Transmission line reserved by a communications carrier for the private use of a customer. A leased line is a type of dedicated line.

link   Network communications channel consisting of a circuit or transmission path and all related equipment between a sender and a receiver. Most often used to refer to a WAN connection. Sometimes called a line or a transmission link.

link-state routing algorithm   Routing algorithm in which each router broadcasts or multicasts information regarding the cost of reaching each of its neighbors to all nodes in the internetwork. Link-state algorithms require that routers maintain a consistent view of the network and are therefore not prone to routing loops.

LLC (Logical Link Control)   Higher of two data-link layer sublayers defined by the IEEE. The LLC sublayer handles error control, flow control, framing, and MAC-sublayer addressing. The most common LLC protocol is IEEE 802.2, which includes both connectionless and connection-oriented types.

LMI (Local Management Interface)   A set of enhancements to the basic Frame Relay specification. LMI includes support for keepalives, a multicast mechanism, global addressing, and a status mechanism.

load balancing   In routing, the ability of a router to distribute traffic over all its network ports that are the same distance from the destination address. Load balancing increases the utilization of network segments, thus increasing total effective network bandwidth.

local loop   A line from the premises of a telephone subscriber to the telephone company central office.

LocalTalk   Apple Computer's proprietary baseband protocol that operates at the data-link and physical layers of the OSI reference model. LocalTalk uses CSMA/CA and supports transmissions at speeds of 230.4 Kbps.

loop   A situation in which packets never reach their destination, but are forwarded in a cycle repeatedly through a group of network nodes.

MAC (Media Access Control)   Lower of the two sublayers of the data link layer defined by the IEEE. The MAC sublayer handles access to shared media.

MAC address   Standardized data-link layer address that is required for every port or device that connects to a LAN. Other devices in the network use these addresses to locate specific ports in the network and to create and update routing tables and data structures. MAC addresses are 48 bits long and are controlled by the IEEE. Also known as a hardware address, a MAC-layer address, or a physical address.

MAN (metropolitan-area network)   A network that spans a metropolitan area. Generally, a MAN spans a larger geographic area than a LAN, but a smaller geographic area than a WAN.

Mb   Megabit. Approximately 1,000,000 bits.

Mbps   Megabits per second.

media   The various physical environments through which transmission signals pass. Common network media include cable (twisted-pair, coaxial, and fiber optic) and the atmosphere (through which microwave, laser, and infrared transmission occurs). Sometimes referred to as physical media.

Media Access Control   *See* **MAC**.

mesh   Network topology in which devices are organized in a segmented manner with redundant interconnections strategically placed between network nodes.

message   Application layer logical grouping of information, often composed of a number of lower-layer logical groupings such as packets.

MSAU (multistation access unit)   A wiring concentrator to which all end stations in a Token Ring network connect. Sometimes abbreviated MAU.

multiaccess network   A network that allows multiple devices to connect and communicate by sharing the same medium, such as a LAN.

multicast   A single packet copied by the network and sent to a specific subset of network addresses. These addresses are specified in the Destination Address field.

multicast address   A single address that refers to multiple network devices. Sometimes called a group address.

multiplexing   A technique that allows multiple logical signals to be transmitted simultaneously across a single physical channel.

mux   A multiplexing device. A mux combines multiple input signals for transmission over a single line. The signals are demultiplexed, or separated, before they are used at the receiving end.

NAK (Negative acknowledgment)   A response sent from a receiving device to a sending device indicating that the information received contained errors.

name resolution   The process of associating a symbolic name with a network location or address.

NAT (Network Address Translation)   A technique for reducing the need for globally unique IP addresses. NAT allows an organization with addresses that may conflict with others in the IP address space to connect to the Internet by translating those addresses into unique ones within the globally routable address space.

NBMA (nonbroadcast multiaccess) Term describing a multiaccess network that either does not support broadcasting (such as X.25) or in which broadcasting is not feasible.

NBP (Name Binding Protocol) AppleTalk transport level protocol that translates a character string name into the DDP address of the corresponding socket client.

NCP (Network Control Protocol) Protocols that establish and configure various network layer protocols. Used for AppleTalk over PPP.

NetBIOS (Network Basic Input/Output System) An application programming interface used by applications on an IBM LAN to request services from lower-level network processes such as session establishment and termination, and information transfer.

NetWare A network operating system developed by Novell, Inc. Provides remote file access, print services, and numerous other distributed network services.

network Collection of computers, printers, routers, switches, and other devices that are able to communicate with each other over some transmission medium.

network interface Border between a carrier network and a privately owned installation.

network layer Layer 3 of the OSI reference model. This layer provides connectivity and path selection between two end systems. The network layer is the layer at which routing takes place.

NLSP (NetWare Link Services Protocol) Link-state routing protocol for IPX based on IS-IS.

node Endpoint of a network connection or a junction common to two or more lines in a network. Nodes can be processors, controllers, or workstations. Nodes, which vary in their functional capabilities, can be interconnected by links, and serve as control points in the network.

NVRAM (nonvolatile RAM)   RAM that retains its contents when a device is powered off.

OSI reference model (Open System Interconnection reference model)   A network architectural framework developed by ISO and ITU-T. The model describes seven layers, each of which specifies a particular network. The lowest layer, called the physical layer, is closest to the media technology. The highest layer, the application layer, is closest to the user. The OSI reference model is widely used as a way of understanding network functionality.

OSPF (Open Shortest Path First)   A link-state, hierarchical IGP routing algorithm, which includes features such as least-cost routing, multipath routing, and load balancing. OSPF was based on an early version of the IS-IS protocol.

out-of-band signaling   Transmission using frequencies or channels outside the frequencies or channels used for transfer of normal data. Out-of-band signaling is often used for error reporting when normal channels are unusable for communicating with network devices.

packet   Logical grouping of information that includes a header containing control information and (usually) user data. Packets are most often used to refer to network layer units of data. The terms datagram, frame, message, and segment are also used to describe logical information groupings at various layers of the OSI reference model, and in various technology circles. *See also* **PDU**.

PAP   Password Authentication Protocol. Authentication protocol that allows PPP peers to authenticate one another. The remote router attempting to connect to the local router is required to send an authentication request. Unlike CHAP, PAP passes the password and host name or username in the clear (unencrypted). PAP does not itself prevent unauthorized access, but merely identifies the remote end. The router or access server then determines if that user is allowed access. PAP is supported only on PPP lines.

partial mesh   Term describing a network in which devices are organized in a mesh topology, with some network nodes organized in a full mesh, but with others that are only connected to one or two other nodes in the network. A partial mesh does not provide the level of redundancy of a full mesh topology, but is less expensive to implement. Partial mesh topologies are generally used in the peripheral networks that connect to a fully meshed backbone. *See also* **full mesh**; **mesh**.

PDU (protocol data unit)   The OSI term for a packet.

physical layer   Layer 1 of the OSI reference model; it corresponds with the physical control layer in the SNA model. The physical layer defines the specifications for activating, maintaining, and deactivating the physical link between end systems.

Ping (packet internet groper)   ICMP echo message and its reply. Often used in IP networks to test the reachability of a network device.

poison reverse updates   Routing updates that explicitly indicate that a network or subnet is unreachable, rather than implying that a network is unreachable by not including it in updates. Poison reverse updates are sent to defeat large routing loops.

port   1. Interface on an internetworking device (such as a router). 2. In IP terminology, an upper-layer process that receives information from lower layers. Ports are numbered, and each numbered port is associated with a specific process. For example, SMTP is associated with port 25. A port number is also known as a well-known address. 3. To rewrite software or microcode so that it will run on a different hardware platform or in a different software environment than that for which it was originally designed.

PPP (Point-to-Point Protocol)   A successor to SLIP that provides router-to-router and host-to-network connections over synchronous and asynchronous circuits. Whereas SLIP was designed to work with IP, PPP was designed to work with several network layer protocols, such as IP, IPX, and

ARA. PPP also has built-in security mechanisms, such as CHAP and PAP. PPP relies on two protocols: LCP and NCP. *See also* **CHAP**; **LCP**; **NCP**; **PAP**; **SLIP**.

presentation layer   Layer 6 of the OSI reference model. This layer ensures that information sent by the application layer of one system will be readable by the application layer of another. The presentation layer is also concerned with the data structures used by programs and therefore negotiates data transfer syntax for the application layer.

PRI (Primary Rate Interface)   ISDN interface to primary rate access. Primary rate access consists of a single 64-kbps D channel plus 23 (T1) or 30 (E1) B channels for voice or data. Compare to **BRI**.

protocol   Formal description of a set of rules and conventions that govern how devices on a network exchange information.

protocol stack   Set of related communications protocols that operate together and, as a group, address communication at some or all of the seven layers of the OSI reference model. Not every protocol stack covers each layer of the model, and often a single protocol in the stack will address a number of layers at once. TCP/IP is a typical protocol stack.

proxy ARP (proxy Address Resolution Protocol)
Variation of the ARP protocol in which an intermediate device (for example, a router) sends an ARP response on behalf of an end node to the requesting host. Proxy ARP can lessen bandwidth use on slow-speed WAN links. *See also* **ARP**.

PVC (permanent virtual circuit)   Permanently established virtual circuits save bandwidth in situations where certain virtual circuits must exist all the time, such as during circuit establishment and tear down.

query   Message used to inquire about the value of some variable or set of variables.

queue   A backlog of packets stored in buffers and waiting to be forwarded over a router interface.

RAM   Random-access memory. Volatile memory that can be read and written by a computer.

reassembly   The putting back together of an IP datagram at the destination after it has been fragmented either at the source or at an intermediate node. *See also* **fragmentation**.

reload   The event of a Cisco router rebooting, or the command that causes the router to reboot.

RFC (Request For Comments)   Document series used as the primary means for communicating information about the Internet. Some RFCs are designated by the IAB as Internet standards.

ring   Connection of two or more stations in a logically circular topology. Information is passed sequentially between active stations. Token Ring, FDDI, and CDDI are based on this topology.

ring topology   Network topology that consists of a series of repeaters connected to one another by unidirectional transmission links to form a single closed loop. Each station on the network connects to the network at a repeater.

RIP (Routing Information Protocol)   A routing protocol for TCP/IP networks. The most common routing protocol in the Internet. RIP uses hop count as a routing metric.

ROM (read-only memory)   Nonvolatile memory that can be read, but not written, by the computer.

routed protocol   Protocol that carries user data so it can be routed by a router. A router must be able to interpret the logical internetwork as specified by that routed protocol. Examples of routed protocols include AppleTalk, DECnet, and IP.

router   Network layer device that uses one or more metrics to determine the optimal path along which network traffic should be forwarded. Routers forward packets from one network to another based on network layer information.

routing   Process of finding a path to a destination host.

routing metric   Method by which a routing algorithm determines preferability of one route over another. This information is stored in routing tables. Metrics include bandwidth, communication cost, delay, hop count, load, MTU, path cost, and reliability. Sometimes referred to simply as a metric.

routing protocol   Protocol that accomplishes routing through the implementation of a specific routing algorithm. Examples of routing protocols include IGRP, OSPF, and RIP.

routing table   Table stored in a router or some other internetworking device that keeps track of routes to particular network destinations and, in some cases, metrics associated with those routes.

routing update   Message sent from a router to indicate network reachability and associated cost information. Routing updates are typically sent at regular intervals and after a change in network topology. Compare with **flash update**.

RSRB (remote source-route bridging)   Equivalent to an SRB over WAN links.

SAP (service access point)   1. Field defined by the IEEE 802.2 specification that is part of an address specification. Thus, the destination plus the DSAP define the recipient of a packet. The same applies to the SSAP. 2. Service Advertising Protocol. IPX protocol that provides a means of informing network routers and servers of the location of available network resources and services.

segment   1. Section of a network that is bounded by bridges, routers, or switches. 2. In a LAN using a bus topology, a segment is a continuous electrical circuit that is often connected to other such segments with repeaters.

3. Term used in the TCP specification to describe a single transport layer unit of information.

serial transmission   Method of data transmission in which the bits of a data character are transmitted sequentially over a single channel.

session   1. Related set of communications transactions between two or more network devices. 2. In SNA, a logical connection that enables two NAUs to communicate.

session layer   Layer 5 of the OSI reference model. This layer establishes, manages, and terminates sessions between applications and manages data exchange between presentation layer entities. Corresponds to the data flow control layer of the SNA model. *See also* **application layer**; **data-link layer**; **network layer**; **physical layer**; **presentation layer**; **transport layer**.

sliding window flow control   Method of flow control in which a receiver gives a transmitter permission to transmit data until a window is full. When the window is full, the transmitter must stop transmitting until the receiver acknowledges some of the data, or advertises a larger window. TCP, other transport protocols, and several data-link layer protocols use this method of flow control.

SLIP (Serial Line Internet Protocol)   Uses a variation of TCP/IP to make point-to-point serial connections. Succeeded by PPP.

SNAP (Subnetwork Access Protocol)   Internet protocol that operates between a network entity in the subnetwork and a network entity in the end system. SNAP specifies a standard method of encapsulating IP datagrams and ARP messages on IEEE networks.

SNMP (Simple Network Management Protocol) Network management protocol used almost exclusively in TCP/IP networks. SNMP provides a means to monitor and control network devices, and to manage configurations, statistics collection, performance, and security.

socket   Software structure operating as a communications end point within a network device.

SONET (Synchronous Optical Network)   High-speed synchronous network specification developed by Bellcore and designed to run on optical fiber.

source address   Address of a network device that is sending data.

spanning tree   Loop-free subset of a network topology. *See also* **Spanning-Tree Protocol**.

Spanning-Tree Protocol   Developed to eliminate loops in the network. The Spanning-Tree Protocol ensures a loop-free path by placing one of the bridge ports in "blocking mode", preventing the forwarding of packets.

SPF (shortest path first algorithm)   Routing algorithm that sorts routes by length of path to determine a shortest-path spanning tree. Commonly used in link-state routing algorithms. Sometimes called Dijkstra's algorithm.

split-horizon updates   Routing technique in which information about routes is prevented from being advertised out the router interface through which that information was received. Split-horizon updates are used to prevent routing loops.

SPX (Sequenced Packet Exchange)   Reliable, connection-oriented protocol at the transport layer that supplements the datagram service provided by IPX.

SRB (source-route bridging)   Method of bridging in Token Ring networks. In an SRB network, before data is sent to a destination, the entire route to that destination is predetermined in real time.

SRT (source-route transparent bridging)   IBM's merging of SRB and transparent bridging into one bridging scheme, which requires no translation between bridging protocols.

SR/TLB (source-route translational bridging)   Method of bridging that allows source-route stations to communicate with transparent bridge stations, using an intermediate bridge that translates between the two bridge protocols.

standard   Set of rules or procedures that are either widely used or officially specified.

star topology   LAN topology in which end points on a network are connected to a common central switch by point-to-point links. A ring topology that is organized as a star implements a unidirectional closed-loop star, instead of point-to-point links. Compare with **bus topology**, **ring topology**, and **tree topology**.

static route   Route that is explicitly configured and entered into the routing table. Static routes take precedence over routes chosen by dynamic routing protocols.

subinterface   A virtual interface defined as a logical subdivision of a physical interface.

subnet address   Portion of an IP address that is specified as the subnetwork by the subnet mask. *See also* **IP address**; **subnet mask**; **subnetwork**.

subnet mask   32-bit address mask used in IP to indicate the bits of an IP address that are being used for the subnet address. Sometimes referred to simply as mask. *See also* **address mask**; **IP address**.

subnetwork   1. In IP networks, a network sharing a particular subnet address. 2. Subnetworks are networks arbitrarily segmented by a network administrator in order to provide a multilevel, hierarchical routing structure while shielding the subnetwork from the addressing complexity of attached networks. Sometimes called a subnet.

SVC (switched virtual circuit)   Virtual circuit that can be established dynamically on demand, and which is torn down after a transmission is complete. SVCs are used when data transmission is sporadic.

switch   1. Network device that filters, forwards, and floods frames based on the destination address of each frame. The switch operates at the data-link layer of the OSI model. 2. General term applied to an electronic or mechanical device that allows a connection to be established as necessary and terminated when there is no longer a session to support.

T1   Digital WAN carrier facility. T1 transmits DS-1-formatted data at 1.544 Mbps through the telephone-switching network, using AMI or B8ZS coding. Compare with **E1**. *See also* **AMI**; **B8ZS**.

TCP (Transmission Control Protocol)
Connection-oriented transport layer protocol that provides reliable full-duplex data transmission. TCP is part of the TCP/IP protocol stack.

TCP/IP (Transmission Control Protocol/Internet Protocol)   Common name for the suite of protocols developed by the U.S. DoD in the 1970s to support the construction of worldwide internetworks. TCP and IP are the two best-known protocols in the suite.

throughput   Rate of information arriving at, and possibly passing through, a particular point in a network system.

timeout   Event that occurs when one network device expects to hear from another network device within a specified period of time, but does not. A timeout usually results in a retransmission of information or the termination of the session between the two devices.

token   Frame that contains only control information. Possession of the token allows a network device to transmit data onto the network. *See also* **token passing**.

token passing   Method by which network devices access the physical medium is based on possession of a small frame called a token. Compare this method to circuit switching and contention.

Token Ring   Token-passing LAN developed and supported by IBM. Token Ring runs at 4 or 16 Mbps over a ring topology. Similar to IEEE 802.5. *See also* **IEEE 802.5**; **ring topology**; **token passing**.

TokenTalk   Apple Computer's data-link product that allows an AppleTalk network to be connected by Token Ring cables.

transparent bridging   Bridging scheme used in Ethernet and IEEE 802.3 networks. Allows bridges to pass frames along one hop at a time, based on tables that associate end nodes with bridge ports. Bridges are transparent to network end nodes.

transport layer   Layer 4 of the OSI reference model. This layer is responsible for reliable network communication between end nodes. The transport layer provides mechanisms for the establishment, maintenance, and termination of virtual circuits, transport fault detection and recovery, and information flow control.

tree topology   A LAN topology that resembles a bus topology. Tree networks can contain branches with multiple nodes. In a tree topology, transmissions from a station propagate the length of the physical medium, and are received by all other stations.

twisted-pair   Relatively low-speed transmission medium consisting of two insulated wires arranged in a regular spiral pattern. The wires can be shielded or unshielded. Twisted-pair is common in telephony applications and is increasingly common in data networks.

UDP (User Datagram Protocol)   Connectionless transport layer protocol in the TCP/IP protocol stack. UDP is a simple protocol that exchanges datagrams without acknowledgments or guaranteed delivery, requiring that error processing and retransmission be handled by other protocols. UDP is defined in RFC 768.

UTP (unshielded twisted-pair) Four-pair wire medium used in a variety of networks. UTP does not require the fixed spacing between connections that is necessary with coaxial-type connections.

virtual circuit Logical circuit created to ensure reliable communication between two network devices. A virtual circuit is defined by a VPI/VCI pair, and can be either permanent or switched. Virtual circuits are used in Frame Relay and X.25. In ATM, a virtual circuit is called a virtual channel. Sometimes abbreviated VC.

VLAN (virtual LAN) Group of devices on one or more LANs that are configured (using management software) so that they can communicate as if they were attached to the same wire, when in fact they are located on a number of different LAN segments. Because VLANs are based on logical instead of physical connections, they are extremely flexible.

VLSM (variable-length subnet masking) Ability to specify a different length subnet mask for the same network number at different locations in the network. VLSM can help optimize available address space.

WAN (wide-area network) Data communications network that serves users across a broad geographic area and often uses transmission devices provided by common carriers. Frame Relay, SMDS, and X.25 are examples of WANs. Compare with **LAN** and **MAN**.

wildcard mask 32-bit quantity used in conjunction with an IP address to determine which bits in an IP address should be matched and ignored when comparing that address with another IP address. A wildcard mask is specified when defining access list statements.

X.121 ITU-T standard describing an addressing scheme used in X.25 networks. X.121 addresses are sometimes called IDNs (International Data Numbers).

X.21   ITU-T standard for serial communications over synchronous digital lines. The X.21 protocol is used primarily in Europe and Japan.

X.25   ITU-T standard that defines how connections between DTE and DCE are maintained for remote terminal access and computer communications in public data networks. X.25 specifies LAPB, a data-link layer protocol, and PLP, a network layer protocol. Frame Relay has to some degree superseded X.25.

zone   In AppleTalk, a logical group of network devices.

Index